THE BUILDING OF
MANHATTAN

The Building of MANHATTAN

by Donald A. Mackay

Illustrated by the author

1817

HARPER & ROW, PUBLISHERS, New York
Cambridge, Philadelphia, San Francisco, Washington
London, Mexico City, São Paulo, Singapore, Sydney

FIRST EDITION

Designer: C. Linda Dingler
Copy editor: William Reynolds

Library of Congress Cataloging-in-Publication Data

Mackay, Donald A.
  The building of Manhattan.

  1. Building—New York (N.Y.)—History. 2. Manhattan (New York, N.Y.)—
History. 3. Manhattan (New York, N.Y.)—Public works—History.
I. Title.
TH25.N5M33   1987   690′.09747′1   87-45069
ISBN 0-06-015788-7   87 88 89 90 91 MPC 10 9 8 7 6 5 4 3 2 1
ISBN 0-06-096268-8 (pbk.) 87 88 89 90 91 MPC 10 9 8 7 6 5 4 3 2 1

CONTENTS

PREFACE

Artists are lucky. Once they are seen to be actually drawing something, they are generally accepted as part of the landscape. Busy Manhattan construction sites are no exception, if the artist keeps out of the way, and once it has been determined he is not an inspector. He can stand around, tolerated, in all kinds of places, for long periods of time, doing nothing but watching other people work. Of course he may not be making any money, but that's another part of being an artist. What he may be doing, even if he's not yet aware of it, is accumulating material for a book like this.

Almost thirty years ago a drawing I made of the construction of the Chase Manhattan Bank in lower Manhattan had been put away and forgotten. By chance, all these years later, I met foundation engineers of the consulting firm that worked on the foundation and they described for me the method used to stabilize the "quick" sand encountered during the excavation. Pure luck, and the drawing is now part of the book.

This is not a textbook, but I hope it is factual enough to please the concrete worker who said he'd like his children to see what it is he does for a living. And repay the ironworker I talked with during his lunch break. Asked how fireproofing is applied to steel framework he said, "I'll show you." You follow, only to be stopped by a supervisor's "What are you doing here?" You show him what you're drawing and he takes you down temporary wooden stairs into the unfinished depths of the sub-basement. There you step into another world, a brightly lit office filled with working drawings and schedules, closed off from all the outside commotion. He has you sign an insurance liability release, tells you always to borrow a hard hat and to come back on Saturday when he'll have time to talk. Not only does he talk, but you see fireproofing being applied. It's slippery and messy, and its application on an off-day doesn't interfere with other work operations. On another Saturday you expect to find out how heavy panels get anchored to the outer frame of the building but the foreman has had to bring in a crew on doubletime pay. It is not the time to ask questions. Later, on a weekday, he sees you and leads you up in the lift, up the outside of the building, to an open upper floor. Here his men are working right on the edge of the building, far above the street, carefully, with much physical effort, anchoring a panel into place. You acquire an admiration for all involved, as you keep away from the edge of the building. You also realize you are no longer just roaming around, you are committed to developing a book.

The quick sketch you make in a situation like that is of details. There probably isn't time even for that. What you saw you write down and sketch when you get out on the street, before you forget it. You may not know yet how it will fit into a drawing or where it will go in the book, or what questions to ask that will give the drawing logic or purpose. You take some quick photos. Only back in the studio can you work out what it is you wish to say and illustrate. It may be a composite drawing, from preliminary sketches and photos of similar work functions.

Sometimes the aspect of the drawing is complete, as in the demolition of the building at 54th Street and Madison Avenue. I first saw this demolition from a bus, made a quick exit, and looked for a way to get above the scene. Around the 53rd Street corner is a tall building built when elevator lobbies had windows. Sure enough, after checking out different floors I found a seldom used level with a perfect view above the entire demolition (page 82). Incidentally, the man who continuously sprayed water on the wreckage to keep down the dust got fifteen dollars an hour, and was waiting for the chance to do some demolition work himself.

I am sure there must be gaps in the writing, from not knowing the right questions to ask. One very cold day I went upstairs in a fast-food place that overlooked a building under construction and a workman was there, having a cup of coffee. He was an inspector temporarily caught up with his work. His job was to climb the steel framework and check all the different size bolts as the steel was being erected, making sure each bolt had its correct number of washers and was tightened to its own exact degree. Until then I had thought all bolts got tightened as tight as possible. Here was an answer to a question I never would have asked. Now I would watch for a worker tightening a bolt with a torque wrench. He's on page 129.

Jumping the tower crane is much more spectacular. I had talked with workmen who'd seen it done but couldn't explain the sequence. I got a handsome booklet from the Iowa manufacturer, but the procedure was somehow incomplete. I waited for days to see it happen. Only then did it all become clear. People in the street smiled after seeing it done.

A lot of wandering about the city is in these pages. It took a long time for it all to come together. The thoughts about the early days of New York began as family research on some Dutch ancestors who were here on Manhattan Island in its earliest days as a tiny settlement. Like the construction sketches, that part just grew in size until one day it seemed fitting to meld it into one bit of allegiance, to the city and its people.

March 1987
Ossining, New York

THE BUILDING OF
MANHATTAN

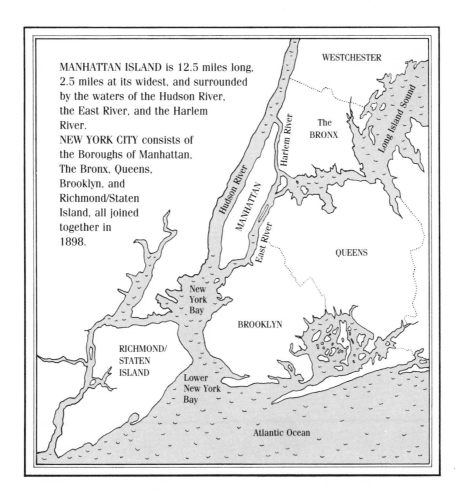

MANHATTAN ISLAND is 12.5 miles long, 2.5 miles at its widest, and surrounded by the waters of the Hudson River, the East River, and the Harlem River.

NEW YORK CITY consists of the Boroughs of Manhattan, The Bronx, Queens, Brooklyn, and Richmond/Staten Island, all joined together in 1898.

No other city in the world has such a concentration of skyscrapers and large buildings as has Manhattan. It is a city always changing: building, tearing down, rebuilding. It digs deep below the surface, it reaches to the sky.

It puts together enormously complex buildings with seeming ease and grace, in the midst of busy streets.

The traffic flows by. New Yorkers hurry on . . . and watch.

It is a scene well worth watching—enormous energy and creative imagination are at work.

New York City—on the Island of Manhattan—in less than 400 years has grown from a small Dutch trading post into today's awe-inspiring panorama of architectural and engineering marvels.

Built on a unique geological underbase, at the head of a great natural harbor, it is one of the wonders of the world.

Four separate ice ages have buried much of North America and Northern Europe under thousands of feet of ice and snow. The last Ice Age, about 10,000 to 18,000 years ago, completely buried Manhattan Island, shown here in its present-day shape and location.

IN THE BEGINNING

Manhattan Island is of very recent origin, in geological time.

Its creation as an island is one of the latest episodes in the long history of the titanic forces that have altered the landscape of New York.

It has been rocked by massive earthquakes, squeezed, shaped, and twisted. Periods of volcanic activity spewed forth molten lava. At one time a vast inland freshwater sea covered the entire area.

Geologists take the birth of Manhattan back more than a billion years. They record three eras of major high-mountain formation. Erosion, wind, rain, and ice slowly reduced those ancient alps in the ongoing process of land transformation.

About 70 million years ago the present island shape of Manhattan began to be formed, well before the great ice ages first appeared two million years ago.

Then, 10,000 to 18,000 years ago, the forward edge of the last great ice sheet ground inexorably southward, pushing gravel and enormous rocks, scouring the earth, and burying Manhattan Island under a massive wall of solid ice. The sheet of ice moved forward onto Staten Island, along the reach of Long Island . . . and stopped.

So great was the amount of water locked into this vast worldwide ice formation that the ocean level at Manhattan was 330 feet—100 meters—lower than it is today.

As this ice slowly melted and the glacial front retreated northward, torrents of rushing water carved the bed of the Hudson River ever deeper, the ocean rose to its present level, and New York's great natural harbor was formed.

The earth's outer, solid continuous crust, its bedrock, now lay just below and sometimes above the surface of Manhattan Island in two distinct areas: the downtown tip of the island and at midtown.

It is primarily on these two areas that Manhattan's skyscrapers have been built. Their tremendous height and weight rest securely on this solid bedrock, which is chiefly a silvery gray rock known as Manhattan schist.

SOUND

ISLAND

about 12,000–16,000 years ago

OCEAN

The earliest people of New York were the Paleo-Indians, descendants of those earlier wanderers who had crossed over into America from Asia by way of the Alaska land bridge. They are believed to have arrived here about 7,000 years ago, probably too late to hunt the mastodon and woolly mammoth. These Ice Age elephants mysteriously vanished, but their fossil remains show that they roamed over New York State and on or near Manhattan Island as late as 11,000 years ago. These great animals weighed between five and six tons and stood nine feet high at the shoulder. Manhattan's climate was very cold. Over thousands of years it would slowly grow warmer as the glaciers vanished.

When the first Europeans arrived in what is now New York Harbor, they found native Indians living on the island. These Algonquin-speaking people, consisting of some twenty-seven groups in about a hundred settlements, called their island Manhattes, variously spelled Manhata, Manahatin, or Manatans, and probably meaning "Island of the Hills."

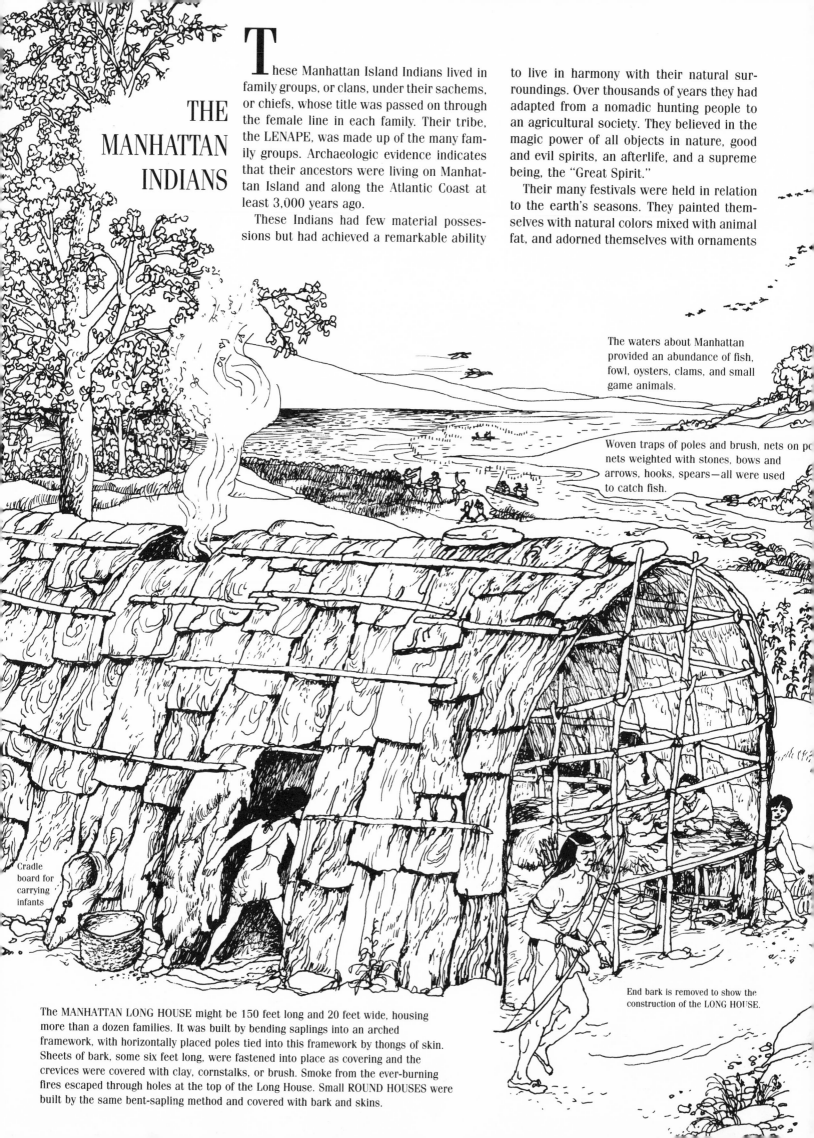

THE MANHATTAN INDIANS

These Manhattan Island Indians lived in family groups, or clans, under their sachems, or chiefs, whose title was passed on through the female line in each family. Their tribe, the LENAPE, was made up of the many family groups. Archaeologic evidence indicates that their ancestors were living on Manhattan Island and along the Atlantic Coast at least 3,000 years ago.

These Indians had few material possessions but had achieved a remarkable ability to live in harmony with their natural surroundings. Over thousands of years they had adapted from a nomadic hunting people to an agricultural society. They believed in the magic power of all objects in nature, good and evil spirits, an afterlife, and a supreme being, the "Great Spirit."

Their many festivals were held in relation to the earth's seasons. They painted themselves with natural colors mixed with animal fat, and adorned themselves with ornaments

The waters about Manhattan provided an abundance of fish, fowl, oysters, clams, and small game animals.

Woven traps of poles and brush, nets on po nets weighted with stones, bows and arrows, hooks, spears—all were used to catch fish.

Cradle board for carrying infants

End bark is removed to show the construction of the LONG HOUSE.

The MANHATTAN LONG HOUSE might be 150 feet long and 20 feet wide, housing more than a dozen families. It was built by bending saplings into an arched framework, with horizontally placed poles tied into this framework by thongs of skin. Sheets of bark, some six feet long, were fastened into place as covering and the crevices were covered with clay, cornstalks, or brush. Smoke from the ever-burning fires escaped through holes at the top of the Long House. Small ROUND HOUSES were built by the same bent-sapling method and covered with bark and skins.

of metal, bone, feathers, and shells. They had great powers of endurance.

We know the names of some of these Manhattan clan groupings: Rechtank, Werpoes, Shepmoes, Sapohanikan, Rechewanis, Conykeeks, Muskuta, Machicanituk, Penadnik, Shorakapkok, Nipnichsen.

They had no concept of owning land, freely using what they needed and moving on to another locality within their tribe's territory when the fertility of the land where they had been living was exhausted. They and their ancestors had lived on Manhattan for untold generations. They would vanish soon after the arrival of the European white man, leaving behind only some artifacts, some trails which would become roadways such as the Bowery and Broadway, and the name of the island—Manhattan.

Major strongholds were enclosed by palisades, and were used for communal living in the winter.

Corn, beans, squash, and pumpkins were cultivated. Wild nuts, tubers, and berries were gathered for food. Prepared pits dug in the ground were filled with food for use through the winter.

Mortar and pestle for grinding corn

Preserving meat by drying and smoking. Fish were sun-dried.

The earliest known depiction of Nieuw Amsterdam: The Hartgers view, 1628

J. Clarence Davies Collection, The Museum of the City of New York

AND THEN THE DUTCH CAME

While Giovanni da Verrazano, for France, and Estavan Gomez, for Spain, had sailed separately into the waters of New York Bay many years earlier, the first European to explore thoroughly the waters around Manhattan Island was Henry Hudson. An Englishman in the service of the Dutch, he came in 1609, looking for a northwest passage to the Orient.

Instead, he found Manhattan Island, heavily wooded, with great stands of hickory, oak, and other hardwoods. Large clams and oysters, as well as much small game, provided food for the Indians, who, it was reported, were dressed in "Mantles of Feathers, and some in Skinnes of divers sorts of good Furres."

The lower tip of the island had many hills, which in later years would be leveled down, while the northern part was of a much greater height, with rocky outcroppings. Small streams, swamps, and ponds were all about. Robert Juet, an officer of Hudson's ship, wrote, "This is a very good Land to fall with, and a pleasant Land to see."

In 1613, Adriaen Block, who had been to the Hudson River in 1611, returned to spend the winter on Manhattan Island on a fur-trading venture. His ship, the *Tyger,* caught fire, and its remains beached at the site of today's World Trade Center Plaza. His men set to work felling trees and built a new ship, of about 18 tons, the first large work of building not by Indians on the Island of Manhattan. Block sailed this new boat into Long Island Sound and then on to Cape Cod.

The first permanent settlement, of huts "of the bark of trees," was begun in 1625. In 1626, on the 26th of May, Peter Minuit, as director general of the Dutch West India Company, bought the island from the Indians—all 20,000 acres—for 60 guilders' worth of cloth, trinkets, and beads. It came to about a penny for each 10 acres.

According to its charter, the Company was to "promote the settlement of fertile and uninhabited districts, and to do all that the service of those countries and the profit and increase of trade shall require." The whole purpose of New Amsterdam, as the tiny settlement on the tip of the island was named, was business.

Ten years passed before private ownership of property was allowed. Then these early Dutch built their own houses, of wood with thatched roofs. Soon brick houses with tile roofs became common. In 1642 the Dutch West India Company built a tavern to accommodate the increasing numbers of people visiting and passing through New Amsterdam. This tavern, which sold the Company's wine and brandy, had its own well and brewhouse. It became the City Hall in 1653.

From its very beginnings, the town had building and land disputes. In 1654 one Frederick Arentsen, a turner of wood, bought a lot from Teunis Tomasen, a mason, who agreed to take part of the price in chairs. Arentsen insisted on having the lot "delivered to him at thirteen inches to the foot."

6

New Amsterdam in 1655:
a town of about 120 houses
and a thousand people

Tomasen protested, in court.

On June 8, 1654, Teunis Tomasen was again in court, demanding 13 florins from Michael Paulisen, for whom he had built a chimney according to contract. The chimney smoked and Paulisen had had it pulled down and rebuilt by someone else, at a cost of two beavers. He said he did not owe the debt. The court decided in favor of Tomasen: since defendant Paulisen "at his own pleasure had the chimney taken down and rebuilt, plaintiff cannot be prejudiced thereby."

Many of these early chimneys were wooden, above thatched reed roofs. Fire was a constant danger to the town. If a house burned down due to the negligence of the owner, he was fined 25 guilders. Four fire-warders were appointed to inspect all chimneys: an unclean one was fined three guilders, with the money used to maintain the town's fire ladders, hooks, and leather water buckets.

Director General Peter Stuyvesant and his council, in 1647, ordered people who had been granted lots to put up proper buildings on them, or the lots would be taken from them and given to people who wanted to build and were in need of a proper place.

All sales of real estate had to be approved by the authorities to prevent fraud. Moreover, in 1655 a commission of four surveyed the entire town, with orders to straighten out streets and fix the location of lots. They not only laid out seventeen streets, they surveyed and fixed prices for the lots.

One building contract is described in I. N. Phelps Stokes' *The Iconography of Manhattan Island:* "Isaac de Foreest registers at the office of the provincial secretary a contract made between him and two English carpenters ... for building for him 'a dwelling house 30 feet long and 18 feet wide with 2 transom windows and 2 round windows, 4 girders with brackets and 2 free girders, one partition, one passage way tight inside and outside, and the entire house tight all around, to construct in the same house a pantry and three doors. Together with a tobacco house 60 feet long with the inside work: 1 small kitchen 20 feet long and 16 feet wide covered with clapboards, also an English chimney. Likewise to cover the dwelling house in such a manner as to be secure against water and snow.' The carpenters are to be paid 300 Carolus guilders for the job."

In the contract for another house, to be 60 feet long by 24 feet in width, Jan Damen agreed to provide builder Jeuriaen Hendricksen and his men "with provisions and drink until the work is completed," in addition to payment.

There was a distinctive feature about these houses that gave New Amsterdam the look of a typical Dutch town—the houses all had steep roofs and many had stepped gables rising right up to the roof peak.

Seal of the Town of New Amsterdam, 1654, showing the beaver, its trading lifeblood. In 1626, 7,258 beaver skins were shipped to Holland. In 10 years that number had doubled. Skins were used as money—one skin was worth eight guilders, a little more than three dollars. Indian wampum, which the Dutch called "seawan," was made from seashells. "Manhattan wampum," which had a value in Dutch coinage, was a superior polished seashell.

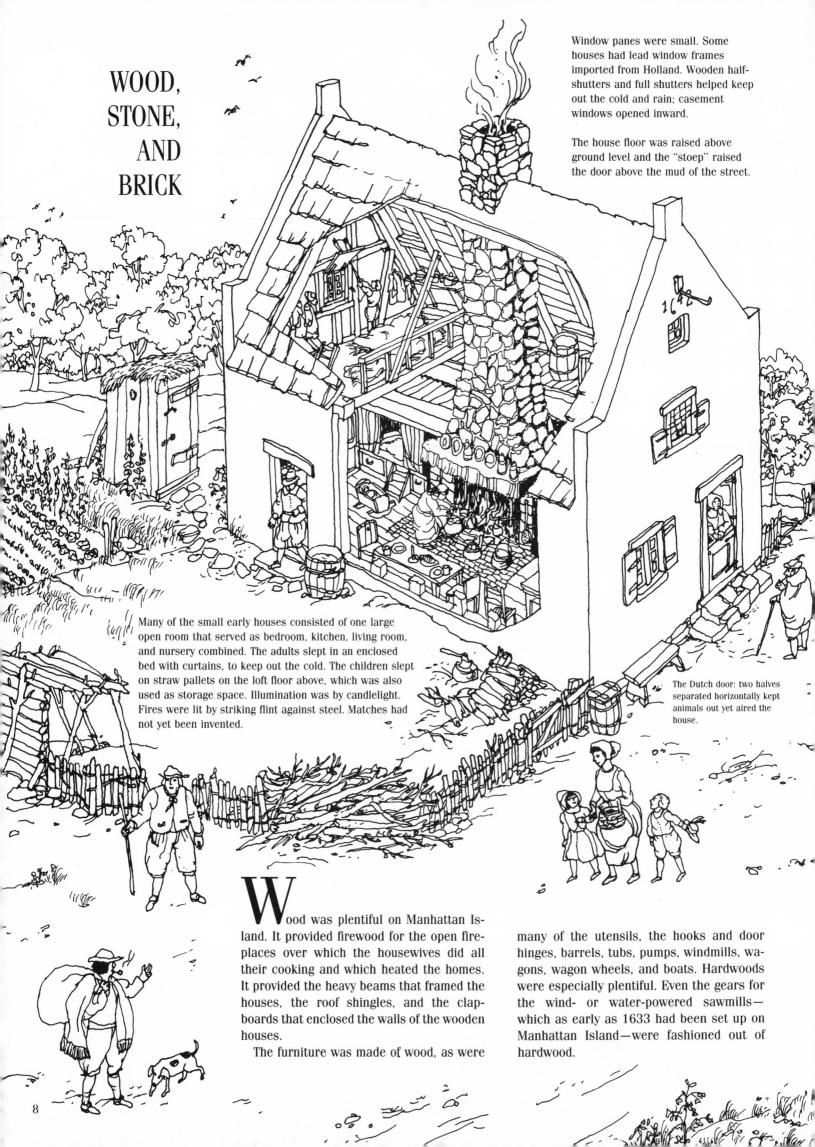

WOOD, STONE, AND BRICK

Window panes were small. Some houses had lead window frames imported from Holland. Wooden half-shutters and full shutters helped keep out the cold and rain; casement windows opened inward.

The house floor was raised above ground level and the "stoep" raised the door above the mud of the street.

Many of the small early houses consisted of one large open room that served as bedroom, kitchen, living room, and nursery combined. The adults slept in an enclosed bed with curtains, to keep out the cold. The children slept on straw pallets on the loft floor above, which was also used as storage space. Illumination was by candlelight. Fires were lit by striking flint against steel. Matches had not yet been invented.

The Dutch door: two halves separated horizontally kept animals out yet aired the house.

Wood was plentiful on Manhattan Island. It provided firewood for the open fireplaces over which the housewives did all their cooking and which heated the homes. It provided the heavy beams that framed the houses, the roof shingles, and the clapboards that enclosed the walls of the wooden houses.

The furniture was made of wood, as were many of the utensils, the hooks and door hinges, barrels, tubs, pumps, windmills, wagons, wagon wheels, and boats. Hardwoods were especially plentiful. Even the gears for the wind- or water-powered sawmills—which as early as 1633 had been set up on Manhattan Island—were fashioned out of hardwood.

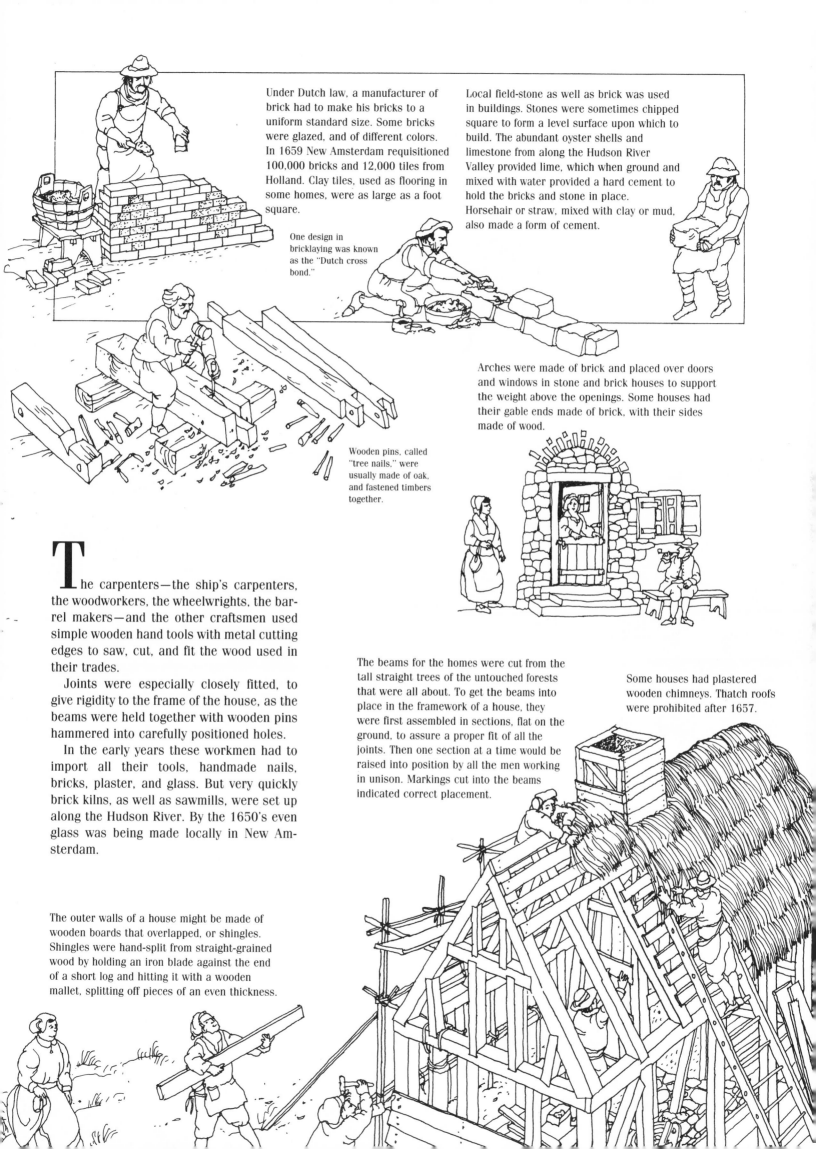

Under Dutch law, a manufacturer of brick had to make his bricks to a uniform standard size. Some bricks were glazed, and of different colors. In 1659 New Amsterdam requisitioned 100,000 bricks and 12,000 tiles from Holland. Clay tiles, used as flooring in some homes, were as large as a foot square.

One design in bricklaying was known as the "Dutch cross bond."

Local field-stone as well as brick was used in buildings. Stones were sometimes chipped square to form a level surface upon which to build. The abundant oyster shells and limestone from along the Hudson River Valley provided lime, which when ground and mixed with water provided a hard cement to hold the bricks and stone in place. Horsehair or straw, mixed with clay or mud, also made a form of cement.

Wooden pins, called "tree nails," were usually made of oak, and fastened timbers together.

Arches were made of brick and placed over doors and windows in stone and brick houses to support the weight above the openings. Some houses had their gable ends made of brick, with their sides made of wood.

The carpenters—the ship's carpenters, the woodworkers, the wheelwrights, the barrel makers—and the other craftsmen used simple wooden hand tools with metal cutting edges to saw, cut, and fit the wood used in their trades.

Joints were especially closely fitted, to give rigidity to the frame of the house, as the beams were held together with wooden pins hammered into carefully positioned holes.

In the early years these workmen had to import all their tools, handmade nails, bricks, plaster, and glass. But very quickly brick kilns, as well as sawmills, were set up along the Hudson River. By the 1650's even glass was being made locally in New Amsterdam.

The beams for the homes were cut from the tall straight trees of the untouched forests that were all about. To get the beams into place in the framework of a house, they were first assembled in sections, flat on the ground, to assure a proper fit of all the joints. Then one section at a time would be raised into position by all the men working in unison. Markings cut into the beams indicated correct placement.

Some houses had plastered wooden chimneys. Thatch roofs were prohibited after 1657.

The outer walls of a house might be made of wooden boards that overlapped, or shingles. Shingles were hand-split from straight-grained wood by holding an iron blade against the end of a short log and hitting it with a wooden mallet, splitting off pieces of an even thickness.

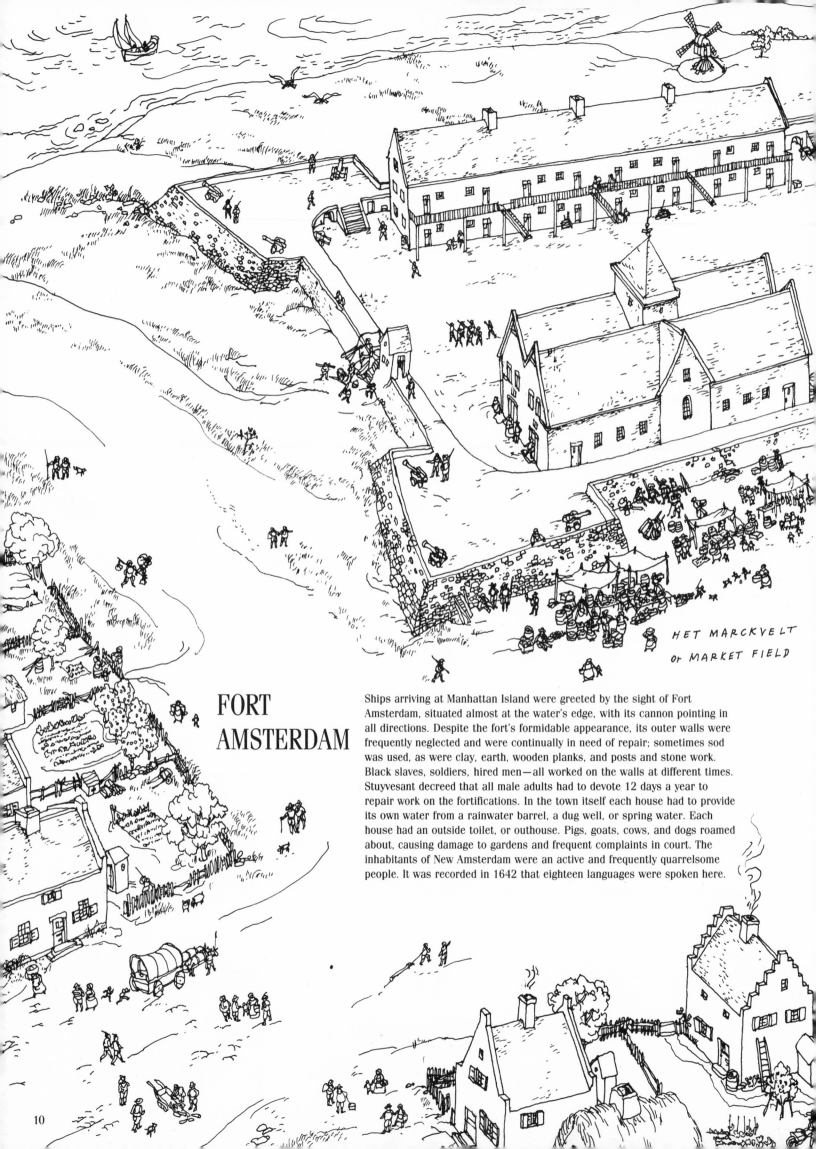

FORT AMSTERDAM

HET MARCKVELT
or MARKET FIELD

Ships arriving at Manhattan Island were greeted by the sight of Fort Amsterdam, situated almost at the water's edge, with its cannon pointing in all directions. Despite the fort's formidable appearance, its outer walls were frequently neglected and were continually in need of repair; sometimes sod was used, as were clay, earth, wooden planks, and posts and stone work. Black slaves, soldiers, hired men—all worked on the walls at different times. Stuyvesant decreed that all male adults had to devote 12 days a year to repair work on the fortifications. In the town itself each house had to provide its own water from a rainwater barrel, a dug well, or spring water. Each house had an outside toilet, or outhouse. Pigs, goats, cows, and dogs roamed about, causing damage to gardens and frequent complaints in court. The inhabitants of New Amsterdam were an active and frequently quarrelsome people. It was recorded in 1642 that eighteen languages were spoken here.

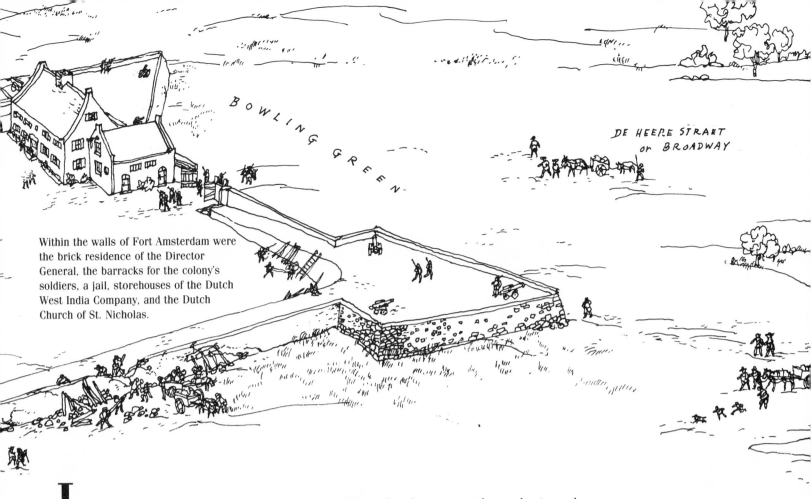

BOWLING GREEN

DE HEERE STRAET or BROADWAY

Within the walls of Fort Amsterdam were the brick residence of the Director General, the barracks for the colony's soldiers, a jail, storehouses of the Dutch West India Company, and the Dutch Church of St. Nicholas.

In 1647, Peter Stuyvesant arrived in New Amsterdam as the new director general of New Netherland, responsible for maintaining authority in all the land between the Delaware River in the south and the Connecticut River in the northeast.

New Amsterdam was the territory's biggest settlement and its center of government. The rest of New Netherland was mostly unbroken wilderness. A few trading posts had been established, notably Fort Orange—now Albany, New York.

These were turbulent years for the Dutch. English settlers were moving onto their land, Indians were sometimes on the warpath, Swedish settlers tried to colonize their Delaware River lands, and they were losing their large colony in Brazil to the Portuguese. In Europe, the Dutch and the English were at war from 1652 to 1654.

In New Amsterdam itself Peter Stuyvesant issued legislation and orders, administered justice, assigned land to the settlers, arranged the daily life of the town, and supervised the militia. His overbearing manner brought protests and, in 1653, a change for New Amsterdam: a city council and a government for the town, to be administered separately from the rest of New Netherland.

These Dutch were good merchants and traders but they had neglected their defenses. One day in 1664, four English ships anchored in the harbor and demanded the surrender of the town "Scituate upon the Island commonly knowne by the Name of Manhatoes."

Faced with this ultimatum, and with inadequate means of defense, the influential men of the town persuaded Stuyvesant to do the sensible thing and turn the town over to the English. Alone in his protestations and with less than a day's supply of cannon shot, the one-legged Stuyvesant surrendered. The English promptly took possession of the town and renamed it New York.

The changeover was an easy one—the Dutch and everyone else retained full property and inheritance rights, and business went right on as usual.

Nine years later, for a few months, the Dutch navy seized the town once more and renamed it New Orange. Finally, by treaty, the English again were in possession of all of New Netherland and the small town on the tip of Manhattan Island.

The Dutch, whose influence would be felt for many generations to come, had ruled for about 40 years. The population of New York was less than 2,000 people.

STUYVESANT SURRENDERS

1664: NEW AMSTERDAM IS NOW NEW YORK

The English had taken possession of a boisterous, contentious, and frequently dangerous town, renamed for their own Duke of York. Properly laid-out streets with their stepped roof houses, vegetable gardens, and grazing areas for domestic animals seemed secure behind the northern defensive "waal," which ran in a straight line from river to river.

Yet only nine years earlier, in 1655, nearly 2,000 Indians of the Hudson River tribes had gone on a three-day rampage, burning farms on Manhattan Island, Staten Island, and New Jersey, and threatening New Amsterdam itself. More than 100 Dutch settlers had been killed; more than 150 others—mostly women and children—had been captured and hundreds of cattle killed or driven off. The outlying settlers had fled to safety behind this wall of the fortified community. By 1699 the Indians had ceased to be a threat and the town had been built beyond the "waal," which was torn down. In 1709, by ordinance, a slave market was erected at the foot of "Wall" Street, "at which place all negro and Indian slaves to be let out to hire, or to be sold, took their stand." Today's Wall Street area is the financial center of the city and the nation.

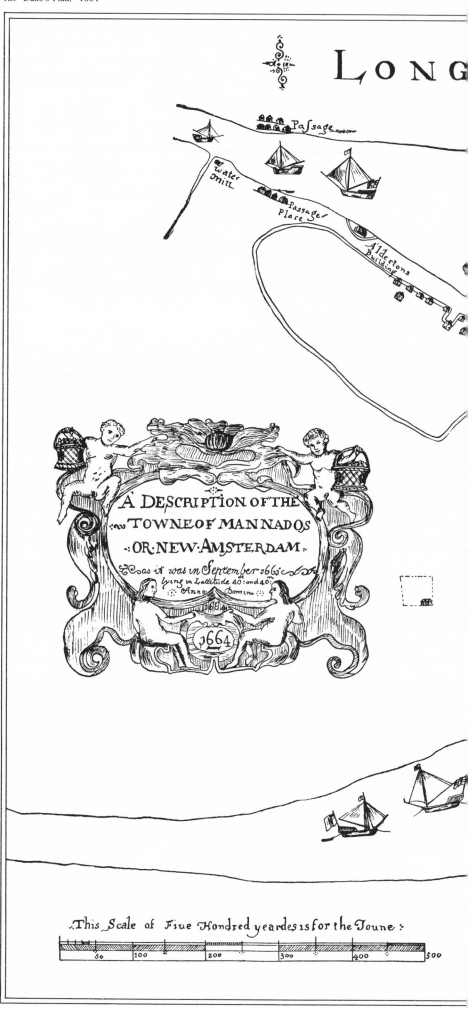

Reaching into the heart of the town is the Dutch-dug canal.
Filled in, it is today's Broad Street. so named for its width.

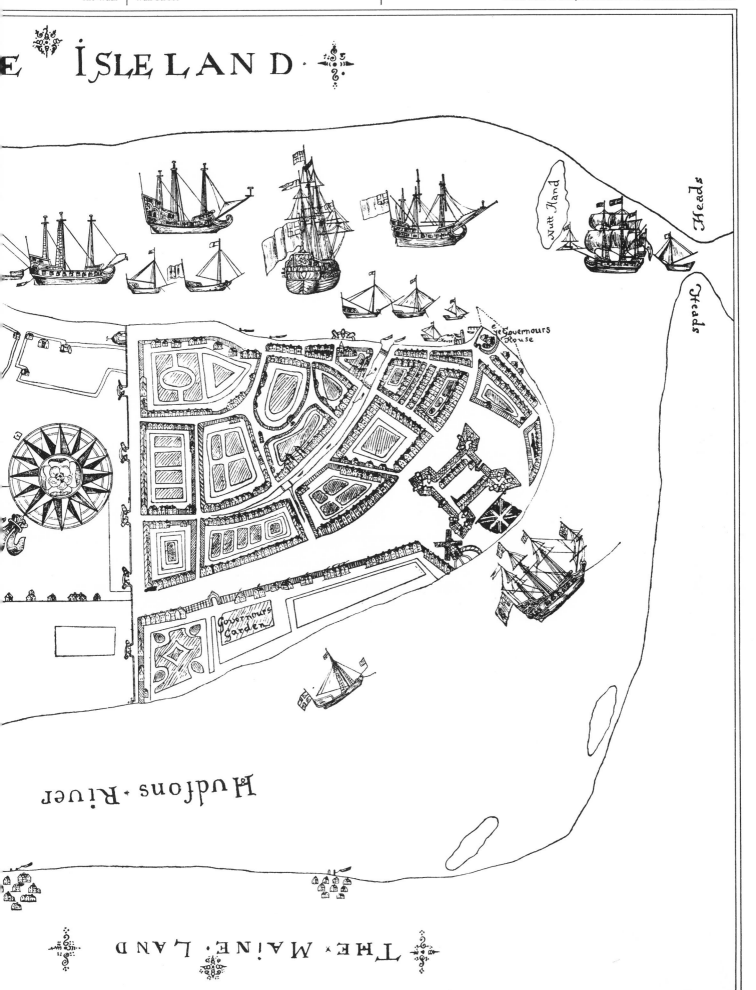

E ÍSLE LAND ·

Nutt Iland

Heads

Heads

ye Gouernours House

House

Gouernours Garden

Hudfons · Riuer

The · MAiNE · LAND

Fire was the great destroyer of early New York. In September 1776, only days after Washington's army had retreated from Manhattan Island, a disastrous fire swept through the city, leaving one-fourth of it in ruins. St. Paul's Chapel, at Broadway and Fulton Street, survived that fire and is today the oldest public building, in continuous use, in the city. It was built in 1766 of Manhattan-mica-schist and brownstone.

COLONIAL NEW YORK: 1664–1783

New York grew slowly under the English: from 1,500 people in 1665 to nearly 25,000 in 1775. It lived through the French and Indian War, epidemics of smallpox and yellow fever, lack of adequate pure water, appalling sanitary conditions, occupation by military forces, and the American Revolution of 1776–83.

Through it all, buildings were torn down, or leveled by fire. Some of the early Dutch stepped-roof buildings would last until the Great Fire of 1845, but the city was now English and it took on a new look as it prospered and expanded.

Areas of the city began to be associated with specific activities: a shipping and waterfront area, a business district, warehouses, a light manufacturing center. The residential areas were divided according to wealth and social position. Obnoxious trades such as tanning and the slaughtering of animals were kept at the far edges of the ever-growing town.

Travel was slow and difficult, hindering the northward expansion of the town. When pressure for building space became insistent, the town even sold lots under the East River. Merchants bought the lots, filled them in with dirt and rubble, and built a new business district. Today, that once underwater area is Water Street, two blocks inland.

During the American Revolution, New York City became the key military position controlling the Hudson River and separating the New England Colonies from the Southern Colonies. As the vital strategic center for fighting the rebellious Americans, New York was occupied by the British for the entire seven years of the war.

War itself came to Manhattan Island on September 15, 1776, when a British naval barrage drove Washington's men from positions along Kip's Bay, between present-day 34th and 42nd streets. Washington reorganized his army at Harlem Heights and held off a British attack there. But within weeks he was outflanked and abandoned the island, leaving the British in control.

Beginning in that year, 1776, New York became a camp for the British army, a prison for captured American soldiers, a haven for runaway slaves, and the refuge for thousands of Loyalists who opposed the Revolution and had left their homes elsewhere in the Colonies for the safety of the city.

It was a city in turmoil, and it was a desperate time for its inhabitants. When the war ended in 1783 with the Americans victorious, the defeated British officers and soldiers, and perhaps as many as 35,000 Loyalists and free blacks, passed through the embarkation port of New York City. Some went north into Canada, some to the West Indies, and some went back to England.

The exodus took eight months, and then on November 25, 1783: "in the Morning the American Troops marched from Haerlem, to the Bowery Lane. They remained there until about One o'Clock, when the British Troops left the Posts in The Bowery, and the American troops marched into, and took possession of the City."

New York city was prostrate—in ruins from Trinity Church to the Battery. Its population was half of what it had been seven years earlier. There was a desperate shortage of housing and of buildings of any kind.

This 1767 map shows the city's old defense fort still standing on the tip of the island. By 1789 most of it had been torn down, allowing use of the dirt to enlarge the Battery, and Broadway to be extended to the water's edge.

Street names in the city often underwent name changes in the early years, sometimes for patriotic reasons. After the Revolution, King's College, which had been founded in 1754, became Columbia College, now Columbia University. King Street became Pine Street, Duke Street became Stone Street, and Little Queen Street became Cedar Street.

Manhattan's largest natural freshwater pond was the Collect Pond, called by the Dutch "Der Kolek"—"Rippling Water." Once full of fish and fed by springs of great purity from a depth of 60 feet, it was surrounded by hills and drained into both the East River and the Hudson. Indians left mounds of shells there.

Tanneries, slaughterhouses, and breweries all helped to pollute the pond; by 1815 the hills had been leveled and the pond was filled in.

15

MECHANICKS, SLAVES, AND APPRENTICES

New York began the task of recovery. As a seaport city of many nationalities it had always attracted people who were eager to show their worth in commerce, the professions, and as craftsmen. It was a city of opportunity. It was also a city of great contrasts.

There were black slaves—14 percent of the population. There were indentured servants and there were apprentices.

Laborers worked from sunup to sundown, with few comforts. Unless they owned land or tenements worth at least £20 in their own or their wife's name they could not vote for city office holders. They also had to be twenty-one, a freeman of the city for the preceding three months, and have had lived in the ward where they voted for at least one month.

The construction workers who had the sheer physical job of rebuilding the city still depended on their own muscle power. They were aided by block and tackle, wheels, pulleys, counterweights, and the pulling power of horses and oxen to move and to raise heavy timbers, brick and mortar, and large blocks of stone. Until 1786 even the nails were handmade.

In England, James Watt had invented his steam engine. In Manhattan, in 1796, an inventor experimented with a steam-powered paddle boat in the city's Collect Pond. But at the end of the 18th century, physical strength was still the force that built the city's new mansions, warehouses, government buildings, and other structures.

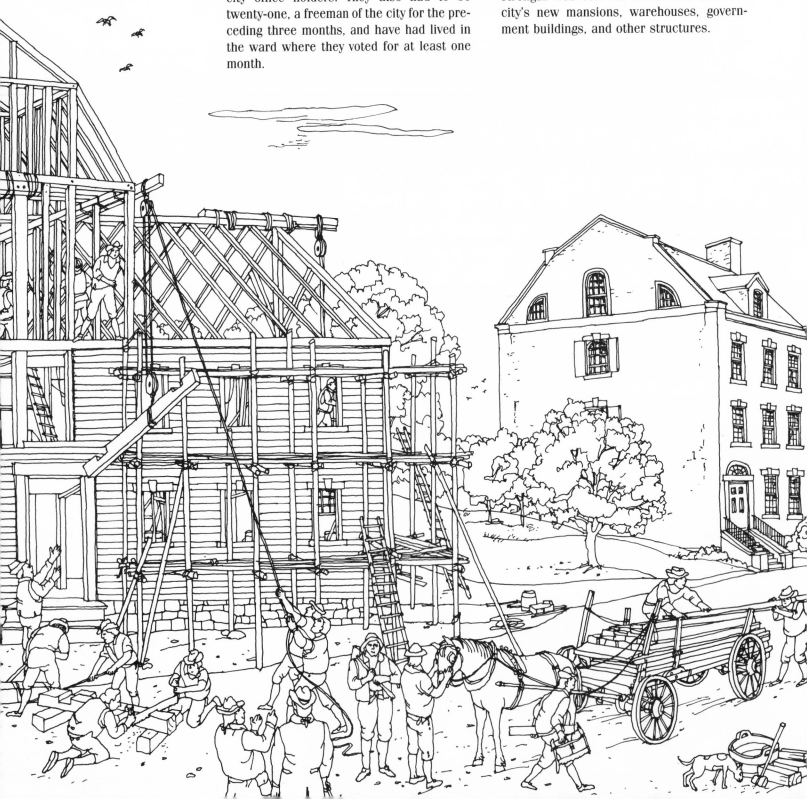

The free laboring man now formed fraternal organizations for particular trades. These were created for social reasons, to improve working conditions, and to help fellow workers in time of illness—even to provide funeral expenses. More than thirty skilled trades were included in The New York Mechanick Society.

THE APPRENTICE

Some families paid for their children to be apprentices. Others, orphans or children unable to care for themselves, were bound to a master for a specified number of years—to live with, and work for, the master while learning his trade or skill.

In 1788 an act was passed to regulate the treatment of apprentices:

"by which it was provided that no master should compel his apprentice to sign any bond or make oath not to set up the same trade, under penalty of £40 fine. An infant was to be bound only until 21 years of age except in the case of binding for the payment of passage money [from Europe], under which circumstances the age limit was extended to 24 years. On the other hand, an apprentice refusing to do his duty was to be committed to the Bridewell [the jail for the poor] until willing to work, and those absenting themselves from work were to serve double the time of their absence or to make satisfaction in some other way."

THE INDENTURED SERVANT

To secure passage from Europe to America, penniless people had to work for those who bought their passage, for a specified number of years. Many ran away before their time was up; rewards were offered for their capture and return.

THE SLAVE

Eleven black slaves were brought to New Amsterdam by the Dutch West India Company in 1626 and their labor helped build Fort Amsterdam. Thereafter blacks as slaves were a part of Manhattan labor and life until July 4, 1827, when New York State declared all slaves within the state to be free.

A slave market existed in the 1700's at the foot of Wall Street. Advertisements for the sale of male and female slaves, with rewards for the return of runaway slaves, were frequent all through the 1700's, while some other owners manumitted—or freed—their slaves. There were freed slaves who were granted land in Manhattan by the Dutch West India Company as early as the mid-1600's.

In 1788 an act was passed by the state regulating the treatment of slaves. Among other things, it provided that:

"every negro, mulatto, or mestee who was a slave at that time, should remain so for life, unless manumitted, and that the children of slave women should be slaves. Selling any slave brought into the state after the 1st of June 1785 was punishable by a fine of £100 and the freeing of the slave. . . . Employing, or harboring a slave without his master's permission was forbidden under a penalty of £5 for every twenty-four hours he was detained up to his value, and if the slave were lost the person harboring him was liable for his value. No one could trade with a slave, without his master's permission, under penalty of forfeiting £5 and three time the value of the goods traded, while selling liquor to a slave, without the owner's permission, was punishable by 40 shillings fine."

Additional provisions of the act stipulated the conditions for freeing slaves: they could not become the responsibility of the city due to age or infirmity, and they had to be capable of supporting themselves.

CAPITAL OF THE NEW NATION: 1785–1790

Seal of the City of New York, 1784

On the 23rd of April, 1789, George Washington made a spectacular entry into New York on a specially built barge, magnificently festooned and rowed across the water from the New Jersey shore by thirteen men in white uniforms. He landed near the foot of Wall Street. Salutes of thirteen guns were fired by boats and shore batteries. The ships, docks, and streets were thick with cheering people.

George Washington had arrived in New York to take up residence and, on the 30th of April, to take the oath of office as the first president of the United States. New York was the capital of the new nation.

It was a short-lived honor. The Constitution had given Congress the power to establish the permanent seat of government—which it did, in the building of a new city for government affairs only: Washington, D.C.

New York was a city of trade, business, and commerce. It was now the largest city in the nation. With its great natural harbor, and freed from the war and its restrictions, it was rapidly overtaking Boston and Philadelphia as the busiest shipping port in the nation. Its merchants were again sailing to far-off lands, even to the tea-ports of China.

Looking up Broad Street toward Wall Street and Old Federal Hall, where, on the upper balcony, Washington took the oath as president. After use as New York's City Hall, the building was torn down in 1812.

Watercolor by George Holland, 1797. I. N. Phelps Stokes Collection, The New York Public Library. Aster, Lenox and Tilden Foundations.

18

ew York City began to expand in size and in population. The census of 1790 for the city and county listed 8,500 white males older than 16 years, 5,907 males under sixteen, 15,254 white females, 1,101 other free persons, and 2,364 slaves.

The city streets were narrow and dirty, and many of them were impassable. New laws imposed a fine of 40 shillings on any householder not keeping his walk and road under repair. The footpath on each side of the street had to be one-fifth the width of the street, paved with brick or flatstone, and curbed. The cartway between had to be arched and paved.

Rents were high. There were now about 4,200 houses in New York. Although the law stated that no house, except one of brick or stone, could be built south of present-day Duane Street, wooden frame buildings with brick fronts were not uncommon.

The house of General Henry Knox, for sale in 1789, was described as being "a four storey brick house on the west side of Broadway, 31½ feet wide by 60 feet deep, containing two rooms of thirty feet in length, one of twenty-six feet, three of twenty-three feet, and two of twenty feet, besides four other rooms with fireplaces, and four smaller ones without them. On the ground floor . . . a large servants-hall . . . a kitchen 20 ft. by 30 ft. in dimension. In the rear of the house there was a piazza thirty feet long by ten feet wide and the back yard contained a good well, cistern, and ash-house. The lots ran back about 500 feet to the end of a wharf on Greenwich Street, and upon one of them, fronting upon Greenwich Street, was a coach-house twenty-eight feet four inches wide."

Pigs still roamed the streets and added to the dirt and confusion. Many households kept all manner of livestock—horses, fowl, pigs, goats. Any goat found roaming the city at large became the property of any person who seized it.

New York City's population had reached 60,515 by 1800. The city was being built up as far north as Canal Street; on the Hudson River side it was reaching out toward Greenwich Village.

New York's seaport streets, shown here about 1797, at the corner of Wall and Water streets, were the scene of most of the city's activities and the center of its financial success. To support its trade the city's merchants built, repaired, and supplied many different types of sailing ships, and in their warehouses they dealt with most of the other ports of the world.

The Tontine Coffee House, by Francis Guy. Courtesy of The New-York Historical Society, New York City.

1811: A PLAN FOR GROWTH

In 1806 the City Council realized that New York needed to plan for its future growth. Industry was taking over more and more residential space in lower Manhattan, while north of Canal Street building lots were being staked out in any empty space. Residential housing was going up on the nearest open land. The development of the island was getting out of control. A commission was appointed to decide what to do.

In 1811, the commissioners presented their "plan," shown on the map below. They observed: "To some it may be a matter of surprise that the whole island has not been laid out as a city. To others it may be a subject of merriment that the Commissioners have provided space for a greater population than is collected at any spot on this side of China. They have in this respect been governed by the shape of the ground. It is not improbable that considerable numbers may be collected at Harlem before the high hills to the southward of it shall be built upon as a city; and it is improbable that (for centuries to come) the grounds north of Harlem Flat will be covered with houses."

At the time, the "plan" was the most far-reaching decision ever taken by the city in shaping its own future. Manhattan Island was now planned as a rectangular grid with wide avenues running north-south, and all streets above 14th Street running east-west from river to river and perpendicular to the avenues.

Avenues were numbered from 1 to 12—four short avenues were lettered A, B, C, and D. The streets were numbered as far north as 155th Street.

No consideration was given to existing roads, property divisions, or the natural variations in the land. Only Broadway, as a major artery already in use, continued as a diagonal road cutting across the grid. Broadway, which got its name from the Dutch *herre wegh*—their "broad way" in lower Manhattan—followed an early Indian trail. The streets below 14th Street, already existing in an irregular manner, were to remain as they were. From now on, New Yorkers would proceed to build at an ever-increasing pace, but always within the confines of the grid plan.

Most of the island was still open land, with farms, squatters, and large estates. There were also many small villages in the undeveloped sections of the island, each with its own name: Greenwich (Village), Chelsea, Yorkville, Murray Hill, Harlem, Carmansville,

How the city grew . . 1650 . . 1750 . . . 1800 . . 1840 . . 1850 . . . By 1864 more than half the city lived above 14th Street.

Central Park was not yet an idea— the city did not acquire the land for the park until 1856.

The Bridges Map, or Randel Survey, 1811. J. Clarence Davies Collection, The Museum of the City of New York.

CITY HALL

The Common Council of April 18, 1803, resolved that, at the laying of City Hall's cornerstone, "the Mayor draw on the City Treasurer for the sum of fifty dollars, and present it to John McComb where the ceremonies are performed, as a compliment to the workmen."

The building's cost was recorded: "The sums expended on this noble superstructure were: from 1803 to 1814 $538,733.45."

Bloomingdale, Manhattanville, Harsenville.

The new City Hall, designed by architects Joseph Mangin and John McComb, was completed in 1812, with the south front and sides built of marble. According to folklore, the north side, which is the back of the building, was of more ordinary red sandstone because the city would never grow beyond that uptown side of the building.

Horses and carriages sometimes competed with livestock, but the new streets were now graded. Collect Pond had been filled in and houses had been built over it. Sanitation was primitive and there were frequent outbreaks of contagious diseases.

Whether rich or poor, all New Yorkers shared problems which had to be solved if the city was to increase in size and prosper. The city had to have a reliable source of pure drinking water, a safe sewage system, and a means of getting about more quickly and more easily.

The grid stopped at 155th Street in Harlem.

The highest point in the city is 280 feet above sea level, at 184th Street and Fort Washington Avenue.

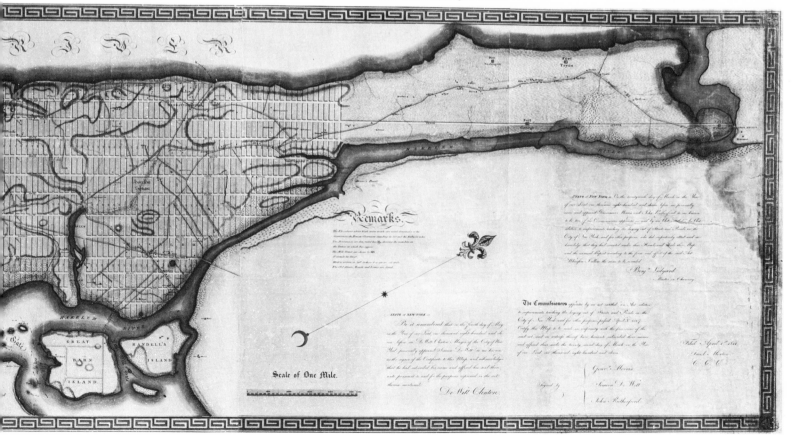

POPULATION PRESSURES: 1811–1850

The problem of getting around the city with ease and speed was not about to be solved easily. Travel in the early 1800's was by horse and carriage—unpredictable and irregular.

Not until 1830 did the first horse-drawn street railroad begin regular service as far north as 15th Street, although by that time a stagecoach was already making the trip from the Battery to Greenwich Village—and taking one hour to get there.

Yearly epidemics caused great distress. Severe outbreaks of mosquito-borne yellow fever killed hundreds yearly. In 1832 Asiatic cholera made its first appearance in New York: 3,500 died. Those who could flee congested lower Manhattan did so. Greenwich Village, already a favorite place in which to live, began to grow in size, and the city as a whole began to move northward. Its population in 1820 reached 120,000—double that of 1800.

The city was growing enormously, financially as well as physically. It weathered the war of 1812–14 with England, when its trade was cut off, and the nation's financial panic of 1837, when all but three of the city's banks failed.

The opening of the Erie Canal in 1825 was a powerful financial impetus to the growth of the city. When first proposed it was considered an act of folly—to carve a canal through 362 miles of wilderness from Albany to Buffalo, making possible a journey by water from New York City to the Great Lakes and to the great American Midwest. There were no highways to that area, and for another quarter-century there would be no railroads. New York was to be the booming transfer center for all goods and travel to the West.

With the canal it took only a third of the time to go from New York to the Midwest and at a twentieth the cost. Fortunes were made by New Yorkers. New villas and mansions were built along Broadway, still a residential street, and along Fifth Avenue, in 1830 built up as far north as 21st Street.

The city, then as now, was continually tearing down and rebuilding. Former mayor Philip Hone wrote in 1831: "The city is now undergoing its usual annual metamorphosis; many stores and houses are being pulled down, and others altered, to make every inch of ground productive to its utmost extent." Eight years later he noted: "The spirit of pulling down and building up is abroad. The whole of New York is rebuilt about once in ten years."

Most of the houses for single families were row houses attached to each other. In 1833 the first tenement, intended exclusively for tenant families, was built. Houses by then were also being built of a brownstone—actually a stone with the name "Jersey freestone."

By 1840 the population had passed the 300,000 mark. The city was growing too fast. Its inhabitants were overwhelming its resources.

The city solved its water problems with one of the great engineering triumphs of the time: the construction of the Croton Reservoir and Aqueduct. This brought clean, pure water to the city from a massive dam on the Croton River, far to the north. Carried only by the force of gravity, the water traveled

In 1807 a historic event took place on New York's Hudson River. Robert Fulton's steam-powered boat, the *Clermont*, made a round trip of 290 miles between New York and Albany at a speed of five miles an hour. First developed in England, the steam engine was a new source of energy. Its development would mean fundamental changes in the life of New York City.

through a 45-mile-long tunnel to Manhattan. On July 4, 1842, the entire city celebrated as this fresh Croton River water filled the newly built reservoir at Fifth Avenue and 42nd Street.

This ready supply of Croton water promised help in combating one of the city's constant dangers: fire. The Great Fire of 1835—the worst in the city's history—had destroyed more than 670 buildings in lower Manhattan. But even with the new reservoir a fire in 1845 again swept lower Manhattan, this time with the loss of nearly 300 buildings and at a cost of many millions of dollars.

Also, with a reliable water supply, indoor plumbing became practical. In addition, by 1850 more than 100 miles of sewer pipes had been installed in the city streets.

Central heating, another innovation that was improving city life, was being built into the more prosperous homes.

It was also becoming easier to get about the city. By 1850 a horse-drawn "railroad" regularly carried passengers all the way from City Hall to a depot on 42nd Street. The streets there were unpaved and most of the land nearby was empty, but the city was expanding into those rectangular street blocks that the commissioners had wisely planned for, years earlier.

New York was called a "semi-barbarous metropolis," and no wonder—it could never catch up with its growth in population. While the city was struggling to accommodate its own people, immigrants were arriving by boat from Europe in record numbers—212,796 newcomers in 1850 alone. The city kept getting bigger but, despite the increasing population pressures, was becoming more livable.

Manhattan was about to undergo a revolution in the way its buildings were built, in their size and height, and in their effect on how the city looked.

In this 1849 view of New York, looking south from Union Square and 14th Street, the most prominent features of the city's skyline are the church spires and ships' masts, with one six-story building in the foreground.

J. Clarence Davies Collection, The Museum of the City of New York

THE CAST-IRON BUILDING

In 1849, James Bogardus, a New Yorker, built a factory for himself at Duane and Centre Streets. It was described in 1858 as "the first complete cast-iron edifice ever erected in America, or in the world."

Bogardus explained his method of cast-iron building construction in a sixteen-page booklet: "The cast-iron frame of the building rests upon sills which are cast in sections of any required length. These sills, by the aid of the planing machine, are made of equal thickness, so as not to admit of any variation throughout the whole: they are laid upon a stone foundation, and are fastened together with bolts. On the joint of the sills stand the columns, all exactly equal in height, and having both their ends faced in a turning lathe so as to make them perfectly plane and parallel; and each column is firmly bolted to the ends of the two adjacent sills on which it rests. These columns support another series of sills, fascias, or cornices, in section, of the same length as the former, but of greater height, according to the design of the architect: they are separately made of equal dimensions, by the planing machine, and are bolted to the columns, and to each other, in the same manner as before. On these again stand another row of columns, and on these columns rests another series of fascias or cornices; and so on, continually, for any required number of stories: the ends of the columns and fascias having been all previously drilled so as to receive the bolts. The arches are bolted, and the spaces between the columns are filled up with windows, doors, and panels, which may be ornamented to any taste."

Since antiquity, buildings had been constructed of stone, brick, wood, and concrete, requiring massive walls and foundations to support the entire weight of the whole structure. Each floor that was added to a building required an increase in the width of the walls at their base, thus limiting every building's height to the width of wall that was practical.

Bogardus' cast-iron frame construction, with his idea of "iron flooring to be supported by iron beams in combination with . . . sectional truss girders," was one early step in the development of the metal skeleton-supported building.

Front and back elevations, and a section of a Bogardus Iron Building, with his method of bolting together the interchangeable columns, beams, and ornamental decoration

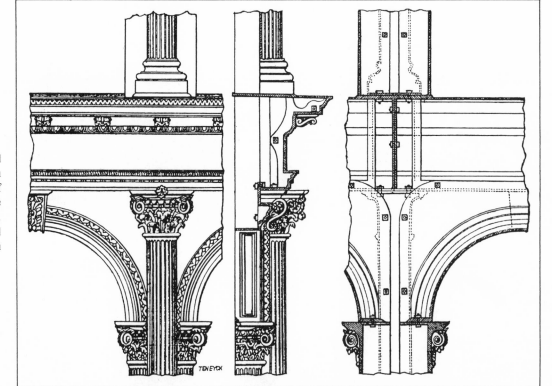

It was a mass-produced, prefabricated structure that "could be erected with extraordinary facility . . . adjusted and secured by the most ignorant workman . . . the building cannot fail to be perpendicular and firm . . . it may be raised to a height vastly greater than by any other known means."

People thought the cast-iron buildings would crash of their own weight, or a fire would melt the structure, or it would be hit by lightning, or the metal would expand and contract and cause the decay of the building. But New York's builders realized the advantages of the speed and economy with which a prefabricated cast-iron building could be erected. They enthusiastically put up cast-iron exteriors, and opened up their interior spaces with delicate iron columns as floor supports. But they still built brick walls behind the cast-iron fronts and used wooden floors and beams.

Cast-iron construction permitted a wide variety of fanciful, inexpensive ornamentation. Faces, flowers, ornate eaves, twisted ropes, scrolls, arches, and columns were all cast in iron.

New York City led the nation in the manufacture and construction of cast-iron buildings. Even today, more than a century after they were built and after thousands have been taken down, almost 300 such buildings are still in use in Manhattan—their cast-iron fronts adding variety and interest to the city's architecture.

Standardized cast-iron buildings, such as this example, could be ordered from Daniel Badger's *Catalog of Architectural Iron Works,* New York City, 1865.

ARCHITECTURAL IRON WORKS,__ NEW-YORK.

THE "SAFETY HOISTER" RAISES THE ROOF

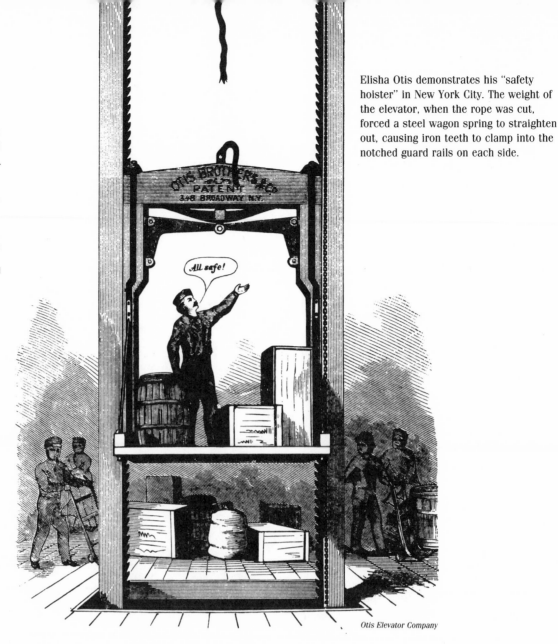

Elisha Otis demonstrates his "safety hoister" in New York City. The weight of the elevator, when the rope was cut, forced a steel wagon spring to straighten out, causing iron teeth to clamp into the notched guard rails on each side.

Otis Elevator Company

Cast-iron buildings had the potential to rise above the customary five or six floors of mid-1800 structures. But there was a real restriction on how high a building would be built—people still had to walk up and down the stairs.

Then, in 1854, Elisha Otis demonstrated his "safety hoister" to an astonished public at New York's Crystal Palace—America's first World's Fair. In a dramatic display of confidence in his invention, while riding his steam-powered elevator he cut the rope which raised and lowered him. Instead of crashing to the bottom, the hoist platform on which he was standing stopped where it was. Otis had invented an elevator braking device.

Steam-powered hoists had been in use before, but this was the world's first practical and safe elevator. Otis continued to improve his elevator as his competitors built their own systems, some driven by counter-weights, vertical screw drives, or hydraulic systems. But the "safety hoister" had become the "safe elevator." No longer would buildings be limited to a height that stairways made practical.

Otis's steam engine, to power his elevator

Larger buildings were being put up higher than ever before, now that the top floors could be reached by elevator and rented as easily as lower floors. A spirit of rivalry seemed to find an outlet in the construction of the city's tallest, or biggest, or most innovative building.

By 1875 the Western Union Building on lower Broadway would reach the height of 10 stories, only to be surpassed by the spire added atop the new Tribune Building that same year.

The 10-story James Gordon Bennet Building on Nassau Street had its top four floors of cast-iron construction added years after the original building had been put up.

By 1889–90, when it was built, the Pulitzer Building, on Manhattan's Park Row, was the tallest office building in the world, at 349 feet. The interior of this building was supported by wrought-iron columns, with the weight of the building supported by very thick outer walls of masonry, in some places more than nine feet thick.

Under the building were great cavernous spaces for equipment plus storage for 500 tons of paper. The electric plant with the "energy of 8,500 incandescent lamps" was in a vault under the sidewalk. The building's boiler room was outside its walls, and its basement was made of solid granite. It was one of the last tall buildings of its kind to be built in New York City.

Builders and architects everywhere were being challenged by new ideas. In England, steel was being made by the new Bessemer process. It was more versatile, harder, and stronger than cast iron or wrought iron. In New York, a method of fireproofing metal beams was being perfected. In America and in Europe engineers were undertaking the building of spectacular new bridges to accommodate the steam railroads expanding across the continents.

The metal beams and arches of these bridges had proved capable of spanning great distances and supporting heavy loads and weights. The load capabilities of the metals under weight, the stresses of shock, and the extremes of temperature and wind velocity were all becoming part of the builder's new technology. What could be done horizontally would have consequences for what could now be built vertically.

In 1955, the once proud Pulitzer Building was demolished to make way for a new roadway approach to the Brooklyn Bridge. In its last days it provided four months of temporary office space for Mayor Robert Wagner and his staff. They had moved there, just across the street, to escape the noise created by the refacing of City Hall's exterior stonework.

Engraving by Charles Graham, Harper's Weekly

Technology can tell you how to build, but to have a vision of what you want to build—something larger and more complex than anyone has ever done before—and then to actually build it, requires a unique person.

For thousands of years the world has looked at the pyramids of Egypt with awe. Their size still astonishes us. We wonder what manner of man conceived of such colossal undertakings.

The builder of the first pyramid, the "step" pyramid, was a man of great daring, imagination, and ingenuity. We know his name, Imhotep, and he was worshiped by the Egyptians as a demigod.

The master builders of the world, in all the different cultures and in all the different historical eras of human endeavor, have built to the limits of their knowledge and the capabilities of their time—and then went beyond those limits.

Manhattan has been built by such men of daring, who upon seeing a challenge took it, and by so doing transformed the city. Two such builders were John Roebling, and after his death, his son, Washington Roebling.

The proposal of John Roebling in 1867 to build the world's largest suspension bridge, the Brooklyn Bridge, across the East River to connect Manhattan with Brooklyn was such a challenge. It was the enormous size of his proposed bridge that excited one's imagination and raised some doubts that it could ever be built.

John Roebling had no such doubts. He had already built suspension bridges, but none to compare with the one he now proposed.

It would be more than a mile long.

Two massive stone towers would have to be built in the turbulent East River. Above water they would be taller than any building yet built in Manhattan.

To reach solid footing beneath the riverbed, men would have to dig from inside an enormous watertight box, called a "caisson," which was about a third the size of a football field and would sink deeper into the river bottom as the men dug. The digging would present many perilous problems. Eventually the depth from high-water mark to foundation bottom on the Manhattan side would be 78 feet, 6 inches.

One massive stone "anchorage" would have to be built on the Manhattan side and one on the Brooklyn side, weighing 60,000 tons apiece and each as tall as an eight-story building.

Four steel-wire cables, each more than 15 inches thick, would be embedded in the Manhattan anchorage, supported across the tops of the two towers, and embedded in the anchorage on the Brooklyn side. Each cable would weigh over 1.7 million pounds and be made of 3,515 miles of twisted strands of wire. From these cables, others would hang down vertically, some diagonally, to support the 85-foot-wide bridge span that would arch at midpoint 130 feet above the East River—high enough for the tallest sailing ship to pass under.

The roadway would have two levels: one for vehicular traffic, and above that an elevated promenade, for pedestrians. Roebling designed the openings through the two towers as soaring Gothic arches more than 100 feet high.

THE WONDER OF THE IMAGINATION

The two arched towers of the Brooklyn Bridge are shown at nearly full height. The steam-powered boom derricks, held in place by guy wires, raise the great granite blocks—some eight tons apiece—to the top of the anchorage, shown here being built. On one occasion, as a granite block was being raised, a guy wire gave way. Two derricks fell from the tower, two men were killed, and several workers were injured.

Iron anchor bars, set into the masonry and fastened to iron anchor plates embedded in the base of the anchorage, tie down the cables that will support the bridge deck. Workmen in the foreground are demolishing old buildings to make way for the approach to the bridge.

Harper's Weekly: *drawn by W. P. Snyder*

THE SKILL OF THE ENGINEER

John Roebling never saw any of his bridge built. His foot was accidentally crushed while he was surveying the waterfront where it was to be built, and the resulting infection killed him.

John Roebling had the vision of the Brooklyn Bridge; his son, Washington Roebling, had the engineering training to build it.

There was now a Society of Civil Engineers, founded in New York City in 1852. Its members specialized in constructing buildings and bridges, and studied the scientific use of materials employed in their profession. Young Roebling had graduated from the first school in the nation to provide engineering training, Rensselaer Polytechnic Institute in Troy, New York. As a Union officer during the Civil War he had built bridges under very difficult circumstances. He had been to Europe to study the innovations in engineering and metallurgy being used there, especially how Europeans built constructions underwater.

The concept of the bridge had been carefully planned, but young Roebling would have to invent solutions to problems of construction that had never been tried before. One problem for which there seemed to be no solution was the "bends." Its crippling effects afflicted some men, but not others. It was caused by too rapid decompression as the workmen went from the compressed air of an underwater caisson back into the natural atmosphere of everyday life.

Harper's Weekly, *1870*

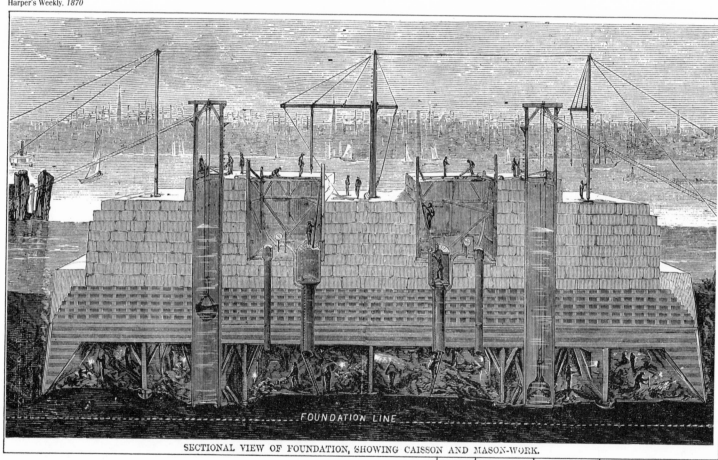

FOUNDATION LINE

SECTIONAL VIEW OF FOUNDATION, SHOWING CAISSON AND MASON-WORK.

AIR LOCK • SUPPLY SHAFT • WATER SHAFT • PARTITION

THE FOUNDATIONS FOR THE BROOKLYN BRIDGE

The problem: to devise a way for men to work underwater while excavating a rectangular area—172 feet by 102 feet, about one-third the size of a football field—down through the mud and debris of the riverbed to a solid base upon which each bridge tower would then rest and be built upon a perfectly level foundation.

The solution: build an upside-down wooden and iron box, open on the bottom, rest it on the riverbed, and keep the water from flooding in by increasing the air pressure within the work space.

As the granite blocks of the bridge tower are placed onto the box, or caisson, the increasing weight will keep pressing the caisson into the river bottom. When the men have dug down so that the caisson has reached a solid bottom—44 feet, 6 inches below high tide on the Brooklyn side; 78 feet, 6 inches on the Manhattan side—cement will be poured through the SUPPLY SHAFTS to fill the entire work area, and the bridge tower will be one solid mass resting on a solid base. Steam-powered boom derricks are on top of the granite blocks.

The AIR LOCK was the means by which men could enter or leave the work chamber, which was always under the pressure of compressed air to keep the river from flooding in. Men entered through a hatchway that was then closed. Then they waited as a valve was opened and the pressure inside the air lock became the same as the pressure below. Finally they climbed through another manhole and down a ladder to the work area. To leave, the process was reversed.

Clam-shell buckets, operated from above, dropped down the WATER SHAFTS to lift out the dirt and rock as it was dug from the riverbed. The water level in the shaft was regulated to an equilibrium with the air pressure in the working chamber to keep the water from dropping down from the shaft and flooding the work chamber.

Roebling himself became an invalid as a victim of the bends. But he continued to direct all work from his home through his wife Edith and by his crew of assistant engineers.

No one knows with certainty, but probably twenty men or more died during the construction of the bridge. The life of the unskilled laborer was a hard one. His pay for a day's work digging underwater in the compressed air of the caissons was at first two dollars; in later years it was slightly higher.

It took 14 years (1869–1883) to build the Brooklyn Bridge. When built, it was considered one of the wonders of the world—a construction concept and feat of overwhelming scale, beautifying the skyline of Manhattan. It is one of the favorite sights in all of New York, and listed as a National Historic Landmark. It is also one of the last of its kind: a construction of massive stone. The next bridges and buildings would make use of steel—a new material of great strength and much promise.

Headroom for the workmen in the digging area was 9.5 feet. The roof above them was made up of five layers of one-foot-square pine timbers, bolted together. All the seams were sealed with thick caulking. A sheet of tin covered the top and sides and was then covered with wood. On top of all this, 10 more feet of timbers were added. The AIR LOCKS, SUPPLY SHAFTS, and WATER SHAFT all passed through this 15 feet of solid timber and into chambers built into the granite. The work area, always damp, was lit by calcium lamps and candles.

WORKING BENEATH SHOE OR EDGE OF CAISSON.

THE IRON SKELETON

Structural iron and steel gave strength without mass. They were versatile in form and use—they could soar upward as well as horizontally, be airy in feeling, curved or straight.

But the transition from masonry-wall buildings to true iron-skeleton construction was a gradual process. Most office buildings built during the transition period used combinations of masonry, ornamental iron fronts, metal beams, and pillars of cast- and wrought-iron.

Many office buildings of the late 1800's still had masonry walls in addition to inner metal supports, for the skeleton frames of these earliest forerunners of today's skyscrapers could not have stood without the support they received from their masonry walls. Both masonry walls and metal supports were built upward simultaneously as parts of the whole, and the metal parts were sometimes not joined to other metal construction.

The metal skeleton would take over more and more of the load-bearing in the gradual evolvement of the tall office building. Eventually it would become, in the words of the 1931 committee examining the method of construction used in Jenney's Home Insurance Building of 1884, "A type of construction in which a metal frame or cage comprised of girders, beams and columns supports all internal and external loads and carries all stresses directly to the foundations."

The style of the new tall buildings was still that of elaborate ornamentation under a wide assortment of historical influences. The elevator had opened up the top floors for ever-higher buildings. Rising land costs made tall buildings practical for the crowded city, and architects were quick to use this new architectural form: the metal-frame iron skeleton. Its horizontal metal beams transferred the weight of the floors to the vertical columns, which, in turn, carried the load down to the foundation. The beams also tied all the uprights together and prevented them from moving sideways.

In Chicago, in 1879, architect William Le Baron Jenney designed a building using cast-iron posts embedded inside the masonry of a conventional masonry building. These posts reduced the need for wide supports between the windows and carried part of the weight of the building. Five years later he designed the 10-story Home Insurance Building, with the first two floors of massive granite masonry. On top of this he built a brick and metal frame structure, which supported all the floor loads and the walls. This building was razed in 1931 and carefully examined during demolition in order to determine its method of construction. It is considered by many to be the first high building to use skeleton construction as a basic design principle.

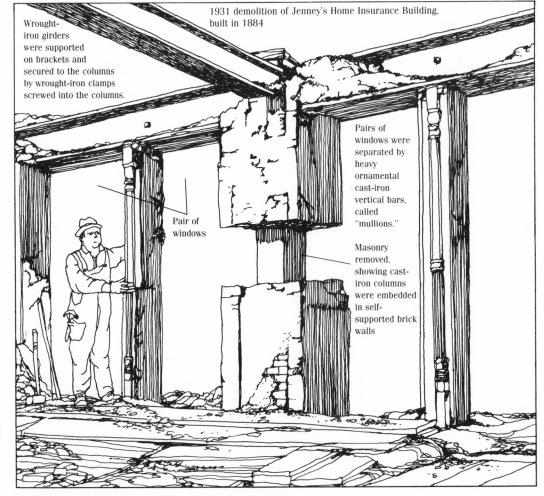

Wrought-iron girders were supported on brackets and secured to the columns by wrought-iron clamps screwed into the columns.

1931 demolition of Jenney's Home Insurance Building, built in 1884

Pairs of windows were separated by heavy ornamental cast-iron vertical bars, called "mullions."

Pair of windows

Masonry removed, showing cast-iron columns were embedded in self-supported brick walls

The Museum of the City of New York

"AN IRON BRIDGE TRUSS STOOD ON END"

In 1888 New York architect Bradford Lee Gilbert designed the Tower Building at 50 Broadway in lower Manhattan. It was 108 feet deep, but had a total available width of only 21 feet, 6 inches. The city's building code stipulated that walls supporting a building's superstructure be of such a thickness that, at street level, all but a little more than 10 feet of the width of Gilbert's building would be solid walls. Gilbert pondered this problem for six months: how to make use of the 21.5-foot width on which his building would have to stand? He later stated in an interview in the *New York Times* that the idea came to him in a flash. "An iron bridge truss stood on end was the solution of the problem." The building code did not limit the height of the foundation of a building, and Gilbert planned to carry his foundation columns—his iron bridge trusses—all the way up his building, 13 stories high. In a windstorm during construction people gathered to see if it would topple over. To calm the fears of the owner of the building, Gilbert himself proposed to occupy the top two floors of the structure. Now torn down, the building had a bronze plaque stating: "the earliest example of skeleton construction in which the entire weight of the walls and floors is borne and transmitted to the foundation by a framework of metallic posts and beams, date 1888–9."

Since ancient times, IRON has been made into tools and weapons by heating and hammering iron ore. When heated to a high temperature, iron becomes molten and, depending on the other components in the mix and the way it is treated, it can be fashioned into cast iron, wrought iron, or steel.

Both wrought iron and cast iron were being used extensively in the construction of large bridges and buildings by the mid-1800's.

WROUGHT IRON has great strength in tension—resistance to forces that would pull it apart—which makes it structurally practical for use in horizontal beams. It is softer than cast iron.

CAST IRON is hard but brittle, and has great strength under compression, making it superior to wrought iron for load-bearing uses, such as vertical supporting beams or pillars.

In 1856, Henry Bessemer, in England, devised a cheap method of fabricating STEEL from pig iron. Steel, due to its greater strength, toughness, and resistance to wear, then began to supplant both cast iron and wrought iron, although both metals are still used in addition to steel for specific purposes today.

Steel is made with many different characteristics, for specialized purposes, by the addition of specific ingredients to iron.

Although nonflammable, all these metals are subject to collapse and potentially dangerous changes from extreme heat, such as fire. Thus they are coated with a fire-retardant protective surface after being put in place on a building project, such as a skyscraper.

1850 TO 1900

New York City was experiencing not only a building boom, but a population explosion as well. In just 35 years, from 1855 to 1890, nearly seven million immigrants arrived in the city from Europe. Since many stayed in New York to live and work, the strain placed upon the city's services was enormous.

Many lived in the most squalid conditions, yet visitors to the city were awed by the splendor of its buildings and the tempo of its life. The "French flat," or apartment, appeared in the city; there were thousands of tenements. Central Park was man-made, created from undeveloped land.

By the end of the century, upper Fifth Avenue from the Fifties to the Nineties would be inhabited by enormously rich people who built their palatial homes on land which had cost them from one hundred to two hundred dollars per square foot. The farms and shanty towns that had been there had long ago been pushed elsewhere. It was reported at the time that ingenious speculators would buy small lots in this fashionable area. Since there were no restrictions on the use to which these lots could be put, a speculator would announce plans to build an objectionable structure, whereupon his irate millionaire neighbor would buy him out at a nice profit. One promoter with a twenty-five-foot lot was described as planning a fifteen-story structure, probably an apartment-house, since it was felt that an office-building in that locality would never find any tenants. An appeal was made to strictly regulate the height and character of buildings on specific streets.

Transportation was still a major problem. Elevated railroad lines with their steam locomotives had opened up both sides of upper Manhattan to development. But until the late

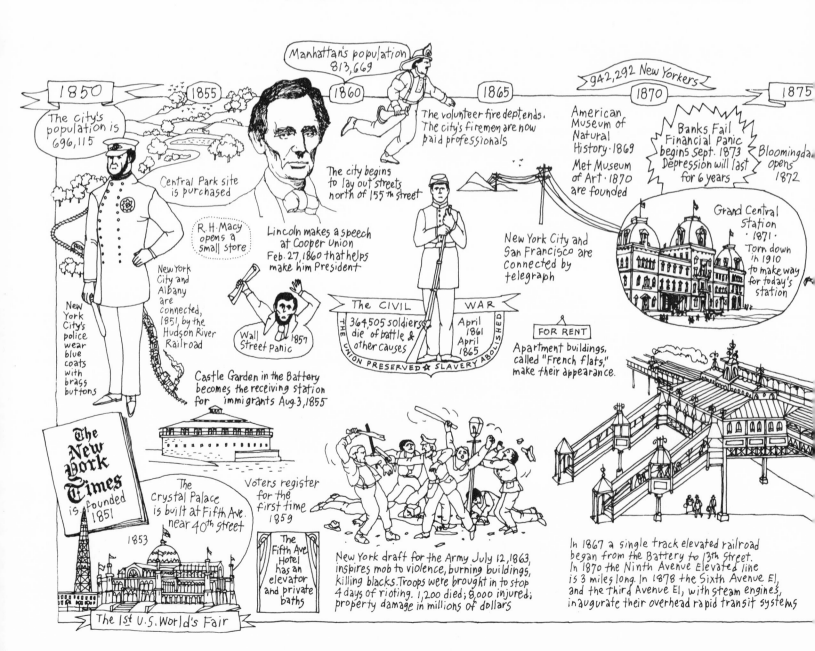

1850 · 1855 · 1860 · 1865 · 1870 · 1875

Manhattan's population 813,669

942,292 New Yorkers

The city's population is 696,115

Central Park site is purchased

The volunteer fire dept. ends. The city's firemen are now paid professionals

American Museum of Natural History · 1869
Met Museum of Art · 1870 are founded

Banks Fail Financial Panic begins Sept. 1873 Depression will last for 6 years

Bloomingdale opens 1872

R.H. Macy opens a small store

Lincoln makes a speech at Cooper Union Feb. 27, 1860 that helps make him President

New York City and Albany are connected, 1851, by the Hudson River Railroad

New York City and San Francisco are connected by telegraph

Grand Central Station · 1871 · Torn down in 1910 to make way for today's station

New York City's police wear blue coats with brass buttons

Wall Street panic 1857

The CIVIL WAR
364,505 soldiers die of battle & other causes
April 1861 April 1865
THE UNION PRESERVED ☆ SLAVERY ABOLISHED

FOR RENT
Apartment buildings, called "French flats," make their appearance.

Castle Garden in the Battery becomes the receiving station for immigrants Aug. 3, 1855

The New York Times is founded 1851

The Crystal Palace is built at Fifth Ave. near 40th street 1853

Voters register for the first time 1859

The Fifth Ave. Hotel has an elevator and private baths

New York draft for the Army July 12, 1863, inspires mob to violence, burning buildings, killing blacks. Troops were brought in to stop 4 days of rioting. 1,200 died; 8,000 injured; property damage in millions of dollars

In 1867 a single track elevated railroad began from the Battery to 13th street. In 1870 the Ninth Avenue Elevated line is 3 miles long. In 1878 the Sixth Avenue El, and the Third Avenue El, with steam engines, inaugurate their overhead rapid transit systems

The 1st U.S. World's Fair

1800's most transport was still provided by horse-drawn vehicles. And the city kept right on growing. In 1870 there were 942,292 people living on Manhattan Island and by 1880 the population total had passed the million mark, to 1,164,673. By 1890 it had reached a million and a half.

As late as 1892 the tallest structure in the city was still Trinity Church with its 25-story-tall spire overlooking Wall Street, but ambitious men were now putting up office buildings with usable floor space at ever-increasing heights.

An explosion of scientific ideas and practical inventions in America and Europe was revolutionizing the way people lived, and where and how they worked. The first commercial oil well was drilled. A railroad now crossed the entire continent. There were fountain pens, typewriters, adding machines, dynamite, and steel alloys, as well as aspirin,

an antitoxin for diphtheria, and a vaccine against rabies. There were gasoline engines and gas and steam turbines. Electricity seemed miraculous. The telephone and telegraph made instant communication possible anywhere in the city.

The value of city land rose dramatically. It was not only possible to build taller and bigger buildings with the new machines and processes that scientists and inventors had provided, it was now profitable to do so.

New Yorkers were accustomed to living in a constantly changing city, the greatest in the nation. Their city had always grown horizontally, sideways to the Hudson and East rivers, and northward to the Harlem River and Spuyten Duyvil. It was now growing vertically, and beginning to give to the world a new vision of a great city—Manhattan, city of skyscrapers.

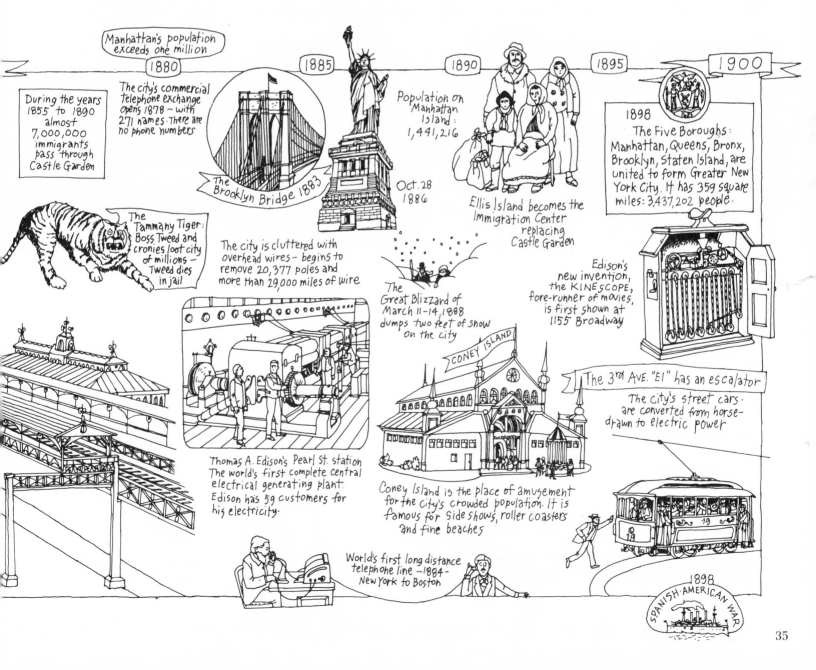

Manhattan's population exceeds one million

1880   1885   1890   1895   1900

During the years 1855 to 1890 almost 7,000,000 immigrants pass through Castle Garden

The city's commercial telephone exchange opens 1878 – with 271 names. There are no phone numbers

The Brooklyn Bridge 1883

Oct. 28 1886

Population on Manhattan Island: 1,441,216

1898 The Five Boroughs: Manhattan, Queens, Bronx, Brooklyn, Staten Island, are united to form Greater New York City. It has 359 square miles: 3,437,202 people.

The Tammany Tiger: Boss Tweed and cronies loot city of millions – Tweed dies in jail

The city is cluttered with overhead wires - begins to remove 20,377 poles and more than 29,000 miles of wire

The Great Blizzard of March 11-14, 1888 dumps two feet of snow on the city

Ellis Island becomes the Immigration Center replacing Castle Garden

Edison's new invention, the KINESCOPE, fore-runner of movies, is first shown at 1155 Broadway

Thomas A. Edison's Pearl St. station The world's first complete central electrical generating plant. Edison has 59 customers for his electricity.

CONEY ISLAND

Coney Island is the place of amusement for the city's crowded population. It is famous for side shows, roller coasters and fine beaches

The 3rd Ave. "El" has an escalator

The city's street cars are converted from horse-drawn to electric power

World's first long distance telephone line –1884– New York to Boston

1898 SPANISH-AMERICAN WAR

35

THE
FLATIRON
BUILDING:
1901

The Flatiron Building, Manhattan's oldest skyscraper landmark, was originally named the Fuller Building for the construction company that built it and owned it. When erected, 1901–1903, it was the world's tallest habitable building, at 300 feet.

It is famous for its unique shape, a triangle formed by the intersection of Broadway and Fifth Avenue at 23rd Street. This piece of land was known as the "flatiron block" well before this building was even planned. The land price in 1901 was "not far from $2 million," and the cost of the new building was another two million dollars.

The new century had just begun. The average life expectancy in the United States for whites was about 47 years: for blacks, only 33 years. There were fewer than 10,000 autos in the whole country. Oklahoma, Arizona, and New Mexico were still territories, not yet states. The Wright brothers would make their first successful flight in an airplane on December 17, 1903; it would last 12 seconds.

In Manhattan, as in the rest of the country, the work week was six days long, 9 or 10 hours a day, and workers received about 12 dollars a week. Child labor and sweatshop working conditions were widespread.

Farther up Broadway, at the corner of 42nd Street, a riveted steel building, the Hotel Pabst, had just been torn down. The journal *American Architect and Building News* noted that "unfortunately for the science of construction, the building removed was built only four years ago, so that it affords little opportunity for studying the effect of time upon metal skeletons cased with masonry." This building had to be taken apart by the "tedious and costly operation of sawing off the heads of the rivets." Would architects, the journal wondered, have to consider how their buildings could be torn down even as they designed them?

Trolley cars and horse and buggy were the means of surface transportation along Broadway when the Fuller Construction Company began to erect its new building. In their brochure for prospective tenants it was described as follows:

"For many reasons this building is unique. It is the cumulative result of all that is known in the art of building, and is equipped with every conceivable convenience that human ingenuity could devise. From a structural standpoint it is the strongest building ever erected.

"It is equipped with six rapid-running Otis hydraulic elevators, and has its own steam and electric plants, furnishing heat and light to tenants free of charge.

"The woodwork is mahogany and quartered oak, and has all undergone a process of fireproofing, in order to eliminate the possibility of fire.

"If early application is made, anyone desiring it may have one or more entire floors arranged and finished in a special manner, without charge, and so make available space otherwise devoted to corridors.

"The offices, as laid out, are very commodious, and, owing to the peculiar shape of the building, have the best of light. The height of the ceilings is as follows: Sub-basement, 10 feet; basement, 12 feet; first floor, 21 feet 6 inches; second, third and fourth floors, 12 feet 10 inches; fifth to fifteenth, inclusive, 11 feet; sixteenth, 11 feet 10 inches; seventeenth and eighteenth, 13 feet; nineteenth, 14 feet 2 inches; twentieth, 10 feet 6 inches."

No mechanical equipment except the derricks is visible in this drawing, based on a photo in the Library of Congress. Two men on the sixth floor are raising a long piece of equipment by hand, using block and tackle. The scaffolding and the enclosed section show how the construction of tall buildings has changed in just a few years. The lower floors are not yet even closed in, while above, supported by the steel framework within, entire floors have been completely enclosed.

Today, the Flatiron Building is still one of the city's most distinguished buildings.

Decorative stonework on the building's exterior

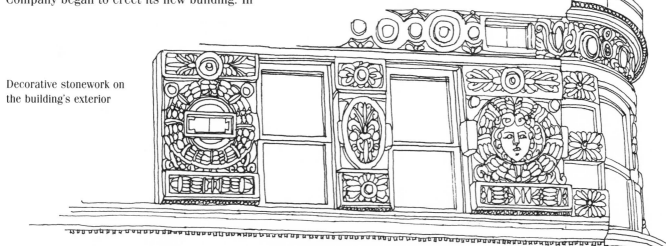

THE WOOLWORTH BUILDING: 1913

*Whoever builds a Bridge or a Building,
Owes an obligation to the Community
That it shall embellish and not deface
the locality.*

Cass Gilbert
* Architect of the Woolworth Building*

The Woolworth Building, considered to be one of the great works of architecture of the 20th century, was given landmark status in 1983 by New York City. It cannot be altered, reconstructed, or demolished in any way without the permission of the city's Landmarks Preservation Commission. The Woolworth Company had just completed a four-year, 22-million-dollar restoration of the building's façade—8.5 million dollars more than the whole building originally cost.

When it was built, in 1913, it was unique in its method of financing. F. W. Woolworth, famous for his five-and-ten-cent stores, paid for the construction of his building as it was being built—without a mortgage or any indebtedness.

Woolworth wanted a building Gothic in style, with a tower. He also wanted the windows arranged so that when any interior space was subdivided, each office would have natural light. There are 60 floors from sub-basement to top, with the average ceiling height being more than 12 feet; this is an esthetic use of space no longer considered economically practical. A skyscraper of the same height—792 feet—built today would have at least 20 floors more than the Woolworth Building.

It was impractical to make a skyscraper with Gothic structural characteristics, so the architect used ornamentation and details to create a "Cathedral of Commerce." Almost the entire building is covered with terracotta ornamentation. The design of everything, from the doorknobs to the lobby's barrel-vaulted ceilings, was carefully thought out to create a feeling of Gothic sculpture. The beauty of its exterior surfaces and of its entrance lobby at street level is unique in New York City.

From 1913 to 1930 the Woolworth Building was the tallest office building in the world, surpassing Manhattan's 47-story-high Singer Building and the Metropolitan Life Insurance Building at 700 feet. How high could architects and builders go without losing stability in their skyscrapers? What would lightning do to such a tall building? What would happen in a violent storm?

The basic skyscraper structure, with its inner steel skeleton and vertical steel columns and connecting steel cross beams, had now been established. In Europe, as well as in the United States, engineers were developing new techniques for strengthening these internal skeletons. One obvious method was to add diagonally placed beams between columns and to add bracing where columns and beams connected.

The many pieces of the skeleton thus joined act as a connected whole to prevent its collapse and to absorb the pressures and stress placed on the building by the great weight of its parts and the force exerted against it by strong winds. The columns and beams all share in distributing the weight and in channeling stresses to the foundation of the building and into the bedrock.

The steel columns used in the Woolworth Building were the heaviest ever used in a building up to that time. All its steel members were riveted together. In addition to diagonal bracing and knee braces, Cass Gilbert, the architect, decided to use a recent development, portal bracing, to strengthen the building. The strength thus achieved allowed for the use of delicate and intricate design units on the exterior of the building, since these elements could then be purely ornamental and would not be required to help support the structure of the building.

One of the foundation girders, fabricated in Pennsylvania by the American Bridge Company, weighs 68 tons. It is 23 feet long, 8 feet deep, and 6 feet wide. This immense girder was taken from a boat to the site on Broadway on a 100-ton truck pulled by forty-two horses.

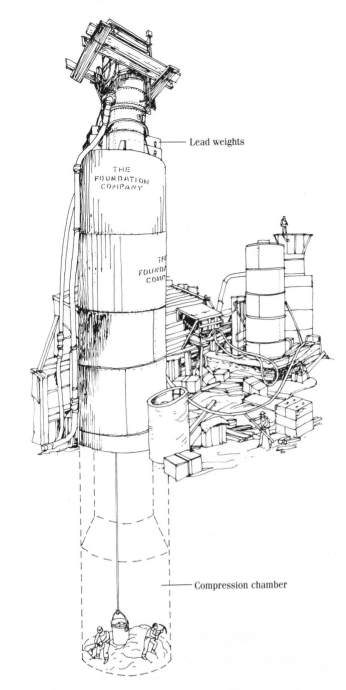

Lead weights

Compression chamber

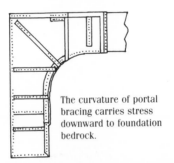

The curvature of portal bracing carries stress downward to foundation bedrock.

The columns are two floors tall.

Beam

Knee brace

Seventeen million bricks were used in the skyscraper, mostly for fireproofing. They were placed between the terra-cotta and the building's steel framework. The original terra-cotta blocks were hooked to the brick back-up and cemented in place.

Because bedrock is so deep at this site, averaging 116 feet below Broadway, the building was built on sixty-nine concrete piers, some of them 19 feet in diameter. Engineers first had to sink metal caissons through loam, gravel stone, shoal water, quicksand, and solid rock, then fill them with concrete. The steel columns of the skyscraper rest on these concrete piers, supporting the building's total weight of an estimated 223,000 tons.

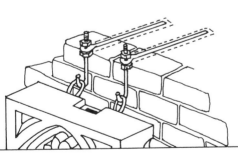

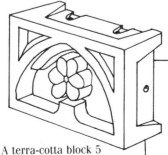

A terra-cotta block 5 inches deep and 14 inches tall, one of the nearly 500 different sizes and shapes used to create the rich detail of the building's exterior

Terra-cotta is clay, baked at a high temperature to create a very hard, lightweight, durable, ornamental tile, or shaped brick. It can be easily modeled into almost any shape: delicate and intricate, or bold and powerful. It can be made to look like sculptured stoneware or enameled metal, and is adaptable to many styles of architecture.

Terra-cotta has been used since ancient times, and in the 19th and early 20th centuries it was widely used as an ornamental façade in the construction of buildings.

In the four-year restoration of the Woolworth Building, the entire terra-cotta exterior was minutely inspected. About 26,000 panels had to be replaced, and some 100,000 others were secured with new stainless-steel anchors.

The replacement blocks are made of concrete—now considered to be better able to withstand the extremes of New York City's weather. They are anchored into the brick masonry and cemented in place with epoxy adhesives, which were unknown in 1913.

BOOK
AND
BUST:
1900–1930

Manhattan had a population of 1,850,093 in 1900 and 2,331,541 by 1910. It was, and is, one of the most densely populated cities in the world.

Horse-drawn vehicles and steam- and electric-powered surface and elevated railroads were inadequate to transport such vast numbers of people about Manhattan and to and from the other boroughs. In the early 1900's the automobile was just beginning to be seen on the city's streets.

On March 24, 1900, work began on a new underground rapid-transit system—now 241 miles long—connecting all the boroughs except the island of Richmond/Staten Island.

By 1904 one could travel rapidly underground all the way from City Hall to 145th Street. Soon the Bronx was connected to Manhattan by a subway tunnel under the Harlem River. By 1908 the subway went deep under the East River to connect Manhattan and Brooklyn.

By 1910 the Williamsburg, Manhattan, and Queensborough bridges had crossed the East River. These bridges, together with the Brooklyn Bridge, provided easier access to Manhattan from Brooklyn, Queens, and Long Island. Penn Station was opened in 1910, and Grand Central Station three years later, in 1913.

With these new transportation lines, many people now worked in Manhattan, but lived and slept elsewhere. Brooklyn, three times the size of Manhattan, would eventually have more homes than Manhattan.

Immigrants from Europe were again pouring through Ellis Island into New York City. In 1907, newcomers set an all-time record: 1,285,349 of them hoping to better their lives in America.

Few cities in the world could equal New York as a financial, manufacturing and commercial center. By the end of the first decade of the century its manufacturing work force totaled almost 700,000. It had more than 23,000 factories and was producing about 10% of the total factory output in the whole country. It was estimated that a ship sailed out of New York harbor about every thirty-six minutes, carrying the city's goods overseas and to domestic ports.

Yet there was no effective government

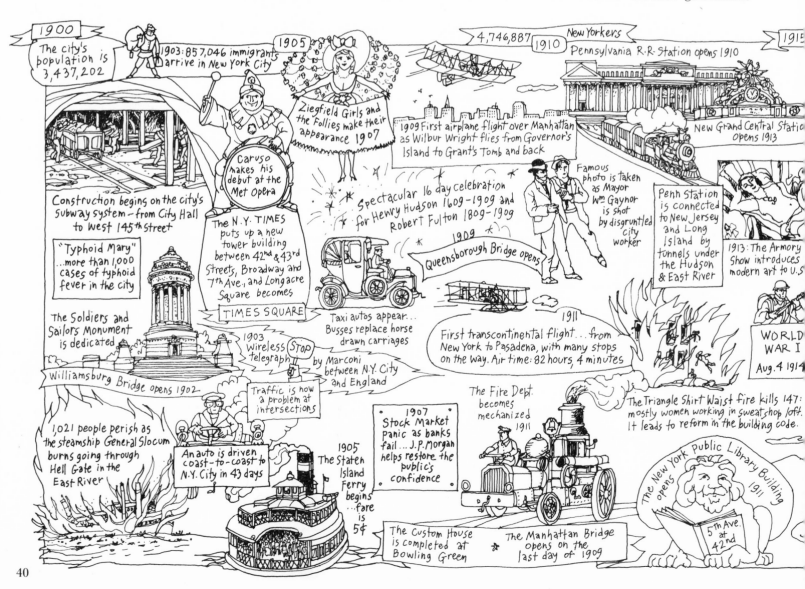

1900
The city's population is 3,437,202

1903: 857,046 immigrants arrive in New York City

1905

4,746,887 New Yorkers 1910

Pennsylvania R.R. Station opens 1910

191

Construction begins on the city's subway system—from City Hall to West 145th Street

"Typhoid Mary" ...more than 1,000 cases of typhoid fever in the city

The Soldiers and Sailors Monument is dedicated

Williamsburg Bridge opens 1902

1,021 people perish as the steamship General Slocum burns going through Hell Gate in the East River

Caruso makes his debut at the Met Opera

The N.Y. TIMES puts up a new tower building between 42nd & 43rd Streets, Broadway and 7th Ave., and Longacre Square becomes TIMES SQUARE

1903 Wireless telegraph Stop by Marconi between N.Y. City and England

Traffic is now a problem at intersections

An auto is driven coast-to-coast to N.Y. City in 43 days

Ziegfield Girls and the Follies make their appearance 1907

Spectacular 16 day celebration for Henry Hudson 1609–1909 and Robert Fulton 1809–1909

Taxi autos appear... Busses replace horse drawn carriages

1905 The Staten Island Ferry begins ...fare is 5¢

The Custom House is completed at Bowling Green

1907 Stock Market Panic as banks fail...J.P.Morgan helps restore the public's confidence

1909 First airplane flight over Manhattan as Wilbur Wright flies from Governor's Island to Grant's Tomb and back

1909 Queensborough Bridge opens

1911 First transcontinental flight...from New York to Pasadena, with many stops on the way. Air time: 82 hours, 4 minutes

The Fire Dept. becomes mechanized 1911

The Manhattan Bridge opens on the last day of 1909

Famous photo is taken as Mayor Wm Gaynor is shot by disgruntled city worker

New Grand Central Station opens 1913

Penn Station is connected to New Jersey and Long Island by tunnels under the Hudson & East River

1913: The Armory Show introduces modern art to U.S

WORLD WAR I Aug.4 1914

The Triangle Shirt Waist fire kills 147; mostly women working in sweatshop loft. It leads to reform in the building code.

The New York Public Library Building opens 1911 5th Ave. at 42nd regulation of safety or health for workers. Young children, as well as adults, worked long hours. In 1914 only about 8% of the nation's work force was unionized. In that year the Ford Motor Company in Detroit raised its basic wage rate to five dollars for an eight-hour day, remarkable for its time. It had been two dollars and forty cents for a nine-hour day. The average man in manufacturing worked a 52-hour week; women, 50 hours.

World War I came and went, with New York City as the nation's seaport, shipping out men and supplies to Europe. The worldwide influenza epidemic of 1918 swept through the city, leaving nearly 13,000 dead. Crime and political corruption were frequently rampant.

To control its growth, in 1916 the city enacted the first zoning code in the nation. It divided the city into use, height, and area districts. The code stipulated the height and bulk of buildings that could be built, by the use of setbacks in a building's construction, as determined by the width of the street on which the building fronts. It regulated the location of trades and industries, and open spaces, to preserve residential districts and stabilize real estate values.

In the Roaring Twenties the city was a boom town. Another migration, of black Americans, was arriving in New York from the South, and Harlem became the nation's greatest black community.

The pace of life had quickened and Manhattan was the place to be. Optimism was contagious, and it was everywhere. Forgotten was the financial panic of 1907 when banks across the country had failed.

A new building, the Chrysler Building, was to be built 77 stories high; it was to be the tallest in the world. Another, the Empire State Building, was to be even higher. The year was 1929.

In that year, on October 29th, the New York Stock Market collapsed. Wall Street was in panic. First New York shuddered . . . then the nation . . . then the world. History's worst financial crisis—the Great Depression—had begun.

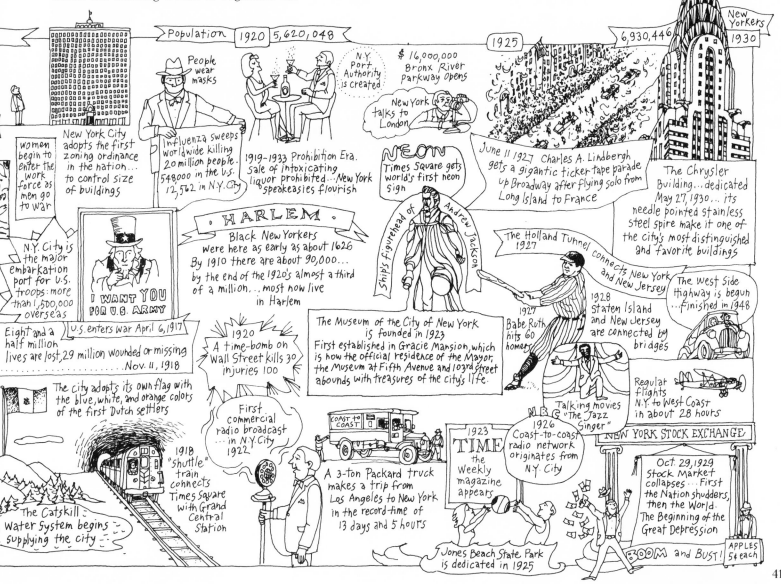

THE EMPIRE STATE BUILDING: 1930–1931

The Empire State Building was built in the earliest days of the Great Depression. More than 20 million Americans were without a job. Hungry men and women waited all day long in breadlines throughout the country—even in the heart of Times Square—just for a free meal.

Early in 1929, the developers of the proposed Empire State Building had decided to spend 44 million dollars on the building's construction. The land cost 16 million dollars, although the site size was only about two acres.

On the site stood the old Waldorf-Astoria Hotel. While it was being demolished the stock market crashed and the world's economy collapsed. But the project went right ahead. Final construction costs were less than 25 million dollars—the Depression had lowered the cost of everything.

The building's design was greatly influenced by New York's building code, which, in 1929, stipulated that no building could be built straight up from the street for more than 125 feet; at that height the building had to be set back from the street baseline. A further setback at the 30th floor would be necessary to comply with the floor size, which at that height could be no more than one-quarter the size of the land on which the building would be built.

It was a monumental task: to design the world's tallest building, create as much usable rental space as possible, plan so it could be built within 18 months, and still have a handsome building. In the end, architect William Lamb worked on fifteen designs before his plan "K" was finally chosen.

Even before demolition of the old hotel had begun, the design of the Empire State Building was ready, together with a complete inventory of all construction needs. So well coordinated were design needs with construction needs that occupancy of part of the building began four months ahead of schedule.

Because of the Depression, the Empire State Building was never fully rented in its earliest years, but it immediately became one of the wonders of New York City and a favorite tourist attraction. Ordinary folk and the famous alike made the trip up to the observation tower and were enthralled by the sheer height of it all.

Today, more than 50 years later, nearly two million people a year ride the 1,250 feet up to its lofty tower to gaze out over Manhattan and marvel at the city scene spread out below them. On a clear day you can see 50 miles away. It is both unnerving and exhilarating to realize that workmen have stood on exposed beams in the open air at this great height to build the very observation platform upon which you are standing.

Clouds and fog may float below you. In a high wind the top of the building actually moves. It is frequently hit by lightning. The tip of the TV tower above you is 1,472 feet above street level, yet the steel skeleton of the building readily absorbs and dissipates both the force of the wind and the electric charge of the lightning. The 365,000-ton weight of the building is anchored into solid bedrock, 55 feet below the surface at Fifth Avenue and 34th Street.

The TV broadcast antenna atop the spire is as high as a 22-story building.

In the 1930's, dirigibles, or airships, as they were also known, were thought to be a future means of international travel. In October 1928 the *Graf Zeppelin* had flown from Germany to Lakehurst, New Jersey—a distance of 6,630 miles—in 4 days, 15 hours, and 46 minutes. It was hoped the top of the Empire State Building could act as a mooring mast. In 1931, the Goodyear blimp *Columbia* lowered a bundle of newspapers to the mooring-mast parapet on the 103rd floor. The rope lowering the newspapers was cut and the papers delivered, but the whole procedure was dangerous. A few other attempts were made by small blimps to attach themselves to the mooring mast but none succeeded and the idea was abandoned.

In 1945 a U.S. Air Force bomber making an approach to a Newark, New Jersey, airport in fog and rain was seen passing over midtown Manhattan at low altitude. Seconds after narrowly missing other buildings, it crashed into the Empire State Building at a speed of more than 250 miles per hour. Three people died in the plane and eleven in the building, but the building stood firm, although extensive damage was done in the impact area at the 78th and 79th floors.

At times, because of wind currents peculiar to areas near skyscrapers, snow will float upward . . . instead of down.

In the past, migratory birds have flown into the Empire State Building at night, confused by the outdoor lighting of the tower. This lighting is now turned off during the migratory season to prevent such occurrences.

THE RIVETER: $1.92 PLUS HALF A CENT AN HOUR

The putting together of the open steel framework of the Empire State Building revealed one distinct difference from the framework of the skyscrapers being put up today.

It was full of rivets.

And its construction was audibly different from today's methods of building.

Riveting made such an infernal racket that New Yorkers wrote angry letters to the newspapers about the noise.

A test had already shown that welded joints were stronger than riveted joints in construction. But, in the 1930's, the riveting gang was still the center of activity in the building of skyscrapers. What they did held everything in place.

There were four men in a riveting gang. According to a news report of that time, they were called the "heater," the "catcher" or "sticker," the "bucker-up," and the "driver" or "riveter." There was also the young helper, or "punk."

The heater cranked the handle of his forge, forcing air up through the coke or charcoal fire, making it flaming hot and heating to an incandescent glow the 10 or more rivet bolts buried in the fire.

When the driver was ready for a new rivet, the heater took a hot cherry-red one out of his forge with his long-handled tongs. And with an underhand toss he hurled the smoking rivet straight at the catcher, who caught it in mid-air in his catching can. The catcher then grabbed it with his tongs, tapped it against a beam to remove any cinders, and jammed it into the waiting hole.

The bucker-up held the rivet in place with his heavy steel dolly bar while, facing him on the opposite side of the pieces being riveted together, the driver pressed the release on his hammer. Within seconds, and with a chattering outburst of noise, his end of the rivet was smashed into a wide cap, permanently bonding together two more sections of the skyscraper framework.

Today, the steel beams and girders of the city's skyscrapers are bolted together with special steel bolts and welded together. Compared with riveting, these connections are stronger, more quickly made, and require fewer men to accomplish.

At the peak of construction on the Empire State Building there were thirty-eight riveting gangs working from 8:30 A.M. to 4:30 P.M.—with half an hour off for lunch. The number of rivets set in place in a day depended on the size of the rivets, and whether the crew was straddling a cold steel beam with nothing much below them or working inside the protection of the building itself. A fast crew might set up to 800 rivets a day. Union scale for riveters was $1.92, plus half a cent, per hour, with double pay for overtime.

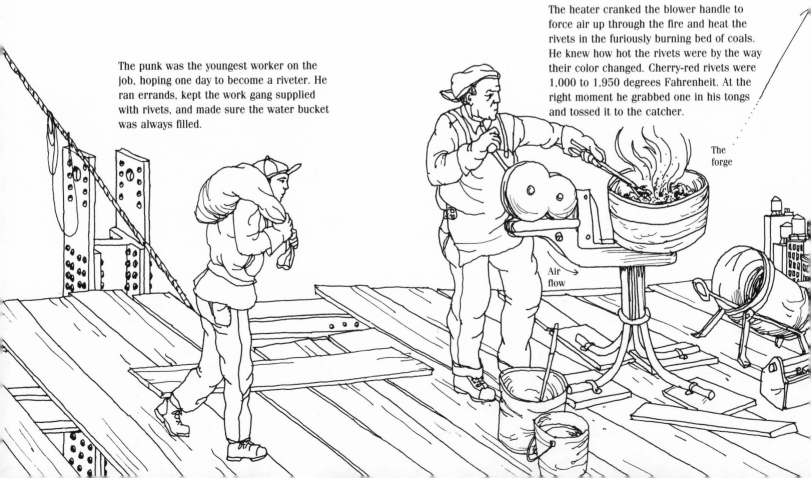

The punk was the youngest worker on the job, hoping one day to become a riveter. He ran errands, kept the work gang supplied with rivets, and made sure the water bucket was always filled.

The heater cranked the blower handle to force air up through the fire and heat the rivets in the furiously burning bed of coals. He knew how hot the rivets were by the way their color changed. Cherry-red rivets were 1,000 to 1,950 degrees Fahrenheit. At the right moment he grabbed one in his tongs and tossed it to the catcher.

The forge

Air flow

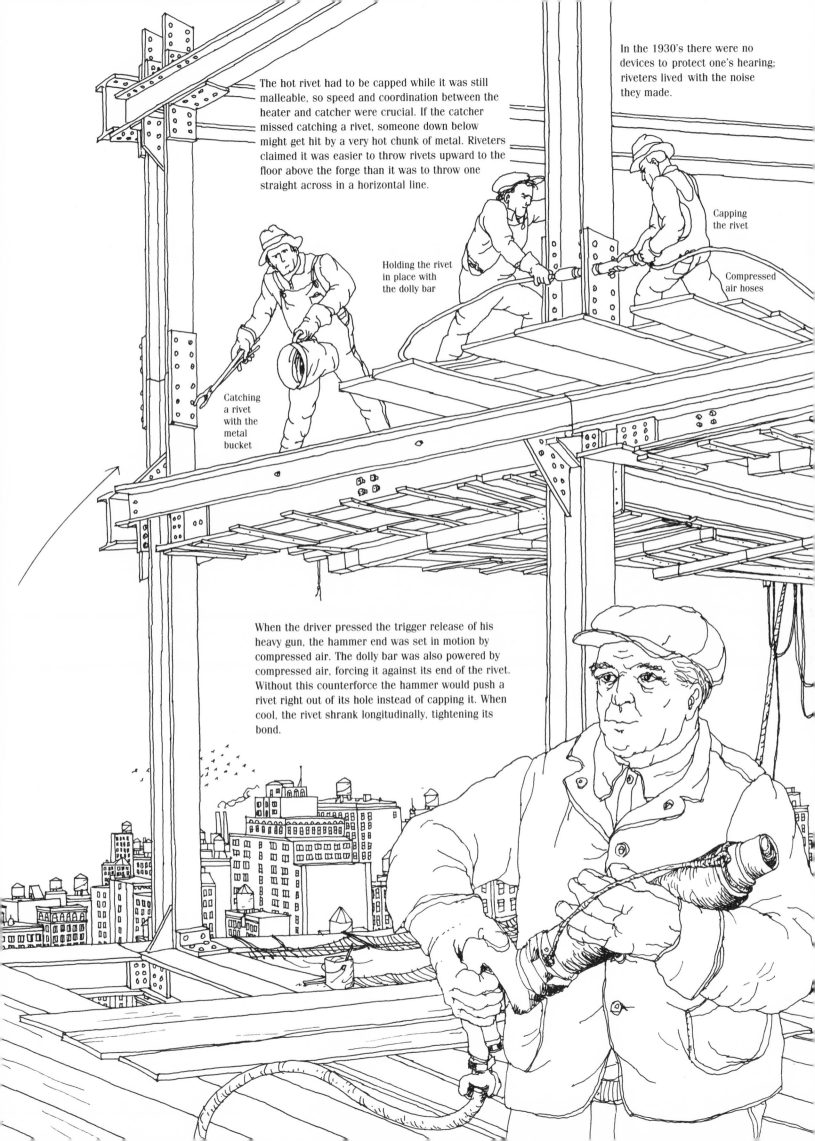

The hot rivet had to be capped while it was still malleable, so speed and coordination between the heater and catcher were crucial. If the catcher missed catching a rivet, someone down below might get hit by a very hot chunk of metal. Riveters claimed it was easier to throw rivets upward to the floor above the forge than it was to throw one straight across in a horizontal line.

In the 1930's there were no devices to protect one's hearing; riveters lived with the noise they made.

Holding the rivet in place with the dolly bar

Capping the rivet

Compressed air hoses

Catching a rivet with the metal bucket

When the driver pressed the trigger release of his heavy gun, the hammer end was set in motion by compressed air. The dolly bar was also powered by compressed air, forcing it against its end of the rivet. Without this counterforce the hammer would push a rivet right out of its hole instead of capping it. When cool, the rivet shrank longitudinally, tightening its bond.

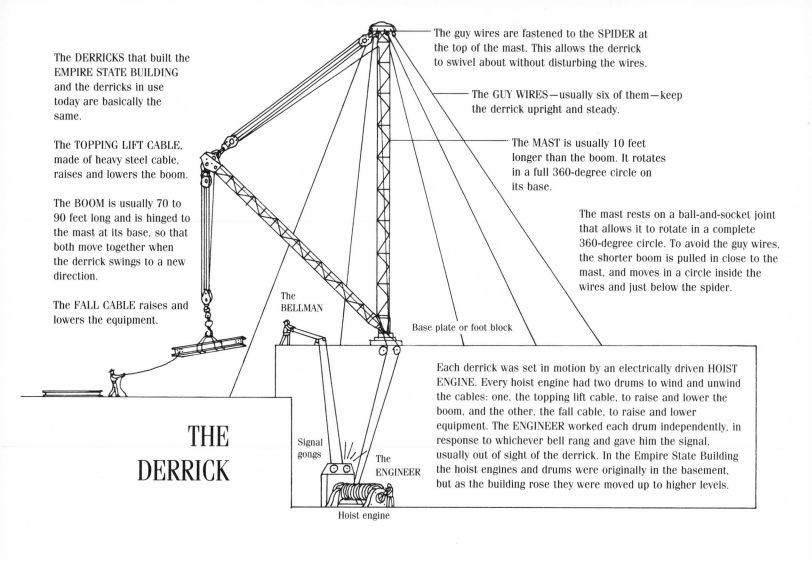

The DERRICKS that built the EMPIRE STATE BUILDING and the derricks in use today are basically the same.

The TOPPING LIFT CABLE, made of heavy steel cable, raises and lowers the boom.

The BOOM is usually 70 to 90 feet long and is hinged to the mast at its base, so that both move together when the derrick swings to a new direction.

The FALL CABLE raises and lowers the equipment.

The guy wires are fastened to the SPIDER at the top of the mast. This allows the derrick to swivel about without disturbing the wires.

The GUY WIRES—usually six of them—keep the derrick upright and steady.

The MAST is usually 10 feet longer than the boom. It rotates in a full 360-degree circle on its base.

The mast rests on a ball-and-socket joint that allows it to rotate in a complete 360-degree circle. To avoid the guy wires, the shorter boom is pulled in close to the mast, and moves in a circle inside the wires and just below the spider.

The BELLMAN

Base plate or foot block

Signal gongs

The ENGINEER

Hoist engine

Each derrick was set in motion by an electrically driven HOIST ENGINE. Every hoist engine had two drums to wind and unwind the cables: one, the topping lift cable, to raise and lower the boom, and the other, the fall cable, to raise and lower equipment. The ENGINEER worked each drum independently, in response to whichever bell rang and gave him the signal, usually out of sight of the derrick. In the Empire State Building the hoist engines and drums were originally in the basement, but as the building rose they were moved up to higher levels.

THE DERRICK

There were as many as sixteen derricks working on the Empire State Building at the same time. Their size and lifting abilities varied, from those limited to a 20-ton load to the biggest—capable of lifting the heaviest load needed, 44 tons.

Wherever possible, the derricks were positioned so that their booms overlapped, allowing material to be placed exactly where needed.

As construction proceeded and the derricks were raised to ever-increasing heights, their cables had to be lengthened to reach the hoist engines down below them. Holes were left in the newly poured concrete floors so the cables would have the most direct link between the hoist engines and the derricks.

The biggest hoist engines were ultimately placed on the 25th floor and the smaller ones on the 52nd floor, where the setbacks in the building's design made it desirable to do so. At the greatest heights, the derricks had to raise the steel beams and columns in two separate liftings—changing over at the 25th floor.

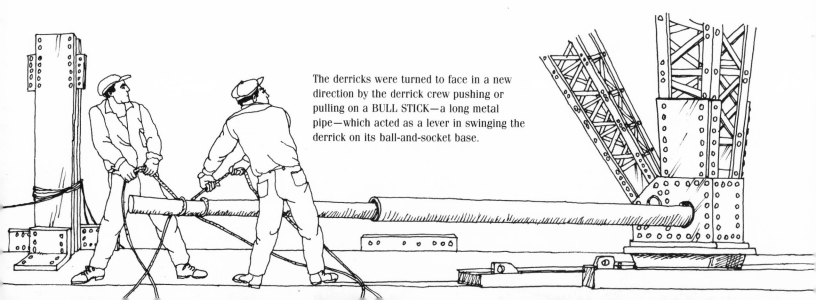

The derricks were turned to face in a new direction by the derrick crew pushing or pulling on a BULL STICK—a long metal pipe—which acted as a lever in swinging the derrick on its ball-and-socket base.

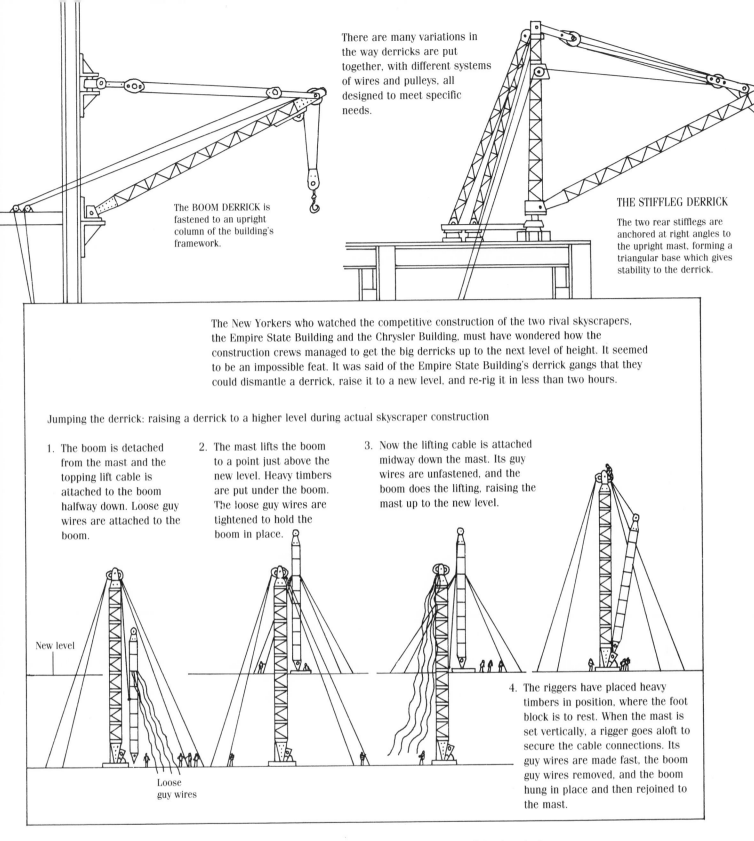

There are many variations in the way derricks are put together, with different systems of wires and pulleys, all designed to meet specific needs.

The BOOM DERRICK is fastened to an upright column of the building's framework.

THE STIFFLEG DERRICK

The two rear stifflegs are anchored at right angles to the upright mast, forming a triangular base which gives stability to the derrick.

The New Yorkers who watched the competitive construction of the two rival skyscrapers, the Empire State Building and the Chrysler Building, must have wondered how the construction crews managed to get the big derricks up to the next level of height. It seemed to be an impossible feat. It was said of the Empire State Building's derrick gangs that they could dismantle a derrick, raise it to a new level, and re-rig it in less than two hours.

Jumping the derrick: raising a derrick to a higher level during actual skyscraper construction

1. The boom is detached from the mast and the topping lift cable is attached to the boom halfway down. Loose guy wires are attached to the boom.

2. The mast lifts the boom to a point just above the new level. Heavy timbers are put under the boom. The loose guy wires are tightened to hold the boom in place.

3. Now the lifting cable is attached midway down the mast. Its guy wires are unfastened, and the boom does the lifting, raising the mast up to the new level.

New level

Loose guy wires

4. The riggers have placed heavy timbers in position, where the foot block is to rest. When the mast is set vertically, a rigger goes aloft to secure the cable connections. Its guy wires are made fast, the boom guy wires removed, and the boom hung in place and then rejoined to the mast.

Today the hoisting, the lowering, and the transfer of loads horizontally may still be done by derrick. The derrick is controlled by an operating engineer who is usually at a lower level of construction and doesn't see the actual loading or unloading of the tons of material he is moving about. In operating his controls, the engineer depends on signals from his loading and unloading bellmen.

During construction of the Empire State Building the bellman pulled on two cables, each attached to a separate bell next to the derrick engineer, who adjusted his winch cables according to the bells.

Today the engineer gets his signals from a bellman pressing buttons on a portable bell box which connects to, and activates, bells and lights at the hoist engine. The bells tell the engineer the function: to raise or lower the boom. The light signal, steady or flickering, is the speed of the function. When raising steel from a delivery truck to the top of an unfinished building, a bellman at street level will give the signals until the steel reaches the top; then a bellman on top takes over. The hoist engineer is located at a lower level, probably in a walled-off enclosure, and cannot see the derrick or the bellman.

Street level bellman

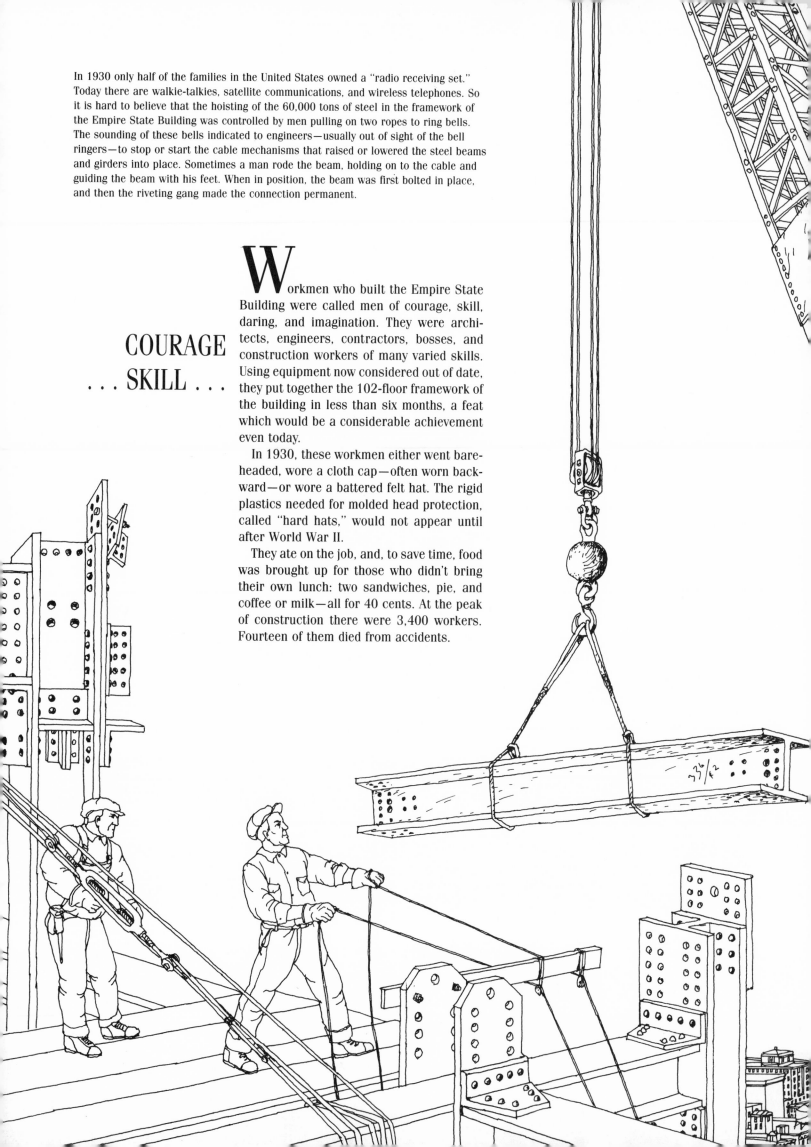

In 1930 only half of the families in the United States owned a "radio receiving set." Today there are walkie-talkies, satellite communications, and wireless telephones. So it is hard to believe that the hoisting of the 60,000 tons of steel in the framework of the Empire State Building was controlled by men pulling on two ropes to ring bells. The sounding of these bells indicated to engineers—usually out of sight of the bell ringers—to stop or start the cable mechanisms that raised or lowered the steel beams and girders into place. Sometimes a man rode the beam, holding on to the cable and guiding the beam with his feet. When in position, the beam was first bolted in place, and then the riveting gang made the connection permanent.

COURAGE ... SKILL ...

Workmen who built the Empire State Building were called men of courage, skill, daring, and imagination. They were architects, engineers, contractors, bosses, and construction workers of many varied skills. Using equipment now considered out of date, they put together the 102-floor framework of the building in less than six months, a feat which would be a considerable achievement even today.

In 1930, these workmen either went bareheaded, wore a cloth cap—often worn backward—or wore a battered felt hat. The rigid plastics needed for molded head protection, called "hard hats," would not appear until after World War II.

They ate on the job, and, to save time, food was brought up for those who didn't bring their own lunch: two sandwiches, pie, and coffee or milk—all for 40 cents. At the peak of construction there were 3,400 workers. Fourteen of them died from accidents.

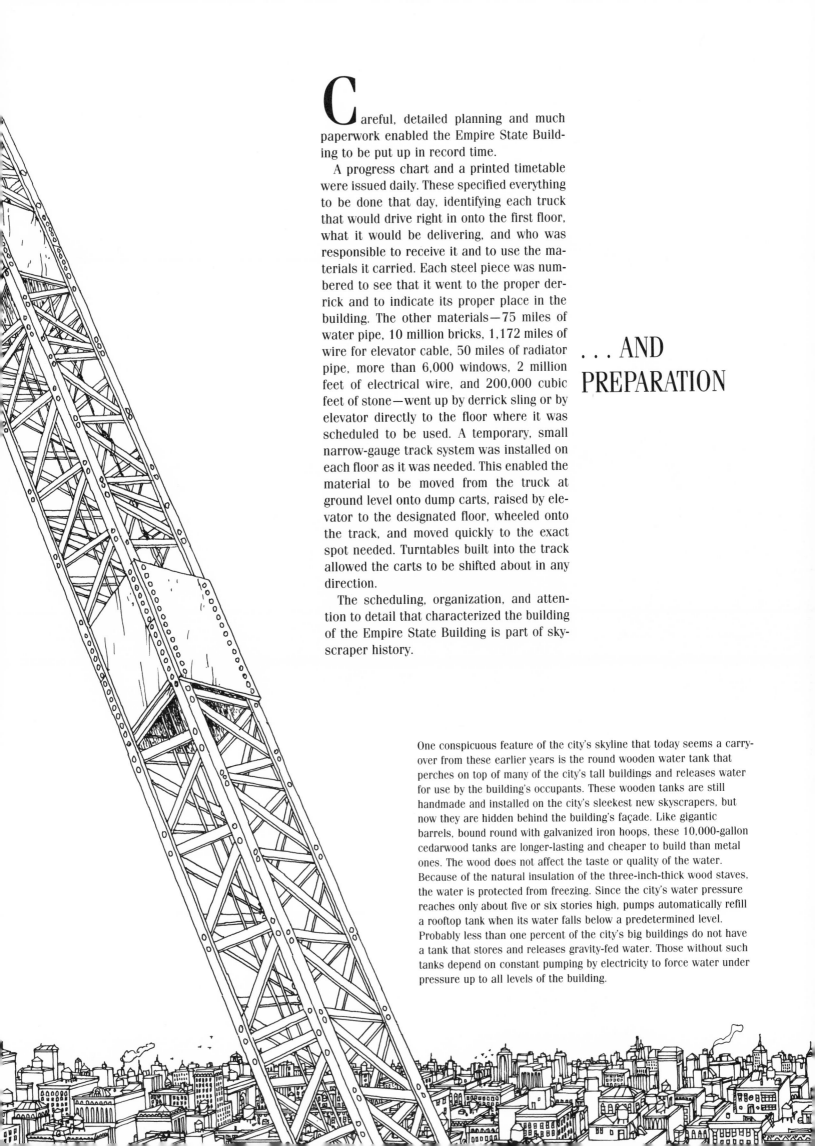

Careful, detailed planning and much paperwork enabled the Empire State Building to be put up in record time.

A progress chart and a printed timetable were issued daily. These specified everything to be done that day, identifying each truck that would drive right in onto the first floor, what it would be delivering, and who was responsible to receive it and to use the materials it carried. Each steel piece was numbered to see that it went to the proper derrick and to indicate its proper place in the building. The other materials—75 miles of water pipe, 10 million bricks, 1,172 miles of wire for elevator cable, 50 miles of radiator pipe, more than 6,000 windows, 2 million feet of electrical wire, and 200,000 cubic feet of stone—went up by derrick sling or by elevator directly to the floor where it was scheduled to be used. A temporary, small narrow-gauge track system was installed on each floor as it was needed. This enabled the material to be moved from the truck at ground level onto dump carts, raised by elevator to the designated floor, wheeled onto the track, and moved quickly to the exact spot needed. Turntables built into the track allowed the carts to be shifted about in any direction.

The scheduling, organization, and attention to detail that characterized the building of the Empire State Building is part of skyscraper history.

. . . AND PREPARATION

One conspicuous feature of the city's skyline that today seems a carry-over from these earlier years is the round wooden water tank that perches on top of many of the city's tall buildings and releases water for use by the building's occupants. These wooden tanks are still handmade and installed on the city's sleekest new skyscrapers, but now they are hidden behind the building's façade. Like gigantic barrels, bound round with galvanized iron hoops, these 10,000-gallon cedarwood tanks are longer-lasting and cheaper to build than metal ones. The wood does not affect the taste or quality of the water. Because of the natural insulation of the three-inch-thick wood staves, the water is protected from freezing. Since the city's water pressure reaches only about five or six stories high, pumps automatically refill a rooftop tank when its water falls below a predetermined level. Probably less than one percent of the city's big buildings do not have a tank that stores and releases gravity-fed water. Those without such tanks depend on constant pumping by electricity to force water under pressure up to all levels of the building.

MIDTOWN MANHATTAN . . . ROCKEFELLER CENTER: 1931

Rockefeller Center is a wonderful place for people-watching. Its Fifth Avenue promenade—the Channel Gardens—and its sunken plaza invite visitor and New Yorker alike to enter, slow down, rest awhile, breathe a bit more easily, and enjoy the visual variety. People from all over the world stop by, carrying cameras. They take pictures of golden Prometheus and his backdrop of cascading water; they take pictures of each other.

They are in a horticultural oasis—unique in the city—where imported exotic greenery changes as the seasons change. Where else would palm trees flourish just off Fifth Avenue . . . or a Christmas tree weighing several tons suddenly appear to signal the beginning of the city's holiday season?

Planned as an integrated complex of buildings for business and entertainment, Rockefeller Center has been expanded since its inception in 1931. Today it has eighteen skyscrapers built about its central skyscraper—the 70-story RCA Building—and it covers almost 22 acres of land in the heart of Manhattan.

Its planners envisioned the site with each skyscraper a unit in relation to each of the other skyscrapers, and to the Center itself. They planned for landscaped areas of open "city space" for light and air, with interconnected patterns of traffic flow, both pedestrian and vehicular, for ease of movement. This design concept was, in 1931, unique for its time, and Rockefeller Center has become a model for similar projects around the world.

Imagine building a cluster of skyscrapers on land you didn't own. Yet that's exactly what happened with Rockefeller Center when construction began on its first 12 acres. Lucky Columbia University owned the land—a gift from New York State in 1814. It had been the site of the Elgin Botanic Garden developed privately by a New York City physician, Dr. David Hosack. Rockefeller Center had a lease to rent the land until 2069. But in 1985, Columbia sold the 12 acres to the Center for 400 million dollars.

Tucked away in parts of the city are private alleys. But where else besides Rockefeller Center is there a private, asphalt-covered street with wide sidewalks in the heart of midtown Manhattan? Rockefeller Plaza extends for three full city blocks from 48th to 51st streets, midway between Fifth and Sixth avenues. Few who travel this street realize that between them and the shopping concourse below there is only a steel framework, steel plates, waterproofing, and 14.5 inches of reinforced concrete. One day each year, in July, for 12 hours, this street is closed to the public to maintain its private status.

One of the most farsighted ideas of the 1930's was Rockefeller Center's below-street-level truck delivery and pick-up, to avoid constant congestion in the streets above. Truck ramps lead to underground depots 30 feet or more below street level, where forklifts, specialized equipment, and turntables service the 700 to 1,000 trucks that arrive daily.

Rockefeller Center underground is a multilevel network of pedestrian facilities, with shop-lined promenades and restaurants—even a U.S. post office. It stretches from Fifth Avenue to Sixth Avenue, with direct connections to the city's subway system.

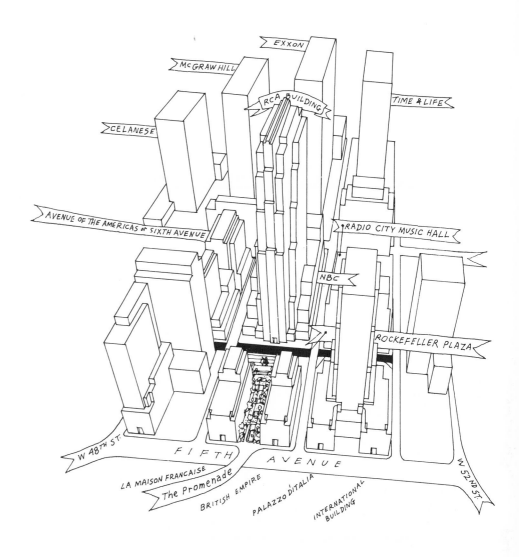

The land on which a large part of the Center is built had already been leased in 1928, to be built upon by private builders. Then came the worldwide depression that began with the 1929 stock-market crash, and any idea of building was abandoned. Millions of people were out of work, and most large-scale construction in New York City—with the exception of the Empire State Building—had stopped. It was a time of despair and of caution. Yet, faced with a costly yearly lease, John D. Rockefeller, Jr., decided to develop the site, personally, as a private enterprise.

In human terms it was an enormous project. Two hundred twenty-eight delapidated tenements, shops, and other buildings had to be demolished and carted away. Four thousand tenants had to be relocated in new living and working quarters.

At a time of vast unemployment, at least 75,000 people were employed at the site, and 150,000 others worked elsewhere, preparing the materials used in the construction.

Rockefeller Center was a civic enterprise on a major scale, as well as a construction project of enormous size.

Its open spaces—nearly one-fourth of the land space has been left unbuilt—with promenades, plazas, trees, flowers, and sculpture, and the lower plaza with its ice-skating rink in winter and outdoor dining in summer, make the Center a focal point in midtown Manhattan. Nearly a quarter of a million people use, or visit, Rockefeller Center daily. The city would be difficult to imagine without Rockefeller Center.

OUT OF THE DEPRESSION: 1930–1965

During the Depression, which lasted through most of the 1930's, about one-fourth of the nation's work force was out of work— 13 million people. A million men were transients, always on the move, homeless. Penniless squatters lived in makeshift shacks in Central Park. Times Square itself was the scene of despair as hungry men and women waited long hours in breadlines for something to eat.

Hamburger steak was advertised for 19 cents a pound, pork chops 25 cents a pound. Trolley cars still ran on tracks along Broadway. Radio was the great unifying link for the whole country with as many as 8 million sets sold yearly. The entire nation listened as President Franklin D. Roosevelt proclaimed at his inauguration, "The only thing we have to fear is fear itself."

In the midst of the despair, the Empire State Building was built, Rockefeller Center was built, the George Washington Bridge opened to traffic, and public-works money built the Lincoln Tunnel under the Hudson as well as public buildings, bridges, sewage systems, and highways. Slowly the city and country began to recover economic strength. In 1939–40, New York City looked to the future with a spectacular World's Fair, just as Hitler engulfed Europe in war.

A year later Pearl Harbor exploded and the nation plunged into World War II. Brownouts dimmed New York's famous skyline as the city shifted to wartime production, and women joined the work force in great numbers for the first time.

New York City was again, as in World War I, the great embarkation port for the troops heading overseas to Europe. Times Square enjoyed one of its greatest boom times, as the mecca for hundreds of thousands of servicemen and women who visited its Stage Door Canteen for entertainment and the chance to socialize with movie stars and celebrities. On August 15, 1945, an estimated two million jubilant New Yorkers jammed the

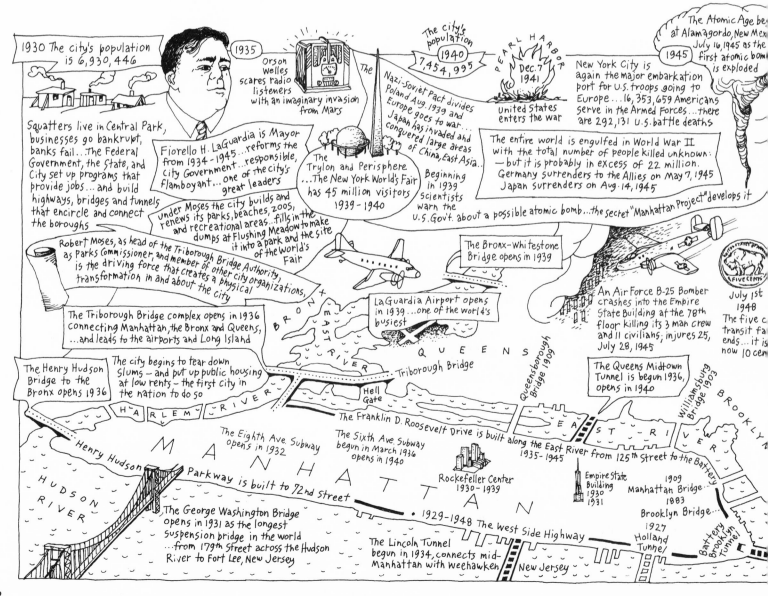

Times Square area as the moving news ribbon on the Times Tower announced Japan's surrender. The war was over.

Veterans returned to find the city with a severe housing shortage. "Cold-water flats," which had hot water but no heat except that provided by the tenant himself, were not uncommon. The biggest city, in the world's most powerful nation, was ready for dramatic change after the hardship years of the Depression and the austerity caused by World War II.

Privately built apartment complexes housing thousands of families were constructed, helped by tax abatements. The city itself sponsored public housing—the first city in the nation to do so.

In the East 40's, where slaughterhouses had just been torn down near the East River, the United Nations headquarters was built, representing all the nations of the world, with a hope for lasting peace.

A building boom put up sleek, air-condi-

tioned buildings, and Sixth Avenue and Third Avenue opened up as the old elevated transit tracks came down. The city became more prosperous than it had ever been. Most of the major corporations of the country had their headquarters in the city. It became a leading center of the world in cultural activities. And far-reaching social changes were beginning as well.

The population figures for 1950–60 remained fairly constant, but a great migration was under way. More than a million middle-class families were moving away from the city to the easily reached suburbs, while more than a million newcomers to New York City—mostly black families from the South and Puerto Rican families from the Caribbean—were moving in.

Complaints heard for more than 300 years—that the city was dirty, dangerous, and always tearing down its buildings, only to rebuild again—were still being heard.

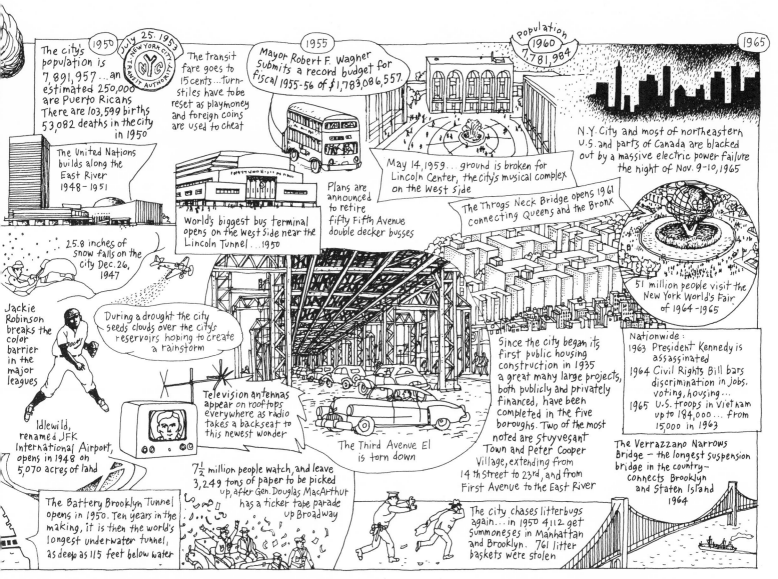

DOWNTOWN MANHATTAN ... THE WORLD TRADE CENTER: 1966–1971

The World Trade Center was conceived in 1960 as central to a plan to develop and rehabilitate the lower tip of Manhattan, which, although it was the financial center of the nation, had many old buildings and a shortage of modern office space.

Residential housing, not available in lower Manhattan for more than a hundred years, was envisaged under the plan. No hotel had been built in the area since 1836.

Unlike the Empire State Building and Rockefeller Center, which were built with private financing, the World Trade Center was built by The Port Authority of New York and New Jersey, an agency of the two states. The World Trade Center brings together in one location more than a thousand government agencies and private businesses engaged in the marketing, financing, processing, documenting, insuring, and transporting of foreign trade. More than sixty nations are represented in the World Trade Center, either by their governments or by private business.

New York City, which began as the tiny Dutch trading port of Nieuw Amsterdam on the tip of Manhattan Island, has one of the world's most famous harbors, with its skyscrapers built right up to the water's edge. And towering over all of lower Manhattan are the twin towers of the World Trade Center, symbols of New York's preeminence as a center of trade and commerce. These towers are two of the world's tallest skyscrapers.

The construction of the World Trade Center is considered to be one of the biggest building projects ever attempted, in the size of its buildings and foundations and the amount of excavation required.

About half of the 16-acre site, including

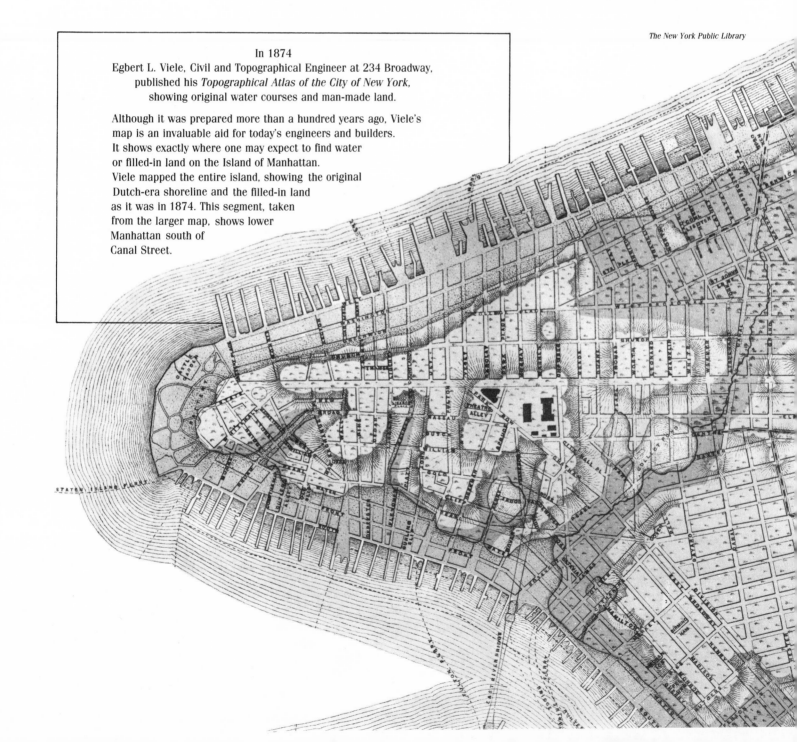

In 1874
Egbert L. Viele, Civil and Topographical Engineer at 234 Broadway,
published his *Topographical Atlas of the City of New York,*
showing original water courses and man-made land.

Although it was prepared more than a hundred years ago, Viele's
map is an invaluable aid for today's engineers and builders.
It shows exactly where one may expect to find water
or filled-in land on the Island of Manhattan.
Viele mapped the entire island, showing the original
Dutch-era shoreline and the filled-in land
as it was in 1874. This segment, taken
from the larger map, shows lower
Manhattan south of
Canal Street.

the two skyscrapers, is built where once there was only water. In that area, landfill—dirt, old bricks, timbers, rock ballast from sailing-ship days—all of these were dumped there during the past 300 years. This fill extended the shoreline about 600 feet into the Hudson River from where it had been when the Dutch first built in Manhattan, in 1625.

The excavation for the World Trade Center was 70 feet below the level of the Hudson River and its five-foot tides. The underground foundation work was six stories deep.

In part of the excavation area, subway trains and an underground railway—moving nearly a thousand trains a day—had to keep running while the excavation was being dug above, around, and below them.

The World Trade Center was a challenge on a gigantic scale: in concept, in engineering, and in construction.

An enormous amount of earth and rock—1.2 million cubic yards—was removed in the excavation of the World Trade Center and deposited behind cofferdams in the Hudson River. This provided 23.5 acres of valuable, vacant, new land where only water had been before. Yet even this gigantic amount of landfill was only about one-fourth of the total movement of soil and sand that has made 92-acre Battery Park City possible. The remaining landfill was sand dredged up from the bottom of lower New York Bay and brought here on scows. Battery Park City Authority, created in 1968 by the New York State Legislature, owns Battery Park City, built its roads and infrastructure, and arranged the long-term land leases under which the developers have built its residential and commercial buildings. The Authority collects land rent and payments in lieu of taxes on these buildings, and uses the revenues to retire its debt. Excess revenues are to be used to pay off 400 million dollars in bonds that will provide financing for 24,000 housing units, for low and moderate income families, throughout the city.

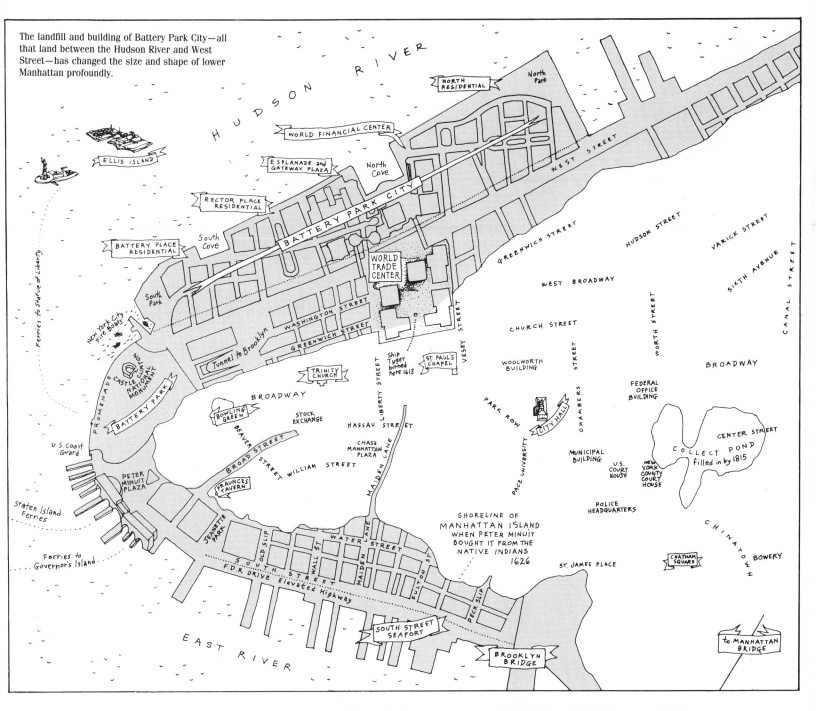

The landfill and building of Battery Park City—all that land between the Hudson River and West Street—has changed the size and shape of lower Manhattan profoundly.

KEEPING THE HUDSON RIVER OUT

The sight of the twin towers of the World Trade Center rising over lower Manhattan is spectacular. What one doesn't see—beneath the buildings—is equally spectacular and a remarkable engineering achievement.

An area of 16 acres, approximately the size of sixteen football fields, had to be dug down six stories below street level, next to and below the level of the Hudson River. A large part of it was filled-in land, above mud and clay, all with a high water content. The excavation and construction of a conventional foundation would have been extremely difficult. Cave-ins would have been likely, and the temporary bracing of the walls would have interfered with the actual construction of the buildings.

It was decided that before any excavation began, a trench would be dug all around the outside of the excavation-to-be, down into bedrock. This trench would be filled with concrete. Then, from inside this enormous bathtub, 1.2 million cubic yards of dirt and rock would be removed.

Not only would the engineers be required to remove dirt, rocks, mud, and debris from the trench as it was being dug, but they would do it without seeing down into the trench, as it was only 3 feet wide, about 70 feet deep, and filled with a bentonite slurry. This slurry, a mixture of a volcanic ash called bentonite, and water, has the unusual capability of preventing cave-ins.

The trench was dug in sections 22 feet in length, by clamshell buckets on digging rigs. The bentonite slurry was poured into the trench as the dirt was removed, keeping the trench always full and the walls supported and intact.

As each section was dug down to bedrock, a prefabricated reinforcing steel cage was lowered into the slurry. Concrete was then tremied, or piped, down to the bottom of the trench, forcing the lighter slurry out at the top, until the entire section was filled with concrete. The slurry was saved, to be used in the digging of the next section of trench.

Initially, every other 22-foot-long section was dug, leaving an undug section between two dug sections. When the concrete sections had hardened on both ends of an undug section, that section was then dug in the same way, and the connecting ends of the sections were joined by a permanent interlocking joint. This was done around the entire perimeter of the World Trade Center, a distance of 3,400 feet.

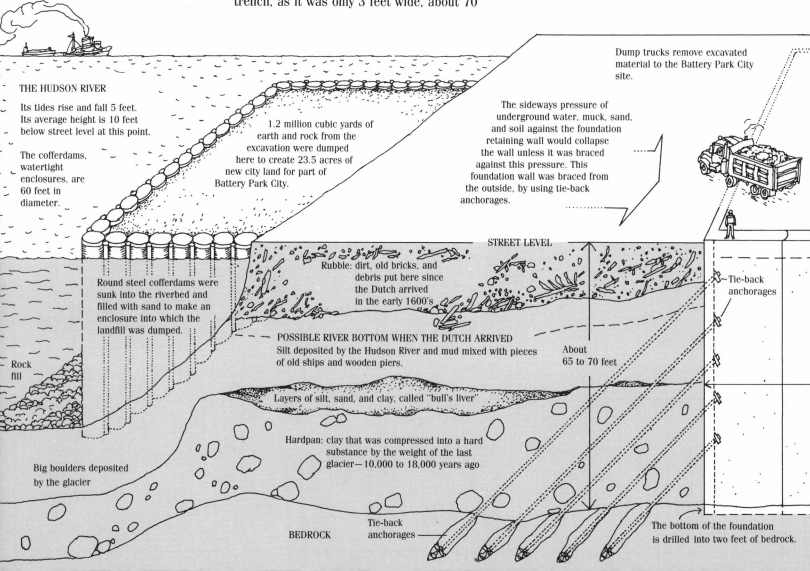

Dump trucks remove excavated material to the Battery Park City site.

THE HUDSON RIVER

Its tides rise and fall 5 feet. Its average height is 10 feet below street level at this point.

The cofferdams, watertight enclosures, are 60 feet in diameter.

1.2 million cubic yards of earth and rock from the excavation were dumped here to create 23.5 acres of new city land for part of Battery Park City.

The sideways pressure of underground water, muck, sand, and soil against the foundation retaining wall would collapse the wall unless it was braced against this pressure. This foundation wall was braced from the outside, by using tie-back anchorages.

STREET LEVEL

Round steel cofferdams were sunk into the riverbed and filled with sand to make an enclosure into which the landfill was dumped.

Rubble: dirt, old bricks, and debris put here since the Dutch arrived in the early 1600's

Tie-back anchorages

Rock fill

POSSIBLE RIVER BOTTOM WHEN THE DUTCH ARRIVED
Silt deposited by the Hudson River and mud mixed with pieces of old ships and wooden piers.

About 65 to 70 feet

Layers of silt, sand, and clay, called "bull's liver"

Big boulders deposited by the glacier

Hardpan: clay that was compressed into a hard substance by the weight of the last glacier—10,000 to 18,000 years ago

BEDROCK

Tie-back anchorages

The bottom of the foundation is drilled into two feet of bedrock.

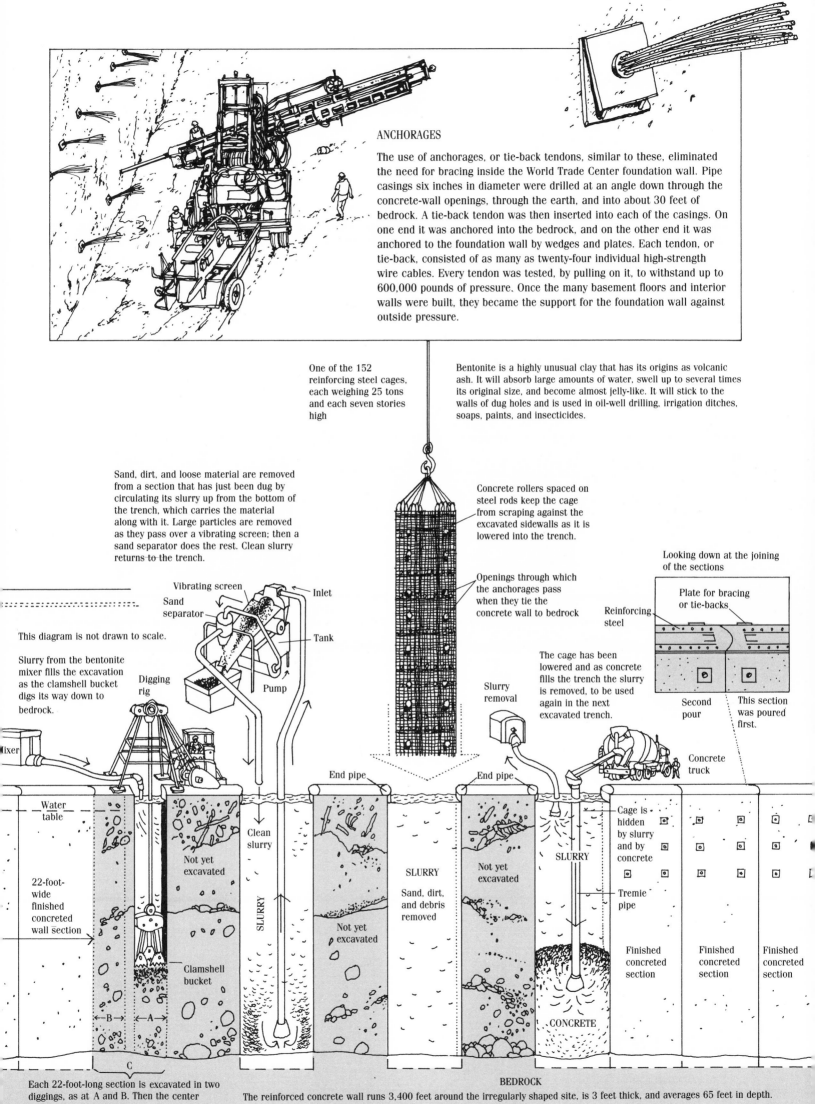

ANCHORAGES

The use of anchorages, or tie-back tendons, similar to these, eliminated the need for bracing inside the World Trade Center foundation wall. Pipe casings six inches in diameter were drilled at an angle down through the concrete-wall openings, through the earth, and into about 30 feet of bedrock. A tie-back tendon was then inserted into each of the casings. On one end it was anchored into the bedrock, and on the other end it was anchored to the foundation wall by wedges and plates. Each tendon, or tie-back, consisted of as many as twenty-four individual high-strength wire cables. Every tendon was tested, by pulling on it, to withstand up to 600,000 pounds of pressure. Once the many basement floors and interior walls were built, they became the support for the foundation wall against outside pressure.

One of the 152 reinforcing steel cages, each weighing 25 tons and each seven stories high

Bentonite is a highly unusual clay that has its origins as volcanic ash. It will absorb large amounts of water, swell up to several times its original size, and become almost jelly-like. It will stick to the walls of dug holes and is used in oil-well drilling, irrigation ditches, soaps, paints, and insecticides.

Sand, dirt, and loose material are removed from a section that has just been dug by circulating its slurry up from the bottom of the trench, which carries the material along with it. Large particles are removed as they pass over a vibrating screen; then a sand separator does the rest. Clean slurry returns to the trench.

Concrete rollers spaced on steel rods keep the cage from scraping against the excavated sidewalls as it is lowered into the trench.

Openings through which the anchorages pass when they tie the concrete wall to bedrock

Looking down at the joining of the sections

Plate for bracing or tie-backs

Reinforcing steel

Second pour

This section was poured first.

Vibrating screen

Sand separator

Inlet

Tank

This diagram is not drawn to scale.

Slurry from the bentonite mixer fills the excavation as the clamshell bucket digs its way down to bedrock.

Digging rig

Pump

Mixer

Slurry removal

The cage has been lowered and as concrete fills the trench the slurry is removed, to be used again in the next excavated trench.

Concrete truck

End pipe

End pipe

Concrete

Water table

22-foot-wide finished concreted wall section

Not yet excavated

Clean slurry

SLURRY

SLURRY

Sand, dirt, and debris removed

Not yet excavated

Not yet excavated

SLURRY

Cage is hidden by slurry and by concrete

Tremie pipe

Clamshell bucket

CONCRETE

Finished concreted section

Finished concreted section

Finished concreted section

←B→ ←A→

C

Each 22-foot-long section is excavated in two diggings, as at A and B. Then the center section, C, is removed.

BEDROCK

The reinforced concrete wall runs 3,400 feet around the irregularly shaped site, is 3 feet thick, and averages 65 feet in depth.

A PROBLEM IN LEVITATION

The vast below-ground excavation of the World Trade Center came to be known as the Big Bathtub. Inside this space would be the large storage areas for U.S. Customs, auto parking, 40,000 tons of air-conditioning equipment, a vast shopping mall, passageways connecting all the buildings, and the PATH commuter railroad from New Jersey.

After crossing under the Hudson River, the commuter railroad from New Jersey, operating since July 1909, ended up exactly where the excavation of the Big Bathtub would have to be dug. Its trains ran inside two parallel cast-iron tubes, each 16 feet, 7 inches in diameter. Five hundred feet of each tube would be exposed during the digging and building of the foundation.

They had been resting there undisturbed for almost 60 years. Now all the dirt, rock, and fill above, around, and below these cast-iron tubes would have to be removed without any interruption to the passengers and trains thundering back and forth inside them.

When the excavation was completed, these heavy tubes were suspended in mid-air about 30 feet above the foundation floor. For two years during this phase of construction they had to be supported against sagging from their own weight, prevented from moving sideways, and protected from train vibrations.

By then a whole new set of tracks and a new terminal had been built, and the old tubes and tracks had been removed.

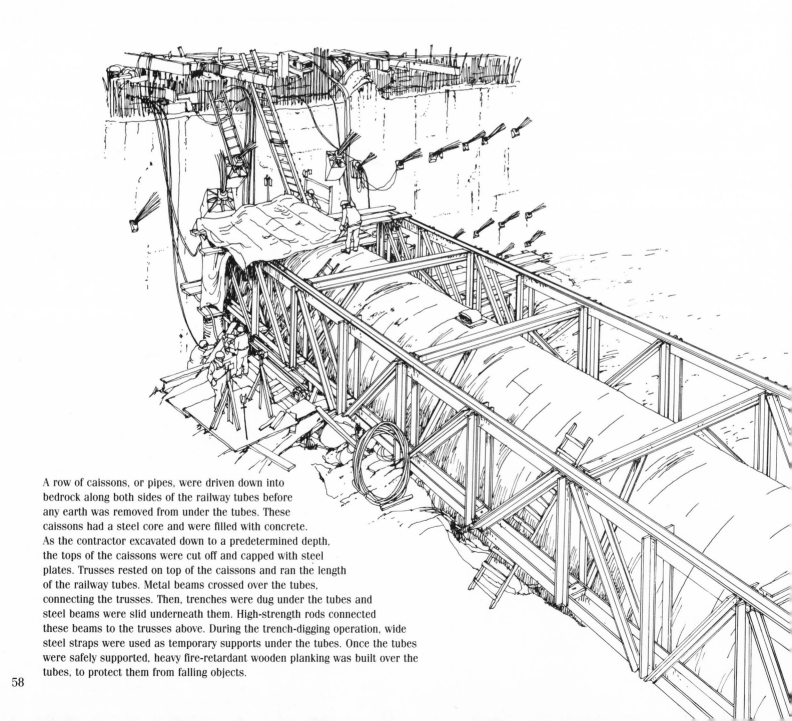

A row of caissons, or pipes, were driven down into bedrock along both sides of the railway tubes before any earth was removed from under the tubes. These caissons had a steel core and were filled with concrete. As the contractor excavated down to a predetermined depth, the tops of the caissons were cut off and capped with steel plates. Trusses rested on top of the caissons and ran the length of the railway tubes. Metal beams crossed over the tubes, connecting the trusses. Then, trenches were dug under the tubes and steel beams were slid underneath them. High-strength rods connected these beams to the trusses above. During the trench-digging operation, wide steel straps were used as temporary supports under the tubes. Once the tubes were safely supported, heavy fire-retardant wooden planking was built over the tubes, to protect them from falling objects.

The twin towers of the World Trade Center weigh more than a million tons; this is the combined dead weight of the structural buildings and the live load—the people using the buildings and their equipment.

The designers of the Center provided enormous reserve strength in the buildings by calculating all the weight-carrying loads and stresses, and by specifying for specific uses, steels with different capabilities. There are twelve different steels used: some are high-strength, others are heat-treated low-alloy steels. Each type has advantages—including, for some, low cost—that determined its use.

Steel may actually compress, or shorten, under heavy weight loads. It was calculated that one type of steel, if used as a column as tall as the World Trade Center, would shorten 16 inches under the stress of 30,000 pounds of pressure per square inch. Some of the steel used in the towers has an ultimate strength of 100,000 pounds of pressure per square inch. Because steels compress dif-

ferently, the engineers had to design the separate components so as to ensure that all the floors would be level under their full loads.

The elevator-stairway core is at the center of each tower, with heavy interior steel columns in and around this core. Four giant kangaroo cranes were positioned in the elevator shafts of each core during construction of the towers. The floor beams—some are more than 60 feet long—extend from the exterior steel wall columns to this central core, leaving each floor, about an acre in size, free of interior support columns. The weight of the floors is carried by the exterior walls of the building and the inner core.

These exterior wall columns are made like long hollow steel tubes, which give them high resistance to wind pressure. The spandrels, horizontal steel beams that form the window frames on each floor, are welded to these box-like support columns, providing rigidity and strength to the towers.

CARRYING THE WEIGHT

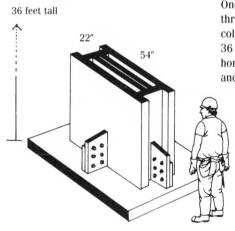

One of the foundation core columns, made of five-inch and three-inch steel, is almost a solid piece of steel. These big core columns, shown cut through, weigh as much as 56 tons and are 36 feet long. They rest on top of a two-layered framework of horizontal steel beams that, in turn, rests on a concrete base anchored into the bedrock.

There are 248 hollow tube EXTERIOR WALL COLUMNS of high-strength steel that form the entire outer surface of the twin towers. You see them as dramatic vertical lines whenever you look at the towers.

Fireproofing protects the steel from damage in a fire and acts as a thermal barrier against hot and cold weather, which, respectively, causes steel to expand and contract.

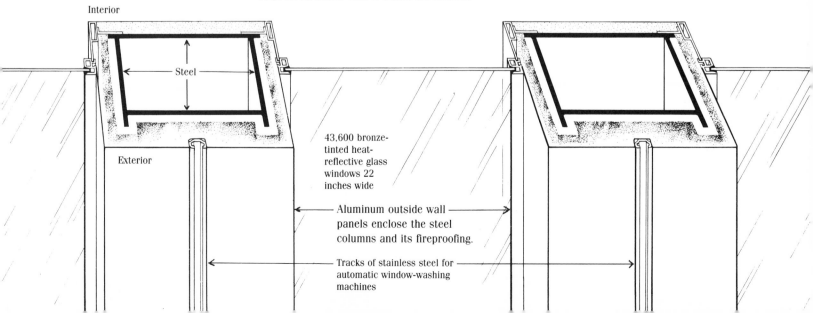

43,600 bronze-tinted heat-reflective glass windows 22 inches wide

Aluminum outside wall panels enclose the steel columns and its fireproofing.

Tracks of stainless steel for automatic window-washing machines

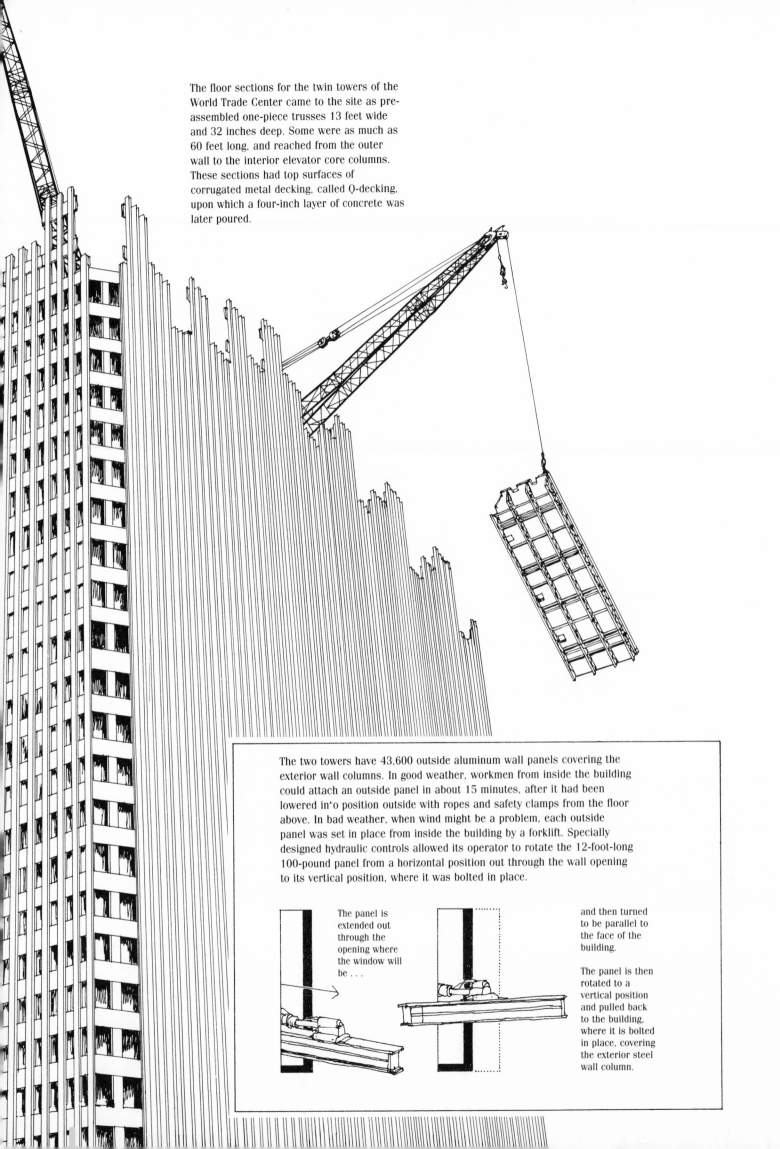

The floor sections for the twin towers of the
World Trade Center came to the site as pre-
assembled one-piece trusses 13 feet wide
and 32 inches deep. Some were as much as
60 feet long, and reached from the outer
wall to the interior elevator core columns.
These sections had top surfaces of
corrugated metal decking, called Q-decking,
upon which a four-inch layer of concrete was
later poured.

The two towers have 43,600 outside aluminum wall panels covering the
exterior wall columns. In good weather, workmen from inside the building
could attach an outside panel in about 15 minutes, after it had been
lowered in·o position outside with ropes and safety clamps from the floor
above. In bad weather, when wind might be a problem, each outside
panel was set in place from inside the building by a forklift. Specially
designed hydraulic controls allowed its operator to rotate the 12-foot-long
100-pound panel from a horizontal position out through the wall opening
to its vertical position, where it was bolted in place.

The panel is
extended out
through the
opening where
the window will
be . . .

and then turned
to be parallel to
the face of the
building.

The panel is then
rotated to a
vertical position
and pulled back
to the building,
where it is bolted
in place, covering
the exterior steel
wall column.

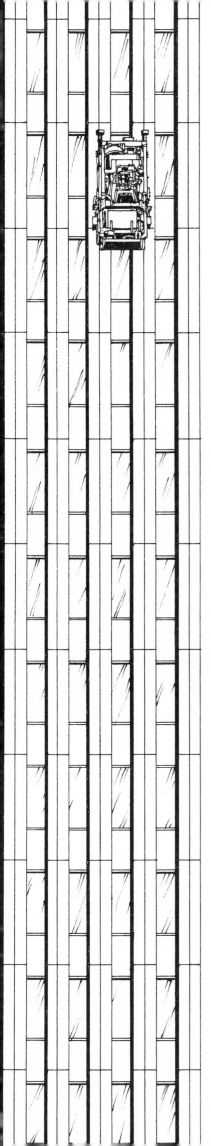

An automatic window-washing machine glides down and up the outside of the World Trade Towers, in grooved stainless-steel tracks built into the outer wall. A window-washing trip down to the 9th floor and back up to the 106th floor takes half an hour. Below the 9th floor the wider windows are washed by men working from steel buckets, lowered from the top of the towers by cables.

A CITY WITHIN THE CITY

The World Trade Center has a daily population of about 130,000 people: tenants, business men and women, and visitors. If it was a city it would be the sixth largest in New York State, next in size to Syracuse and bigger than Albany, the state capital—all on a plot of land only 16 acres.

The twin towers alone contain 192,000 tons of structural steel, 3,000 miles of electrical wiring, 43,600 windows, 4,000 doors, 7,000 plumbing fixtures, 198 elevators, and 50,000 telephones. The World Trade Center itself has the largest enclosed shopping mall in Manhattan, offering more than sixty shops and services, and an underground parking area for nearly 2,000 autos. There are 9.5 million square feet of office space and more than twenty restaurants in this one development. And it has its 130,000 people constantly on the move, and generating nearly 60 tons of trash a day, all of which has to be carted away.

Such a concentration of office space and of people, with their everyday needs for transportation, food, water, sanitation, electricity, and breathing space—all the services that make Manhattan livable—places extraordinary demands upon the city.

Zoning laws control what can be built. Before 1963 there were no restrictions on what could be torn down. But in that year Pennsylvania Station was demolished and the public awakened to the need to preserve its historical and architectural treasures. The Landmarks Preservation Commission was created, its members appointed by the Mayor. They identify and protect buildings of esthetic, cultural, and historical value to the city, and monitor compliance with a building's landmark designation to prevent unauthorized reconstruction, alteration, or demolition. They designate historical districts and protect landscape features of the city. They may, when hardship can be established, allow variances within the landmark designation.

Grand Central Station is one of Manhattan's landmark buildings.

ZONING: AN ATTEMPT TO SET RATIONAL LIMITS

Zoning is a method of controlling land use by law: it regulates the height and form of buildings and the amount of land to be built upon, establishes commercial and residential districts, and seeks to promote growth as well as assure livable surroundings for the city's inhabitants.

It is said that before the arrival of the first Europeans, the Algonquin Indians on Manhattan Island paid tribute to the more powerful Mohican Indians for the privilege of living on the island.

The first Dutch settlers lived there only by the consent of the Dutch West India Company. Private ownership of land was not permitted for the first 10 years of the tiny settlement on the tip of Manhattan.

As the settlement grew, Dutch laws were established to govern the sale of land and the types of building material to be used, all affecting the individual household for the general good. Chimneys, front stoops—or steps—were among the things controlled by Dutch law, with fines imposed to achieve compliance.

As the population increased and the town became a complex city, old laws were changed to meet the new conditions, resulting in a patchwork of regulations. In 1867 New York City passed laws dealing with fire and ventilation. In 1899 it adopted a building code, and in 1901 a tenement-house law was enacted.

By then critics in the city had begun to attack the size and the bulk of the new skyscrapers being built, for they were creating dark and cheerless canyons in lower Manhattan. It is a complaint still heard today.

In 1913–15 the Equitable Life Assurance Company built, on lower Broadway, a building that overwhelmed the area. It rose straight up from the sidewalk to a height of 40 floors, and contained 1.4 million square feet of office space. Whether or not this building was the cause, in the next year, 1916, New York City became the first city in the nation to enact a comprehensive zoning ordinance regulating the use, bulk, and height of buildings.

This 1916 code, an eighty-five-page document that would be amended more than 2,500 times, remained in effect until 1961, when a completely revised zoning code was enacted. So many amendments have now been added to the 1961 code that it requires two thick volumes to list them all.

Zoning requirements change as the city changes, and when experience shows the laws are not working as planned. So complex are these laws that specialized lawyers and architects are needed to guide proposed projects through the many requirements, and to ensure that the building will indeed be allowed to be built as planned.

Suppose you as an individual want to build a skyscraper in Manhattan. Or perhaps you are a large corporation and want to have a new headquarters building in New York City.

Where will you build it?

Lower Manhattan? Midtown Manhattan? The East Side? Or the West Side, where the city may offer you benefits because it wants to attract new construction and businesses to that area?

Every bit of land already has something built upon it, but New York is always ready to tear down its buildings. You will have to assemble a site—by buying all the buildings that occupy the area you want. Since millions of dollars are involved, if this procedure isn't kept a secret, you will be forced to pay exorbitant sums to owners who realize what your plan is and who won't sell unless you meet the price they want.

Sometimes an alternate solution is achieved. One recent skyscraper had to be built around and above an established and busy restaurant, whose owner wanted to remain in business where he is. An agreement was negotiated—the developer acquiring air rights above the restaurant, and its owner staying in business during the construction, and getting additional space in the new building, to expand his restaurant. There is no tenant relationship. They are neighbors, the building enclosing most of the restaurant.

Building a skyscraper today in Manhattan requires dealing with a multitude of different city agencies. Plans must be filed, permits sought, variances asked for, fees paid, forms filled out—all requiring large amounts of time and paperwork. The developer and the architect will have to meet zoning requirements, building codes, fire laws, and a myriad of other city regulations before they receive approval for the proposed building.

The contractor for the actual construction must deal with the city at a more immediate level. In addition to permits and official approval, he must use the city streets as work space, temporary storage space, and unloading depot for the enormous vehicles that will arrive with concrete, steel beams and columns, and all manner of other material.

It is a complex task that is being planned—with high risks. Delay must be avoided, for time is money. Experts are needed, and people and machines must be chosen carefully, as part of a highly coordinated enterprise.

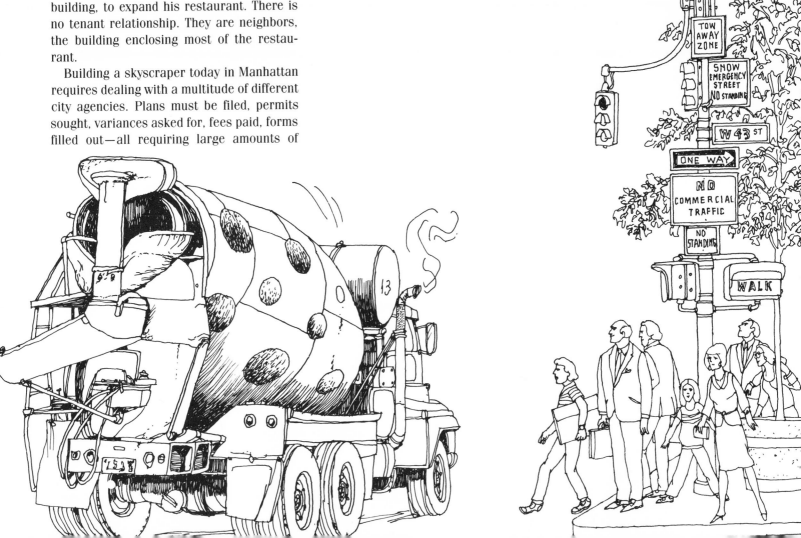

The design of a building requires a team of architects and engineers. But the esthetic vision and expression of an architectural style can establish the building as the achievement of the person designated as the architect. The scale model aids in the design process, enabling the architects, owners, and sometimes the public to envision the building in three dimensions and in relation to its surroundings, and in deciding if changes are desirable. Many skyscrapers in Manhattan are built by large corporations such as IBM, AT&T, and Chase Manhattan for their own use as world headquarters. Others are built by developers as speculative ventures.

THE ARCHITECT: CONCEPT AND DETAIL

The architect is responsible for the design concept and the procedures to be followed in the construction of the building. It is his or her name that is associated with the completed building. In addition, the architect may provide preliminary drawings and cost estimates to the developer, even before the building-site land has been completely assembled.

The architect will get the opinions of structural, electrical, and mechanical engineers, and of the contractor who has been chosen to put up the building, before the design details have been completely worked out on paper. Their practical experience and exchange of ideas result in simplified construction and aids the architect in the design decisions. The structural, electrical, and mechanical engineers are responsible to the architect for the detailed working drawings for each of their specialties.

The amount of paperwork the architects must produce is staggering. Everything that goes into the construction of the building—from the positioning of a 50-ton steel column to the location of the roof drains—must be indicated on the plans. It may take two, three, or more years to design a major project.

Today, construction is begun on many skyscrapers even before the plans are complete, because it is very costly to wait. Once the major elements in the building's design are decided upon, work can begin. The less critical details of the architect's plans can still be completed before the construction workers will need them.

Meanwhile, samples of all types of fixtures and material are studied, enabling the corporation or developer to secure bids from subcontractors, which will add up to the total cost.

CITY OF NEW YORK APPROVAL PROCESS OF A MAJOR PROJECT

Plans must be filed with, and approval obtained from, some or all of these agencies: Department of Buildings, for compliance with zoning, construction, plumbing, mechanical, and elevator codes; local community boards; Board of Estimate, if it's a major project; Board of Standards and Appeals, if a variance from the code is required; the Landmarks Commission. Also needed: street obstruction bond for storage of materials, crane permits, demolition permits.

DEMOLITION
of buildings on the site will be done by demolition companies.

THE DEVELOPER
has assembled the site and decided on the kind of building he wants to build. Money has been borrowed from banks and other lending sources to pay for construction of the building.

THE CONTRACTOR-BUILDER
will actually build the skyscraper as the construction company responsible for, and coordinating all work activity on, the building; and will also point out advantages and disadvantages of certain ways of doing things.

THE ARCHITECT
puts on paper the actual design of the building in accordance with the developer's wishes, or for the company that is erecting the building, and specifies building materials and consults with engineer advisors.

CONSTRUCTION MANAGERS
advise on prices, methods of construction, scheduling, and review contracts before they go out for bids.

SUBCONTRACTORS
are hired by the builder to perform specific types of work. Subcontracting companies are specialists, such as steel erectors, concrete and stone men, electricians, plumbers, sheet-metal workers, interior finishers, and painters.

FOUNDATION ENGINEERS
make soil tests, evaluate construction procedures dealing with underground water and difficult below-ground-level conditions. They design specialized foundations.

STRUCTURAL ENGINEERS
take the architect's drawings and make detailed plans showing where and how the skeleton of the building will be constructed.

MECHANICAL & ELECTRICAL ENGINEERS
determine on paper exactly where all the utilities will be placed within the building, including electricity, communications, heat, ventilation, elevators, plumbing, air conditioning.

The developer has acquired the piece of Manhattan real estate on which to build his skyscraper, the architects' final plans have been approved, and the contractor has been chosen. But without the services that only the city can provide, the skyscraper cannot become a functioning, living entity, busy with thousands of people.

It needs pure water, sewage disposal, electricity, telephones, surface drainage, possibly natural gas and steam heat, and access to rapid transportation. These vital lifelines are all part of the city's underground.

Maps and diagrams locating these underground utilities are indispensable for those who must repair or install them. Their job is made all the more difficult because rarely does one map show all the various cables, wires, and pipes at any specific location. The city maintains the water, sewers, and subways. The other services are supplied by public utilities. Each has its own maps. Some water mains are generations old. Streets have been dug up, refilled, and dug up again. Today, as new work is done, the maps and data are updated, making future repair sites easier to deal with.

THE CITY'S VITAL SERVICES

Somewhere under this asphalt there is a small shut-off valve to a water line. It should be four feet from the curb but the curb has been rebuilt and the street repaved, covering the valve with the asphalt. As it passes over the valve, this metal detector, good for shallow detection underground for 10 inches or so, will pinpoint the valve with telltale beeps.

THE BUSY UNDERGROUND

Manhattan Island, 2.5 miles wide and 12.5 miles long, has more than 500 miles of paved streets.

Beneath these streets and jammed into whatever space can be found is a maze of wires, pipes, cables, tubes, sewers, tunnels, passageways, vaults, and subway systems. These supply to the city electricity, gas, steam, telephone and cable service, sewage disposal, transportation, and water.

Many of the water mains are made of very old cast-iron, with some dating from the early 1900's. Overhead, the city's heavy truck and auto traffic pounds the pavement, causing vibrations and stress—and breaks in the water lines. Streets are flooded, businesses disrupted, and electrical and telephone lines short-circuited by the escaping water. Subway trains rumble below, adding vibrations and strain on the underground utilities.

More than 100,000 manholes and vaults give below-ground access to the city's utilities. They are everywhere. When open, they are the dark holes into which repair crews disappear. They can be dangerous. If a telephone manhole has been closed for a long time, fresh air is pumped into it for five minutes by an electric or propane blower. Next, an explosimeter is lowered into the manhole to indicate that there are no noxious gases below. Only then does a worker go down the ladder and begin work.

Along Manhattan's waterfront there are manholes called "tide holes." These contain water that increases and decreases every six hours with the tides. To work in a tide hole, the water level must be kept as low as possible. This requires portable pumps operating in adjacent tide holes while the workers go about their job.

Every day, somewhere in the city, emergency crews are at work—in the bitter cold of winter, or in the hot humid days of summer. Breakpoints have to be found, holes dug, wires spliced, pipes and mains replaced, and services maintained.

Plastic pipes for natural gas are never buried closer than 15 feet to a hot steam pipe.

No one knows how many Norway rats live underground in Manhattan—probably millions. About a foot and a half long from nose to tip of tail, and weighing about a pound, these rats can eat almost anything, gnaw through cinder blocks, chew through lead insulation, climb walls, swim, and breed so rapidly that the city must wage a ceaseless battle to control them.

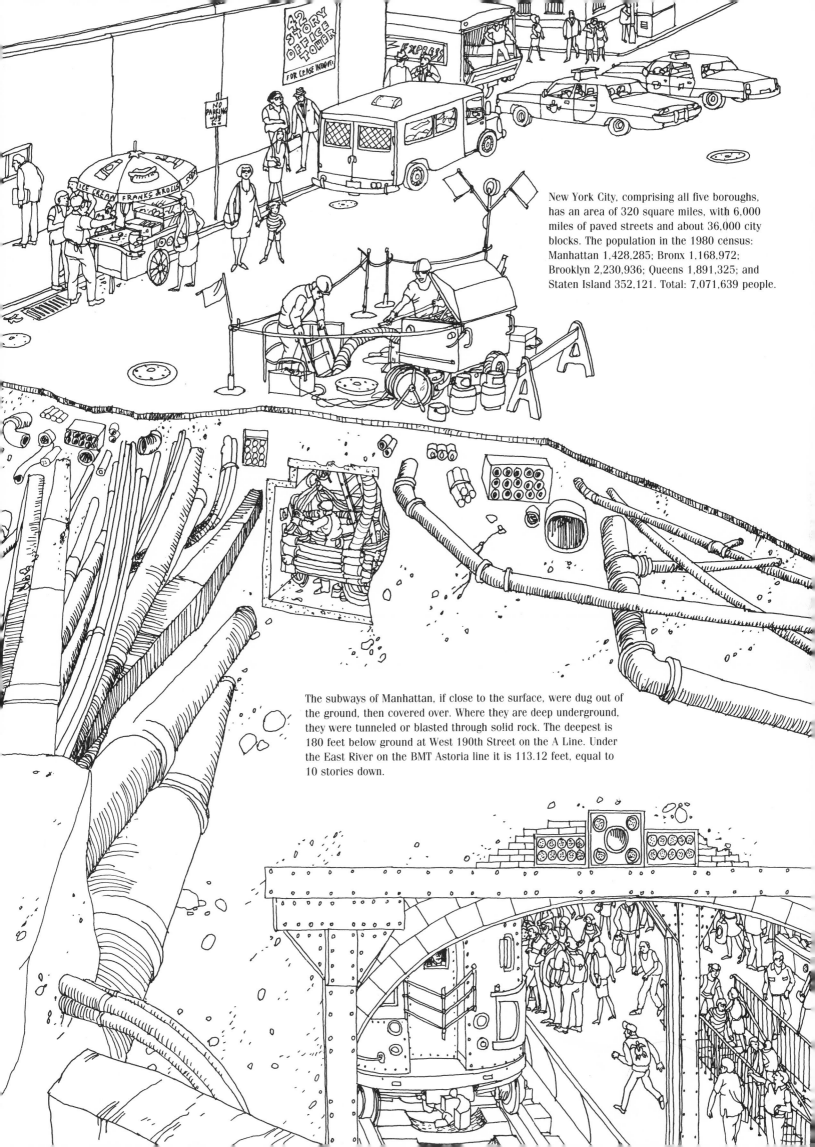

New York City, comprising all five boroughs, has an area of 320 square miles, with 6,000 miles of paved streets and about 36,000 city blocks. The population in the 1980 census: Manhattan 1,428,285; Bronx 1,168,972; Brooklyn 2,230,936; Queens 1,891,325; and Staten Island 352,121. Total: 7,071,639 people.

The subways of Manhattan, if close to the surface, were dug out of the ground, then covered over. Where they are deep underground, they were tunneled or blasted through solid rock. The deepest is 180 feet below ground at West 190th Street on the A Line. Under the East River on the BMT Astoria line it is 113.12 feet, equal to 10 stories down.

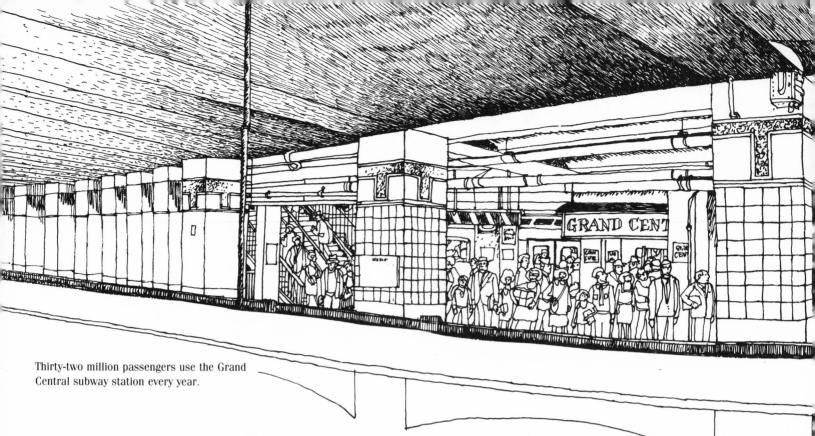

Thirty-two million passengers use the Grand Central subway station every year.

THE SUBWAY

There are New Yorkers who never go down into the subway. Its stations are sometimes dirty, abused, and may be in need of renovation. And when a train arrives—as it surely will—it may be crowded to the doors, claustrophobic, hot, and covered with graffiti. Fortunately, the anti-graffiti crusade has begun to show results, and it is a distinct pleasure to find oneself in a clean, fresh-looking train, speeding uptown or downtown at an express speed of 45 miles an hour.

You have not lived as a Manhattanite until you have taken the Lexington Avenue Express from Grand Central Station to Wall Street during the morning rush hour. Or, at five o'clock, taken the shuttle train from Grand Central to Times Square on a hot summer's day. In the Times Square station, savor the smells of frying foods from the subterranean Nedicks, mingled with the concentrated energy of hordes of determined homegoers, crisscrossing underground on their accustomed ways to uptown trains, downtown trains, and crosstown trains. Overhead is sinful West 42nd Street, its reputation seeping down around and all about you. It is essential New York City.

And the subway system is essential to Manhattan and to all New York City. Its statistics are impressive. It provides swift transportation over routes covering 230 miles. You can ride 32.39 miles without changing trains. If all the tracks were laid end to end they would reach from New York to Knoxville, Tennessee, a distance of more than 700 miles. The system uses 130 billion dollars' worth of electricity a year to trans-port more than a billion passengers a year—3.4 million on any average workday. There are 463 subway stations, 753 token booths, and 2,832 turnstiles.

It takes 46,000 New York City Transit Authority employees to run the subways as well as to operate the city-owned buses in the five boroughs. The fare was five cents when the first city subway began operating October 27, 1904, from City Hall to Broadway at 145th Street. Within living memory, until July 1, 1948, the subway fare was still only a nickel.

Older New Yorkers can remember riding high above ground on the Third Avenue El and the Sixth Avenue Elevated, catching glimpses into the old run-down apartments that once lined those avenues. The streets below, darkened by all the overhead tracks and supporting steel girders, didn't become avenues of wealth with skyscrapers and corporate headquarters until the overhead tracks came down in the 1940's and 1950's.

The subway system, which extended out into the Bronx in 1905, Brooklyn in 1908, and Queens in 1915, still hasn't reached its ultimate destination in terms of additions to its underground tunneling in Manhattan. But digging subways is expensive. Work stopped long ago on the Second Avenue subway, which was begun in 1972. The 63rd Street crosstown, which was dug under Central Park and connects Manhattan and Queens, was on hold—is now scheduled to open in late 1989.

Many of the subway tunnels in Manhattan are very deep indeed, they are real tunnels.

They were drilled, blasted, and dug through solid rock. Wherever possible, the subway was built by "cut and cover," with deep trenches being dug from the surface level down. Tracks were laid and supporting walls with steel girders were built up and roofed over. Dirt and fill were added on top of this, up to street level, and then paved over.

With so many subway tunnels already in existence under the city streets, and so many new deep excavations being dug for big new buildings, it is inevitable that the two should meet. Passersby have seen such a juxtaposition on Lexington Avenue opposite Bloomingdale's. There one could look down into a block-long excavation from 59th Street to 60th Street and see past the exposed steel girders of the removed outer wall section of the subway, onto the underground platform of the busy 59th Street station itself. Inside, on the platform, temporary plywood panels separated the excavation from the passengers waiting for, and using, trains. Outside, beyond the panels, vertical steel beams braced the subway's exposed structure until the subway wall was rebuilt and the new building's foundation was built up against it.

How to minimize vibrations from the subway into the new building? Put a sandwich layer of styrofoam between both new walls. How to protect the subways from any interference by outside construction? All such work must be approved by the Transit Authority. One specialized group of its 1,000 engineers has as its responsibility the analysis of plans and blueprints, and when approved, the monitoring of all work down in,

or adjacent to, the subway structure or tunnels.

Sometimes a developer receives a benefit if he renovates a subway station or builds a new entrance. The city may give him a construction bonus, allowing him up to 20 percent more floor space in his new building than is normally allowed. At the Lexington Avenue 59th Street station, instead of a bonus there was a trade-off between the city and the developer.

Midway in this city block was a stairway that would have led from the subway station into the new building, a feature the developer didn't want. As the mixed assortment of old buildings was torn down, this entrance was closed off. In exchange, the developer was committed to build a new subway entrance at 60th Street, and when that was done, renovate the 59th Street entrance.

Another construction, of much greater magnitude, is the underground pedestrian passageway that now connects two separate subway lines at 51st Street and 53rd Street. It was also dug out beneath busy Lexington Avenue. Every kind of utility was in the way and had to be moved or built around. The passageway goes down 40 feet and has an elevator and an escalator. The developer who built it got a bigger building, and now people can walk underground and transfer from the IRT station at 51st Street to the IND station at 53rd. And the city got a sparkling new addition to its subway system.

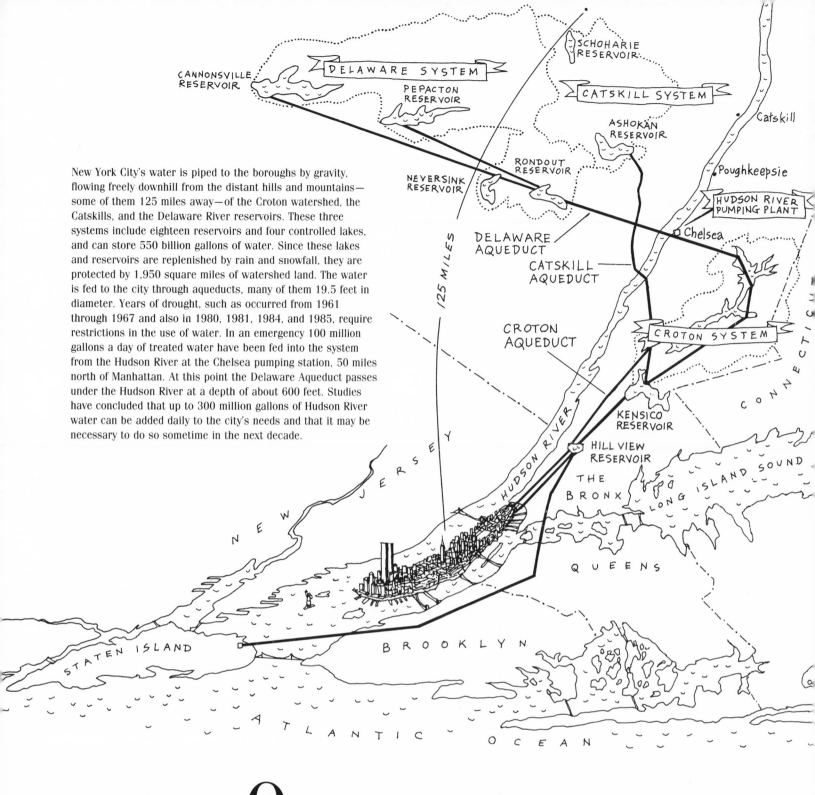

New York City's water is piped to the boroughs by gravity, flowing freely downhill from the distant hills and mountains— some of them 125 miles away—of the Croton watershed, the Catskills, and the Delaware River reservoirs. These three systems include eighteen reservoirs and four controlled lakes, and can store 550 billion gallons of water. Since these lakes and reservoirs are replenished by rain and snowfall, they are protected by 1,950 square miles of watershed land. The water is fed to the city through aqueducts, many of them 19.5 feet in diameter. Years of drought, such as occurred from 1961 through 1967 and also in 1980, 1981, 1984, and 1985, require restrictions in the use of water. In an emergency 100 million gallons a day of treated water have been fed into the system from the Hudson River at the Chelsea pumping station, 50 miles north of Manhattan. At this point the Delaware Aqueduct passes under the Hudson River at a depth of about 600 feet. Studies have concluded that up to 300 million gallons of Hudson River water can be added daily to the city's needs and that it may be necessary to do so sometime in the next decade.

WATER FIT TO DRINK

One of the unseen marvels that New Yorkers take for granted is the city's magnificent water-supply system.

It is the result of planning and construction that began in 1837 with the creation of the Croton Reservoir and Aqueduct project. It continues today with the digging deep within Manhattan and the Bronx of Tunnel Number 3, the first section of which is scheduled to be in operation in 1990. This water tunnel will connect all five boroughs of the city, have underground control centers, and is expected to take care of the projected growth in the city's population—up to 9.4 million by the year 2010. This new tunnel,

24 feet in diameter, will improve the distribution of water, but it will not increase the basic supply.

Much of the city's water is supplied to its users unmetered. All new buildings are metered, as are all commercial and industrial buildings, paying 62 cents per hundred cubic feet of fresh water delivered. Unmetered buildings pay according to a formula based on the width of the building, its height or number of stories, the number of taps, toilets, shower heads, and other water-using fixtures, and the number of dwelling units. New Yorkers use about 1.36 billion gallons of fresh pure water every day. The city's 10-

year program to install meters in all residences may cut this amount by more than 100 million gallons a day.

When the water reaches the city it has been chlorinated, fluoridated, and sometimes aerated. It has been in the reservoir system for several months. Within the city it will be distributed through 6,300 miles of pipes and 184,000 valves, and provide water to about 800,000 separate buildings.

Water is to drink, and is used for many other purposes. One major need is to fight fires, if necessary. Tall buildings have powerful pumps to provide water under pressure at the highest level of the building. Some may have pumps about every tenth floor to maintain this pressure as needed.

Some skyscrapers not only have a water tank up on top, but an intermediary tank lower down in the building. A reserve tank may be in the basement, to feed fire sprinklers.

Maintaining different pressures for different areas of the city is done by releasing more water into the system or by reducing the flow through valves and regulators at trunk mains and zone valves.

Excessive demands can reduce the water pressure in an area, ringing an automatic alarm in one of the control centers that monitor pressures in the system 24 hours a day. A build-up in pressure also triggers the alarm, which, with its continuous readings and printouts, alerts the center to a potential problem.

Wherever there's trouble, out come the street water maps with their different colors indicating low-, intermediate-, and high-pressure areas, and showing where the shut-off valves can be found. Sometimes the problem is easily found—escaping water will probably already have dug a big hole.

Manhattan gets it water from Tunnel Number 1, running the length of the island, deep in the bedrock. Vertical shafts with risers bring the water up to the large trunk mains, some of which are 84 inches in diameter. Every riser has an automatic regulator at the top to control the pressure, and is inspected regularly by a special crew. Regulators can be found at Bryant Park, near Rockefeller Center, and in other public places, but usually go unnoticed.

The city has a grid of these trunk mains, operating at high pressures and distributing water to fifty different zones established by the topography of the land. Regulators reduce the pressure as the trunk mains feed water into the street mains, which are 6 to 20 inches in diameter. These street mains are the iron pipes from which the skyscrapers and apartments—all the buildings of the city—draw their water.

In a system as big as New York City's, where some of the underground pipes may be a hundred years old, breaks are inevitable and occur almost daily. Usually age, brittleness, traffic vibration, or a change in pressure causes a break—which can disrupt subway service, flood basements, damage nearby utility lines, and close off entire areas. Big leaks make their general location known immediately. To locate underground pipes, the source of leaks, or covered-over shut-off valves, the repair crews use specialized detection equipment.

There are thousands of shut-off valves in the system, some of which may have accidentally been paved over. To locate these hidden valves, workers use a DIP NEEDLE. This small leather case has a double compass in it. As a worker points the case true north and swings it over the pavement from side to side, the other compass needle will center on the 90-degree mark when it passes over metal. If it indicates an area three feet across, the worker has found the shut-off valve in its circular "box."

In all new construction the water pipe leading from a building's basement out to a street main must be installed at a right angle to the main. The pipe from an old building often goes off at a different angle, making it difficult to locate outside its building. One operator inside the basement attaches a battery-powered transmitter to the pipe, sending vibrations along the pipe. Outside, his partner moves his receiver along the ground. When his receiver sends out beeps, he knows he has located the missing buried pipe and he traces the beeps to the city main where the shut-off tap for the building is located.

The aquascope: a battery-powered leak detector. Its operator first puts the end to the metal and then turns up the volume. He can hear the leak.

Leaking water makes its own distinctive sounds, which are transmitted by metal objects in the vicinity of the leak. A trained investigator can use this phenomenon to listen with various devices and judge how powerful the leak is, its direction, and how far away it is. These detection devices have thin diaphragm discs that pick up and amplify sounds in the same way a doctor's stethoscope picks up heartbeats and breathing.

INSIDE THE BASEMENT

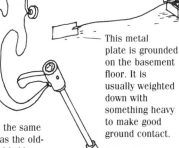

This metal plate is grounded on the basement floor. It is usually weighted down with something heavy to make good ground contact.

The transmitter sends out vibrating impulses.

The transmitting wire is clamped to the water pipe leading to the street outside.

The geophone detects underground leaks. A long hollow transparent plastic tube extends from each earpiece to a heavy disc sandwich of brass and steel. The discs are placed on any surface. Thin membranes stretched tight inside the hollow discs pick up vibrations which are amplified in the earpieces.

Put the spike end against metal and your ear to the other end and listen for running water.

The aquaphone is the same size and shape as the old-fashioned hand-held telephone receiver.

This metal detector has a battery and register gauge on its handle. It will detect metal, giving a steady high-pitch beep.

ELECTRICITY ... LIFELINE OF THE CITY

There are 66,000 miles of electric cables buried beneath the streets of New York City—17,000 miles in Manhattan alone. The city could not function without electricity.

In 1965 there was a massive power failure blanketing the entire northeastern United States and part of Canada. In New York City subways and elevators stopped running, traffic lights went dead, machinery and office equipment became silent, and the city was plunged into darkness. Manhattan was instantly transformed into another dimension, with its masses of towering buildings silent and black, and its millions of people groping their way in eerie darkness. There was danger, excitement, and shared companionship as the city waited for the lights to come back on.

Again, in 1977, the city experienced a total blackout when lightning repeatedly hit Con Edison's high-tension lines in Westchester, shorted the power, and a series of overloads caused the system to shut down.

These blackouts were stark reminders of the city's dependence on a constant source of electricity—which cannot be stored, but must be used as it is generated.

Con Edison, the public utility that provides New York City with its electricity, gas, and steam, generates most of this electricity in its own plants in Manhattan, Queens, Brooklyn and Staten Island, and its nuclear power plant at Indian Point in Westchester. It also buys electricity from other utilities when it is less expensive to do so than to produce its own electricity.

Electricity is created when a magnet rotates inside a coil of wire. A turbogenerator makes electricity when steam—created by heating water with oil, coal, or gas fire, or by nuclear fission—is forced through the turbine, spinning its fan-like blades, and rotating the magnetic core inside the generator. Hydroelectric power uses the force of falling water to spin the blades.

At times almost one-quarter of the city's electricity comes all the way from northern Canada, where giant dams provide cheap hydroelectric power. This is possible because of a grid system that reaches to the Rockies, with regional networks of electricity-generating systems that can feed into each other whenever it is economical or necessary.

Con Edison constantly monitors its needs at its energy control center in Manhattan, which shows its generating plants, transmission lines, and substations on a visual display of the whole system. In an emergency the voltage can be reduced city-wide by up to eight percent, and parts of Westchester, Queens, and Brooklyn temporarily shut down to prevent an overload while standby oil-burning generators are fired up to increase the supply of electricity.

The demand is never constant. It varies with the time of day and with the weather. Hot summer days create a need for air conditioning, which puts enormous demands on the system. The city's subway system alone uses in excess of 4.5 billion kilowatt hours of electricity a year. In Con Edison's control center the operators and computers maintain the balance between supply and demand.

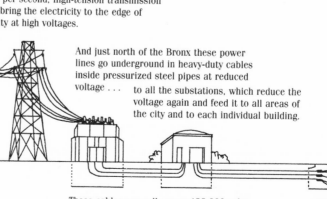

A generator produces electricity at 22,000 volts of power.

A transformer steps up the voltage to as high as 765,000 volts for efficient transmission.

Traveling at the speed of light, 186,000 miles per second, high-tension transmission lines bring the electricity to the edge of the city at high voltages.

And just north of the Bronx these power lines go underground in heavy-duty cables inside pressurized steel pipes at reduced voltage ...

to all the substations, which reduce the voltage again and feed it to all areas of the city and to each individual building.

Con Edison's Indian Point nuclear-power center 30 miles north of New York City on the Hudson River had the first commercial nuclear plant license in the United States. Indian Point supplies 26 percent of Con Edison's power. The utility also has two jointly owned non-nuclear plants north of the city on the Hudson, at West Haverstraw, and near Newburg.

amps: units to measure electric current
volts: units to measure electric potential
watts: units to measure electric energy
kilowatts: how Con Edison measures the use of electricity. Ten 100-watt light bulbs burning for one hour equals one kilowatt of energy.

These cables normally carry 138,000 volts.

The largest voltage transmitted in Manhattan is 345,000 volts—the most common carried underground is 13,000 volts before it is distributed to the customer at lower voltages of 460 and 120 volts.

Manholes and vaults give access to the buried cables between the substations and buildings.

The building's vault varies the voltage needed within the building.

Manhattan is divided into a grid of thirty distribution districts with twenty-three substations. Each district has its own network of cables and its own power source from one of the substations. Each substation has several transformers. Should a break occur within the system it will show up on Con Edison's master control panel and the power will be rerouted, providing uninterrupted service. In the event of a massive power failure, such as occurred in 1983 in the garment district when a city water main broke and a resulting fire damaged a substation, other networks are spliced into that network. A break in a cable from a manhole to a customer, or to a building, doesn't show up on the master control panel. Then Con Edison's repair crews have to test for the cause and repair it, usually down a manhole.

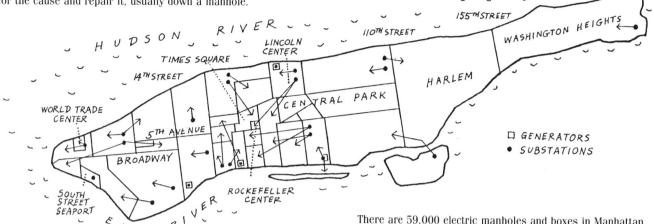

There are many cables of different types and voltages in an underground vault, manhole, or service box. These cables range in voltage from 120 to 15,000 volts, and in size from ¼ to three inches in diameter. The larger, high-voltage cables take up to 12 hours to splice together, depending on the desired configuration. The lead sleeve being prepared by the kneeling worker will be used to cover the splice, and solder wiped in place to protect it from the elements. The crew must know how to construct more than 1,000 different types of splices.

There are 59,000 electric manholes and boxes in Manhattan. Some are as deep as 30 feet below street level, but most are 8 to 12 feet below ground. Water seepage does not usually affect the well-insulated cables, but any water is pumped out and the underground vault is checked with a sensitive meter before workmen enter. Not only must there be no deadly gases down there, but the workmen must be sure there is sufficient oxygen to breathe.

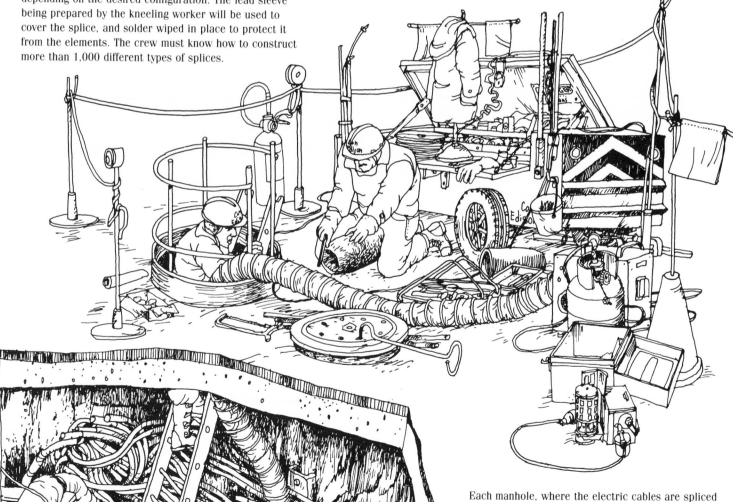

Each manhole, where the electric cables are spliced together, is connected to the next manhole by a group of duct pipes, buried under the streets and encased in concrete, through which the electric cables are carried.

Clouds of steam rising up out of a New York City manhole indicate a probable leak, or water hitting hot pipes. Until repaired, the manhole is vented to let trapped heat escape, as this might damage underground cables or nearby basements.

STEAM

The Metropolitan Museum of Art is heated and cooled by Con Edison's steam. So are the Empire State Building, the twin towers of the World Trade Center, Rockefeller Center, and most of the skyscrapers in Manhattan. The perfectly formed smoke rings that once puffed across Times Square from a billboard advertising cigarettes were steam.

More than a hundred years ago it was realized that piped-in steam could heat buildings and eliminate furnaces. It would be clean, there would be no fuel deliveries or waste removal, and no work crew would be needed. By 1882 an enterprising New Yorker was piping steam to his first customer, a 10-story building half a mile away on lower Broadway.

Today, Con Edison produces 28 billion pounds of steam a year, all of it exclusively for consumers in Manhattan, and most of it a by-product in the manufacture of electricity.

When water is heated until it boils, it turns to steam. While making electricity at its power plants, Con Edison heats water in its boilers to a temperature of 1,000 degrees Fahrenheit under a pressure of 2,400 pounds per square inch. As the steam rushes to escape, it spins hundreds of turbine-fan blades that rotate the generators at tremendous speed, creating electricity. Some of this steam is allowed to cool, condense back into hot water, and is reused.

The rest leaves the generator, its pressure and temperature having dropped, and is fed directly into the pipes and mains under Manhattan's streets. The temperature of the steam is now about 385 degrees Fahrenheit with a pressure of about 150 pounds per square inch. It will travel as fast as 75 miles through the pipes, to heat, to run air conditioners, machinery, and equipment in hotels, factories, apartments, and the tallest skyscrapers.

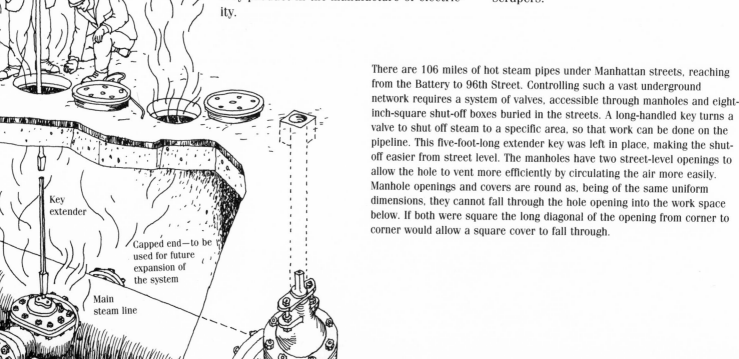

There are 106 miles of hot steam pipes under Manhattan streets, reaching from the Battery to 96th Street. Controlling such a vast underground network requires a system of valves, accessible through manholes and eight-inch-square shut-off boxes buried in the streets. A long-handled key turns a valve to shut off steam to a specific area, so that work can be done on the pipeline. This five-foot-long extender key was left in place, making the shut-off easier from street level. The manholes have two street-level openings to allow the hole to vent more efficiently by circulating the air more easily. Manhole openings and covers are round as, being of the same uniform dimensions, they cannot fall through the hole opening into the work space below. If both were square the long diagonal of the opening from corner to corner would allow a square cover to fall through.

Key extender

Capped end—to be used for future expansion of the system

Main steam line

Shut-off valve

A leak has been detected in this manhole. The entire roof has been excavated and a workman has removed the pipe insulation and is cleaning out the rubble. The shut-off valves have been closed to isolate the leak and the defective fitting will be replaced. Not all manholes have drainage pipes to the city's sewer system, but this one does and is therefore completely dry.

Underground steam pipes, some as big as 30 inches in diameter, are covered with insulation and protected by various types of masonry, cast-iron, or steel housings. They are buried at least two feet underground. In some areas of Manhattan, depending on the congestion of other utilities in the subsurface, they may be as deep as 30 feet underground. There are Park Avenue steam tunnels so deep that they cross the street below the Metro-North railroad tunnel, at 58th and 60th streets.

Some older fittings are of cast iron, about a half-inch thick and susceptible to cracks when subjected to water from external sources, such as a water-main break. Now all the new pipes and fittings are made of steel.

Wherever possible, sections of pipe are welded together, the welds are X-rayed to ensure there are no defects, and the pipe is delivered to the job site. Some fittings are fabricated with flanged ends which are then bolted to pipe flanges; gaskets inserted between the flanges prevent leakage.

Because condensation forms within the steam pipes, there are steam traps situated at low points along the mains. These traps operate on thermodynamic principles, opening to pass the water from the condensation, and closing to prevent steam loss. After this condensate passes through the traps, it flows into a steel pipe chamber where it remains until it has cooled sufficiently to be discharged into the sewer system.

Blower provides cooler air to workmen

There are more than 3,000 expansion joints in the city's steam-pipe system to allow for expansion and contraction of the mains due to temperature changes. The majority of expansion joints contain a bellows element which flexes to absorb the pipe movement, as shown here. Some joints consist of telescoping pipe contained within a packing chamber which prevents a loss of steam should movement occur.

Expansion joint . . . .

Blowouts may occur, with spectacular results— breaking through the pavement and sending steam and sand backfill hundreds of feet into the air. Thanks to the system of shut-off valves, the broken main can be quickly isolated and crews can go underground to make repairs with new steel pipe and fittings.

When Con Edison replaces older cast- or wrought-iron gas pipe with plastic pipe, it cuts and joins the plastic right on the job site. One end of the pipe to be joined is clamped in a movable frame; the other end is placed in a fixed-position clamp. Here the workman holds the two-sided electrically powered cutting tool. As the two pipe ends are forced together, the cutting tool is inserted between them, trimming the two plastic ends exactly, for a perfect fit.

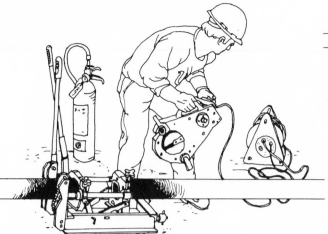

Next, the heating element, also electrically operated, is inserted between the two just-trimmed ends. As heat and pressure are applied, the plastic softens, at a temperature of 500 degrees Fahrenheit.

GAS

Today, the natural gas used in New York City is piped in, under pressure, from Texas and Louisiana, 1,800 miles away—over and under all types of terrain and obstacles. Moving along at about 15 miles per hour through pipes as large as 3.5 feet in diameter, it takes about five days to reach New York City.

With more than a million gas users, Con Edison provides New York City with 98.5 billion cubic feet of gas in a year. It is odorless, tasteless, and colorless, the product of natural forces that over a period of millions of years left vast pockets of the gas trapped underground. It can be explosive. It will kill you if you breathe enough of it. But it is also a clean, practical source of energy, a fuel for industrial and home use—heating, cooling, cooking—performing efficiently and cleanly.

The use of gas in Manhattan, initially for street lighting, goes back to the 1820's. Then it was manufactured from coal, tar, rosin, and even fish oil. Competition among the companies producing gas was fierce, as New Yorkers welcomed this new method of illumination.

Then, in 1882, Edison's Pearl Street station produced the first commercial illumination by electricity. From that time on, New York City would be lit by electricity, not by gas. But the use of manufactured gas for heating and cooking increased as the population of the city grew.

This gas was produced from coal, requir-

ing huge conversion plants in Manhattan and the other boroughs. It was not until 1945, with the development of natural-gas fields and improved pipelines, that Con Edison shut down its last gas-conversion plant in Manhattan.

The switchover to natural gas was a complicated one, since natural gas burns hotter and with a bigger flame than manufactured gas. Every gas-burning appliance and piece of equipment in New York City had to be converted to the requirements of this new gas. All underground mains and pipes had to be purged completely of the manufactured gas, a task that took about 10 months in Manhattan.

Since natural gas is odorless, an artificial odor is added as the gas is piped into the system. This alerts users to its presence, and makes detection of leaks easier. Not unexpectedly, this added ingredient, mercaptan, is nicknamed "skunk oil."

As the gas flows under pressure through the nearly 7,000 miles of gas mains and service pipes in the city, automatic regulators installed in manholes maintain proper pressure. Within each manhole is a filter on the gas line to collect impurities, and a venting pipe to release any gas given off by the regulator. Shut-off valves and bypass pipes allow gas to be diverted around any trouble spots if repairs are needed.

Now the heating element has been removed and the workmen quickly bring the two ends together with maximum pressure, holding them until they fuse together and the plastic cools. The two sections are now permanently joined. As many lengths as are needed are joined the same way. To join larger plastic pipe a mechanically operated unit trims, heats, and fuses the pipe in a similar fashion.

Before plastic pipe is covered over and buried underground, a copper wire is placed along the top of its length, so that a metal detector can locate it should the need arise.

These workmen shown below have put in a bypass line to provide gas to an apartment house while they replace old iron pipe with smaller plastic pipe. They have inserted a balloon stopper inside the plastic pipe and expanded it with a bicycle pump, sealing the open end of the pipe and preventing the escape of gas. The worker in the other pit watches the pressure gauge as gas flows to the apartment. The open end of his pipeline has been turned off by a key in the sidewalk. The old iron pipe has also been exposed about 100 feet further up the street and a section cut away, similar to this end. After all gas has been vented from this separated section, the plastic pipe that has been fused together—more than 100 feet long—will be slid along inside this old iron pipe, eliminating a lot of digging. When coupled at both ends, the bypass line will be removed.

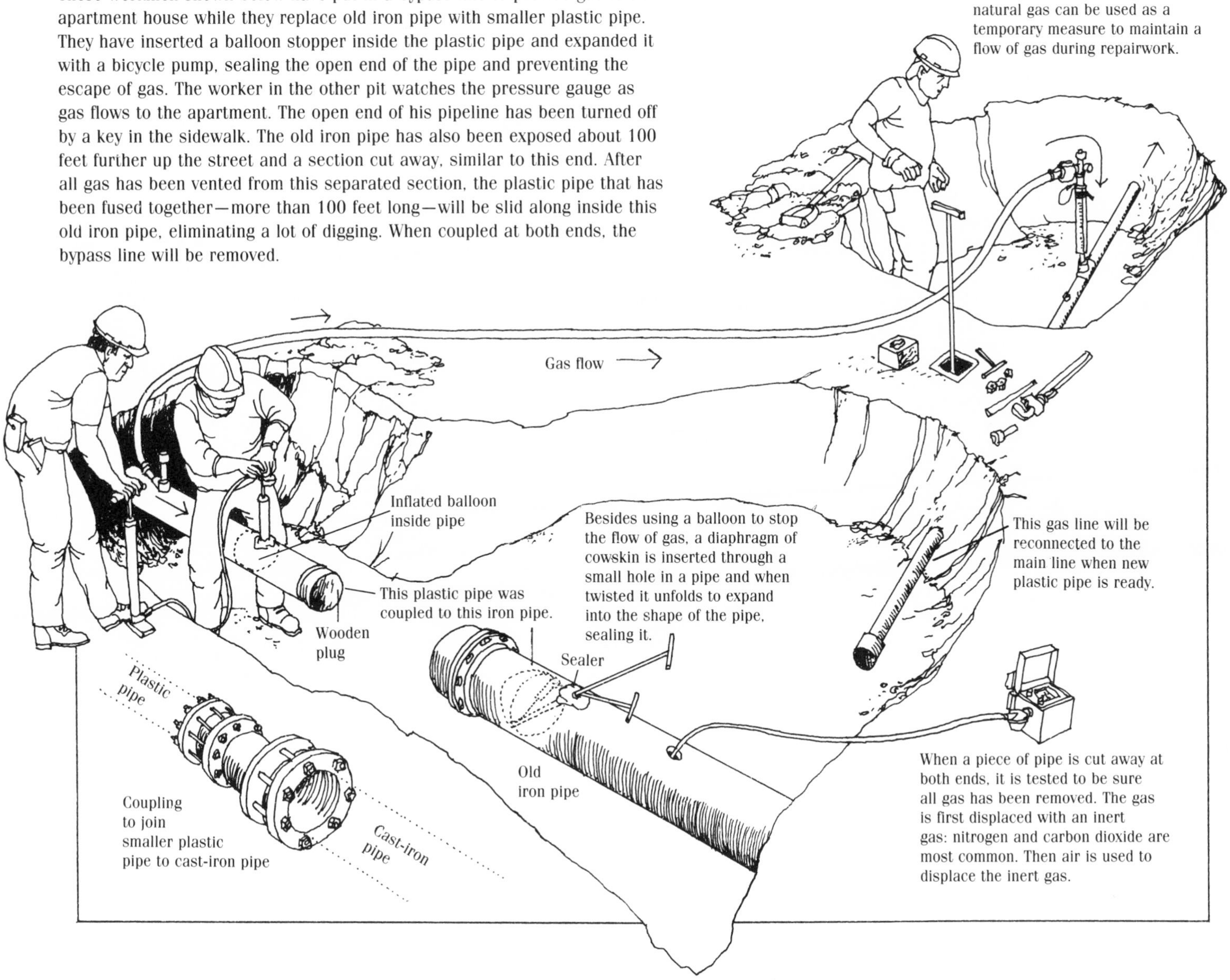

Portable bottles of compressed natural gas can be used as a temporary measure to maintain a flow of gas during repairwork.

Gas flow →

Inflated balloon inside pipe

This plastic pipe was coupled to this iron pipe.

Wooden plug

Plastic pipe

Coupling to join smaller plastic pipe to cast-iron pipe

Cast-iron pipe

Besides using a balloon to stop the flow of gas, a diaphragm of cowskin is inserted through a small hole in a pipe and when twisted it unfolds to expand into the shape of the pipe, sealing it.

Sealer

Old iron pipe

This gas line will be reconnected to the main line when new plastic pipe is ready.

When a piece of pipe is cut away at both ends, it is tested to be sure all gas has been removed. The gas is first displaced with an inert gas: nitrogen and carbon dioxide are most common. Then air is used to displace the inert gas.

The flow of natural gas from Texas and Louisiana to New York City continues unabated, day after day, even though New Yorkers use less, or more of it, depending on the time of day and season of the year.

To build up a ready reserve for the winter heating season, when the demand is greatest, Con Edison liquefies vast amounts of the gas in summer and stores it in a double-walled steel tank in Queens. At this plant the gas is cooled to minus 260 degrees Fahrenheit. As it changes from a gas to a liquid, it shrinks dramatically in volume—requiring only 1/600th the space it had before. The Astoria, Queens, tank holds the equivalent of one billion cubic feet of gas.

TELEPHONE

It is possible to be stuck in traffic on the West Side Highway, inching along toward the 57th Street exit, and see the solitary driver in a nearby car steering with one hand and, with the other, holding a telephone. He is talking into an expensive electronic marvel—the cellular phone—transmitting his two-way conversation into the city's telephone network. But, in spite of cellular and cordless phones, satellites, and space-age technology, telephone communication in Manhattan still ultimately relies on direct cable connections.

If, as you drive along, the traffic lights on nearby Riverside Drive go out of synchronization, it may be because of a flooded manhole, and the temporary failure of a telephone cable there connecting the lights with computers at the city's traffic control center in Long Island City.

Manhattan and the rest of New York City depend on their 14,446 miles of underground cables, of which 387 miles are optical fiber, for instantaneous transmission of voices, electronic data, and information exchange. This enormously long and complex underground system has transmitted as many as 27 million exchanges of information in Manhattan in a single day.

Maintaining it is a never-ending job. Still in the system, still operating, are old lead-encased copper cables, perhaps 50 or 60 years old. Whenever and wherever possible they are removed and replaced by newer plastic-coated copper cable. And whenever possible, not copper but optical fiber cable is placed underground. These hair-thin strands of glass are lighter than copper, take up much less space, are impervious to interference by water or electrical currents, and can carry an almost limitless number of calls simultaneously. Eventually all underground telephone cable in Manhattan will be optical fiber.

Unfortunately, glass fiber and copper wire cannot be spliced together. Optical fiber can only be placed into the underground system where glass joins glass, such as from a substation to a customer or from a substation to a substation.

Meanwhile, copper wire is replaced with copper wire. It is so heavy that its segments are no longer in length than the distance between two manholes. A single piece stretching from just one manhole to the next manhole—perhaps 1,000 feet—may weigh a ton and a half. In contrast, optical fiber is so much lighter that it may extend in an uncut segment stretching a distance of six manholes.

Disruption of service has shown the need for copper cable replacement here at Vesey Street. Just up Broadway is the next telephone manhole. Down inside it is a repairman working at removing an old faulty piece of heavy copper cable. First, he cuts through the cable and separates it from the network of other cables. Then he drills a hole through the cable, which is about three inches thick. He inserts a wire hook through the hole and attaches a heavy yellow nylon rope to the hook. The cable is now ready to be pulled through its underground pipe-like duct to this manhole by this specialized equipment. The cable has also been cut loose down in this manhole, and the claw end of this big rig has clamped onto it. A powerful tug brings up about 10 feet or so of the cable, loosening it in the duct, and winding the cable onto the big spool. Now the big spool takes over and winds away until the entire cut piece is above ground. It has pulled the yellow nylon rope with it. The new piece of copper cable will be drilled, fastened to this nylon cord, and pulled back through the same duct. Down in both manholes the repair crews will then splice the new wires into the system. They may be as deep as 30 feet below ground in some manholes.

VESEY ST   BROADWAY

Each piece of equipment has its own controls.

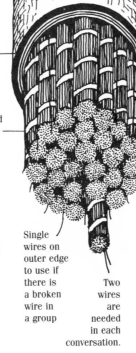
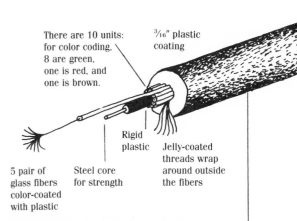

Cooper cable is protected with plastic and thin layers of steel, aluminum, and paper.

Colored plastic binder

Different copper cables have different diameters. The most common diameter in use in Manhattan is twice the size shown here. It contains 2,700 paired wires in twenty-seven groups. Each group is wrapped with a different-colored plastic binder. Each pair of wires in its group is twisted together and easily identified. To maintain integrity in the entire system, each section of cable must match exactly the section to which it is joined. The color coding is organized to easily determine which is the top key color in a cable. Water seepage and a break in the protective shield are the usual causes of disruption in service. Compressed air is continuously forced through the cables to keep out water. If there is an interruption in a line, a technician at the nearest central office can locate it with a hand-held computerized fault locator. This measures a signal sent in a good pair of wires against one sent in the pair not working, to determine where the break is located. The cable illustrated here can carry 2,700 simultaneous conversations.

Single wires on outer edge to use if there is a broken wire in a group

Two wires are needed in each conversation.

There are 10 units: for color coding, 8 are green, one is red, and one is brown.

3/16" plastic coating

Rigid plastic

Jelly-coated threads wrap around outside the fibers

5 pair of glass fibers color-coated with plastic

Steel core for strength

OPTICAL FIBER CABLES are lightwave cables, thin hair-like strands of glass that operate with light pulses generated by laser beams. These pulses transmit voices, computer data, and TV and video messages in digital form using on/off light beams representing ones and zeros. These pulses travel at incomprehensible speeds of 405 million pulses of information per second. This SIECOR 100 fiber cable can carry 302,400 conversations at the same time: 6,048 voice contacts per pair of fibers.

Few people have ever heard of the Empire City Subway Company, Ltd. Yet it has performed a vital service for the inhabitants of Manhattan and the Bronx since 1891. Its workmen dig beneath these city streets, in and around all the underground utilities, and lay the ducts—pipes or conduits—through which are threaded all the low-tension communications cables: telephone, Western Union, cable TV, and connections to fire alarms, police call boxes, and to traffic lights.

Older than the New York Telephone Company, it was one of that company's subsidiaries, but is now an independent company. Under an agreement with the city, it alone does this digging, which gives the city tight control over its own streets.

When something, such as a new skyscraper, has a need for new conduits, the city approves, and then notifies Empire. Empire meets with the Mayor's Traffic Coordinating Committee, supplying a sketch with details: where? how big a job? how long will it take? Only when it gets permission can it begin to dig.

Most ducts are plastic. Some, in unusual places, are steel, which is difficult to shape, and is costly. In lower Manhattan, where underground congestion is very tight and there are lots of steam pipes, the ducts are made of fiberglass. Sometimes diggers find very old ducts made of creosoted wood, still almost as good as when they were buried; others have crumbled to sawdust. All are replaced.

Once the ducts are buried, Empire moves on and the phone company, or another company, such as Western Union, installs its own cables through the conduits.

AND EMPIRE CITY SUBWAY

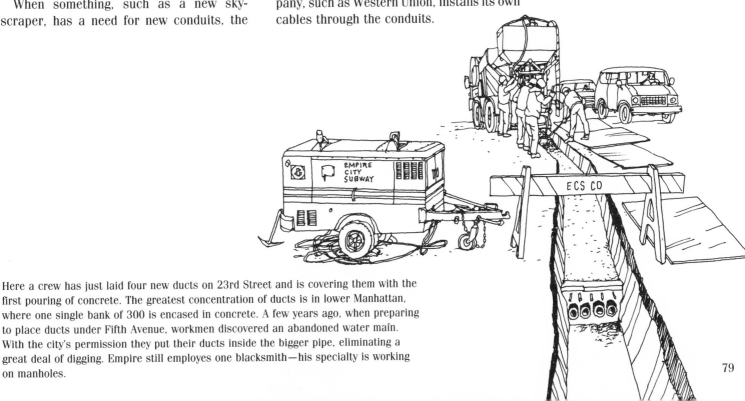

Here a crew has just laid four new ducts on 23rd Street and is covering them with the first pouring of concrete. The greatest concentration of ducts is in lower Manhattan, where one single bank of 300 is encased in concrete. A few years ago, when preparing to place ducts under Fifth Avenue, workmen discovered an abandoned water main. With the city's permission they put their ducts inside the bigger pipe, eliminating a great deal of digging. Empire still employes one blacksmith—his specialty is working on manholes.

SEWAGE

Even the earliest Dutch, when the population of New Amsterdam was only a few thousand, had problems with sewage. They complained that their dug canals stank frequently with obnoxious odors.

A hundred and fifty years later, when New York City was the capital of the newly formed United States, the city's sewage system was still extremely primitive. According to accounts written in 1789, it consisted of a long line of slaves who nightly carried tubs of waste to the river.

Indoor plumbing did not exist until the city had an adequate supply of piped water. In 1842 the Croton Reservoir and Aqueduct began to supply the city with pure fresh water and by the late 1850's the city had about 100 miles of sewer pipes.

Fortunately for Manhattan it is an island, surrounded by tidal water—the Hudson River and the East River, emptying into the harbor. As recently as 1985, not just Manhattan, but all of New York City was discharging about 200 million gallons of untreated sewage daily into these waters.

But consider that the city uses 1.36 billion gallons of water a day. Where does it all go after it is used? Most of it goes down into the underground sewer pipes: 6,500 miles of them, servicing all the boroughs. Once in the pipes, the sewage passes into main lines and then into the big trunk lines until it reaches one of the city's fourteen treatment plants.

Upon entering a treatment plant the sewage flows through and past two series of upright bars spaced an inch apart. These isolate large objects such as tin cans, plastics, and pieces of wood, which are then removed by automatic raking devices and carted off to sanitary landfills.

The sewage moves on into a settling tank, where it sits for about an hour, allowing suspended organic matter, sand, and dirt to settle to the bottom of the tank. Here they are removed by pumps, and any oily material that floats on the surface is skimmed off.

Now the sewage flows into an aeration tank, where it remains for several hours. Here it is agitated with compressed air, sent up through the bottom. This increases the oxygen supply, which allows bacteria to thrive on those impurities that are still suspended in the liquid. The bacteria break the impurities down into chemical compounds, which cluster together.

Manhattan's huge 33-acre, 1.1-billion-dollar North River Sewage Treatment Plant began operating on December 30, 1985, with the capacity to treat 150 million gallons of raw sewage a day. The plant's superstructure was built on a platform above the Hudson River's edge, from 135th to 145th streets. This colossal plant services an area reaching from Bank Street in Greenwich Village to Spuyten Duyvil in the north, and east to Fifth Avenue down the middle of the island. Covered with concrete and with soil varying in depth from a foot to four feet, the entire roof of the plant was designed as a state park, complete with a football field, softball fields, basketball courts, indoor and outdoor swimming, a skating rink, a running track, and other recreational facilities.

Once this has happened, the whole mixture, liquid and clusters, flows into another settling tank; these tanks are huge. Here, in a few hours, the clusters settle on the bottom of the tank, forming a mass of shapeless matter called "sludge." Sludge contains most of the impurities that are being removed from the sewage. The liquid that is left, after being treated with chlorine to kill any remaining bacteria, is discharged out into the waters about the city as clarified effluent.

What to do with the leftover sludge—thousands of tons of it every day? First a special tank removes as much remaining water from it as possible, returning this water to the first settling tank to be reprocessed.

The thickened sludge goes into a large circular enclosed tank and will stay there for a few weeks with the temperature at about 95 degrees Fahrenheit, perfect for the growth of another type of bacteria. These thrive on sludge at this temperature, breaking down the solids in the sludge and converting half of the mass into gases, mostly methane. This gas is used to generate some, or all, of the power needs of the plant itself.

The digested sludge is then loaded onto self-propelled sludge boats and is dumped out at sea in an area specified by the federal government.

That takes care of the nearly 1.4 billion gallons of sewage each day.

How to pay for it? The city's sewer rates are 60 percent of the water rate charge a building's ownership must pay.

And what of all the water that falls on the city as rain, into about 125,000 of its storm-water catch basins? Its removal is also part of that same 6,500-mile sanitary sewer system. All but about 2,000 miles have double-duty pipes carrying combined sewage and rainwater to the treatment plants. During a storm this increased volume sometimes creates a sudden overload on the system, causing regulating devices to divert both rainwater and sewage directly into the rivers and the harbor. Separate sewers for each function—sewage and rainwater—is the goal of the city.

The Hudson and the East River rise and fall with the tides, not yet completely free of pollution. But they are cleaner than they have been in a long time.

And the fish are coming back.

GOING . . .
GOING . . .

Any piece of land in Manhattan that can be built on, has been built on. Almost always, before something new can be built, an existing structure has to be torn down. Or the exterior of an old building is removed from its steel skeleton, the insides gutted, and a new skyscraper is erected on the framework of the old. These are jobs for wrecking companies and demolition workers.

City regulations govern demolition. Yet traffic is disrupted, clouds of dust irritate pedestrians, and the dismantling is noisy. It is also a spectacle for passersby as unexpected vistas of the city suddenly appear—exposing the rich variety of architectural design that exists high on the tops of Manhattan's buildings. Strange patterns of construction, fanciful arrangements of air conditioners, bricked-over windows, water towers, pipes and vents, gargoyles and ornamentation are now revealed.

A few weeks earlier this had been a 17-story brick-and-masonry office building on a busy midtown corner of Madison Avenue and 54th Street. Now the wreckers are down to the fifth floor. Despite the look of chaos and destruction, this is a very controlled operation. Two tall office buildings adjoin the site, pedestrians are walking the streets below, and the flow of traffic is unceasing. It is a densely congested area.

The outer faces of the building were first covered with scaffolding—a network of colored pipes, 17 stories high, with built-out platforms at the top, and a roofing of heavy timbers at street level, above the sidewalks and heads of people.

On 54th Street, at street level, an enormous hole has been battered in the building and the insides carted away, leaving a cavernous opening big enough for large dump trucks to drive into.

A crew of more than thirty men are at work here, tearing the building down. Men working in pairs, taking turns with jackhammers and crowbars, clean away the metal beams, exposing them so the cutters with acetylene torches can cut through the metal and drop each beam like a dead tree onto the rubble-strewn floor. One worker sprays water on the growing piles of old brick, plaster, cinder blocks, and other debris to keep the dust down. The small, agile bulldozers push everything on the floor into a big pile near the drop chute. The wooden drop chute begins at the floor being demolished and ends at the street level, going down the old elevator shaft. To minimize dust and noise, the debris is not dropped down the chute continuously, but in big bunches, with the chute's trap door closed on the bottom and with large canvas tarps enclosing the entire area.

This loading area has a bombed-out look, with
dangling wires, broken plaster, and twisted pipes; it is
dark, damp, and dusty. A big bulldozer is there,
loading the wreckage onto the trucks after it comes
crashing down the wooden chute. On some jobs a big
crane or derrick with a claw or a clamshell
attachment will batter through a floor, knock down
walls, and remove steel beams. Small crawler tractors
with steel hammers break up concrete floors. It is
dirty and hazardous work.

Here you won't get to see the spectacular
demolition scene you might expect—a four-ton steel
ball being swung back and forth by a big crane
crashing into the building, battering whole walls into
debris. This requires large areas of operating space,
something rarely available in crowded Manhattan.

Scrap-metal beams
are cut up by acetylene torch for ease of handling.
The pieces will be carted to the steel mill, resmelted,
and refabricated as usable metal.

...GONE

Twenty-ton trucks haul away the debris of demolition. Each load must be driven to dump sites in Staten Island, Queens, Brooklyn, or New Jersey, as there are no landfill sites on Manhattan Island.

The basements of the demolished buildings which stood on this site have been filled in with rubble and packed down flat, level with the street.

Once completely cleared, flat, open spaces like this often become temporary parking lots . . . but not for long. Drilling crews are waiting to move in with their boring rigs. They will set up their rigs and begin to make test borings in a regular pattern all over the now empty lot.

A timekeeper with a clipboard
keeps a record of truck
departures and returns.

NO ADMITTANCE
Authorized
Personnel Only

DANGER

The flagman warns
pedestrians and stops traffic
when trucks leave or enter
the site.

Permanently attached tarpaulins
are unrolled to cover dirt and
debris before filled trucks drive
through city streets.

POST
NO
BILLS

TEST
BORINGS

The truck-mounted drilling rigs do their
test borings and bring up soil samples
before the excavation of the site begins.

No one knows exactly what is under the rubble-filled basements of the old buildings that have just been torn down. Is it crumbly rock or granite, sand, soil, dirt with a high water content, gravel, filled-in earth? Is there water and mud down there? How far down is bedrock? The architects and engineers who are designing the building, planning the time schedule, and estimating the costs have a good idea what to expect but must know precisely. The core samples taken by this drilling rig will help these architects and engineers determine the type of foundation to be designed. The contractors will interpret the core samples to determine the construction methods to be used in building the foundation.

The drillers force pipe casings down into the bore holes as they drill. By keeping the casings filled with water and watching the color and type of soil that rises to the top of the water, the driller can tell that there has been a change in the composition of the earth below his rig. Or he can sometimes tell by the way his rig is drilling. He stops drilling, pulls out the drill, lowers a cylinder inside the pipe casing, and brings up a sample of the material for analysis. Samples from all over the site give a profile of its geology.

AND
DRILLING
ROCK

The bedrock that underlies Manhattan is not one great enormous homogeneous mass of rock. It has areas that crumble, it has different degrees of hardness, fracture lines, and intrusions of rock that erode more easily then others. More than 170 minerals have been found in the rock of Manhattan. The men working these drilling rigs and jackhammers are breaking up the rock or drilling blast holes. It has begun to snow and if it continues, work will stop because of the danger of accidents and injuries. Under some union contracts, workers who show up on a day when the weather prohibits any work at all will get show pay, equal to two or three hours' wages. In other unions, there is no pay if the weather prohibits work.

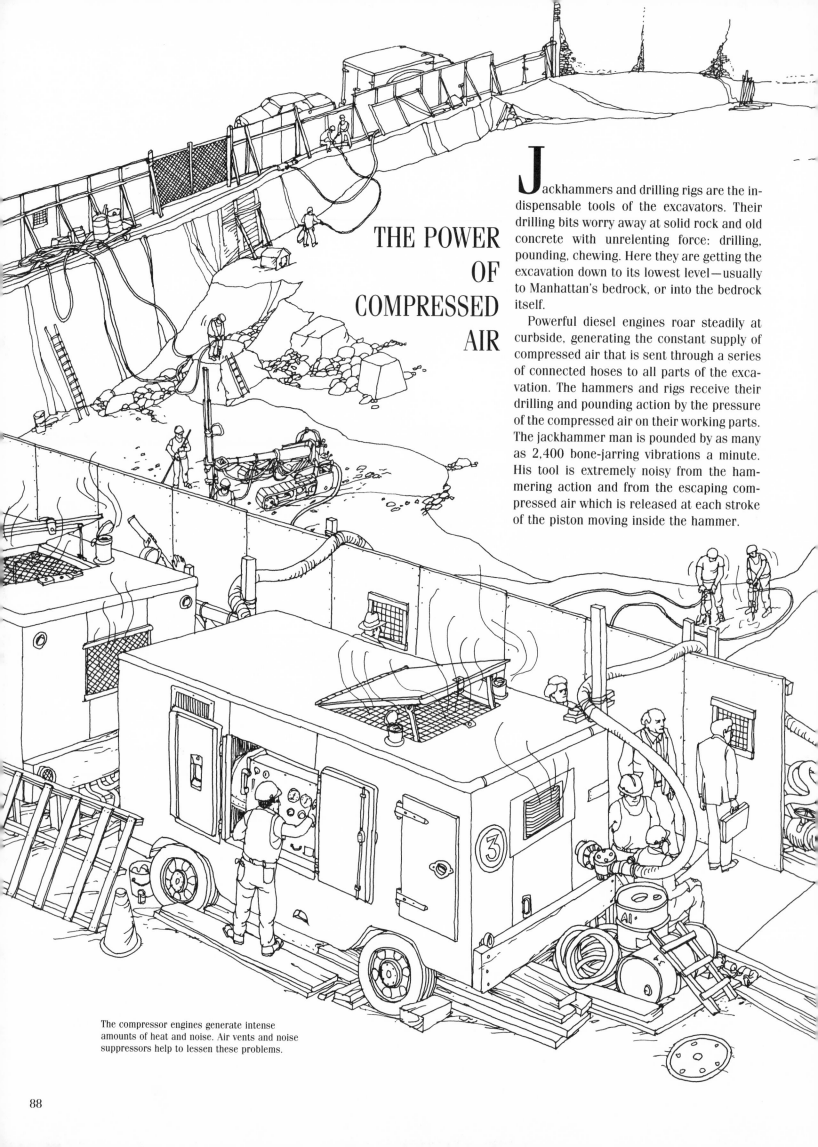

THE POWER
OF
COMPRESSED
AIR

Jackhammers and drilling rigs are the indispensable tools of the excavators. Their drilling bits worry away at solid rock and old concrete with unrelenting force: drilling, pounding, chewing. Here they are getting the excavation down to its lowest level—usually to Manhattan's bedrock, or into the bedrock itself.

Powerful diesel engines roar steadily at curbside, generating the constant supply of compressed air that is sent through a series of connected hoses to all parts of the excavation. The hammers and rigs receive their drilling and pounding action by the pressure of the compressed air on their working parts. The jackhammer man is pounded by as many as 2,400 bone-jarring vibrations a minute. His tool is extremely noisy from the hammering action and from the escaping compressed air which is released at each stroke of the piston moving inside the hammer.

The compressor engines generate intense amounts of heat and noise. Air vents and noise suppressors help to lessen these problems.

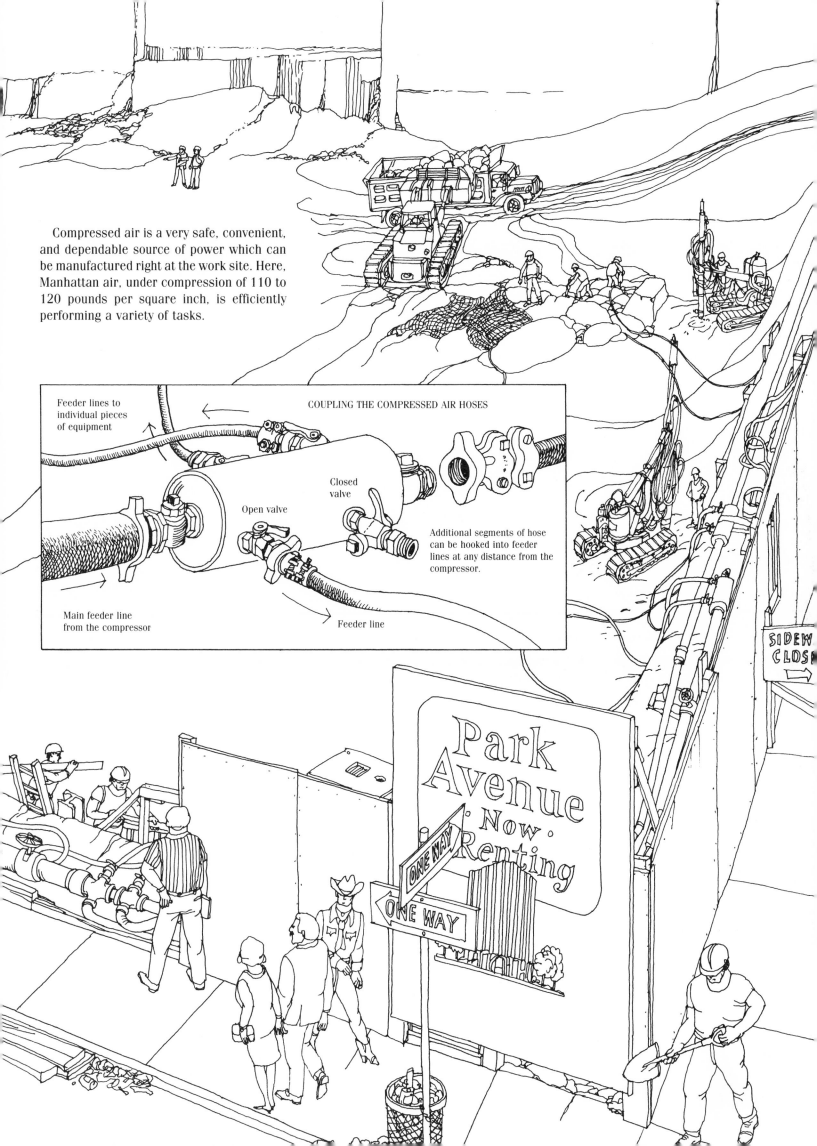

Compressed air is a very safe, convenient, and dependable source of power which can be manufactured right at the work site. Here, Manhattan air, under compression of 110 to 120 pounds per square inch, is efficiently performing a variety of tasks.

COUPLING THE COMPRESSED AIR HOSES

Feeder lines to individual pieces of equipment

Closed valve

Open valve

Additional segments of hose can be hooked into feeder lines at any distance from the compressor.

Main feeder line from the compressor

Feeder line

SIDEW CLOS

Park Avenue Now Renting

ONE WAY

ONE WAY

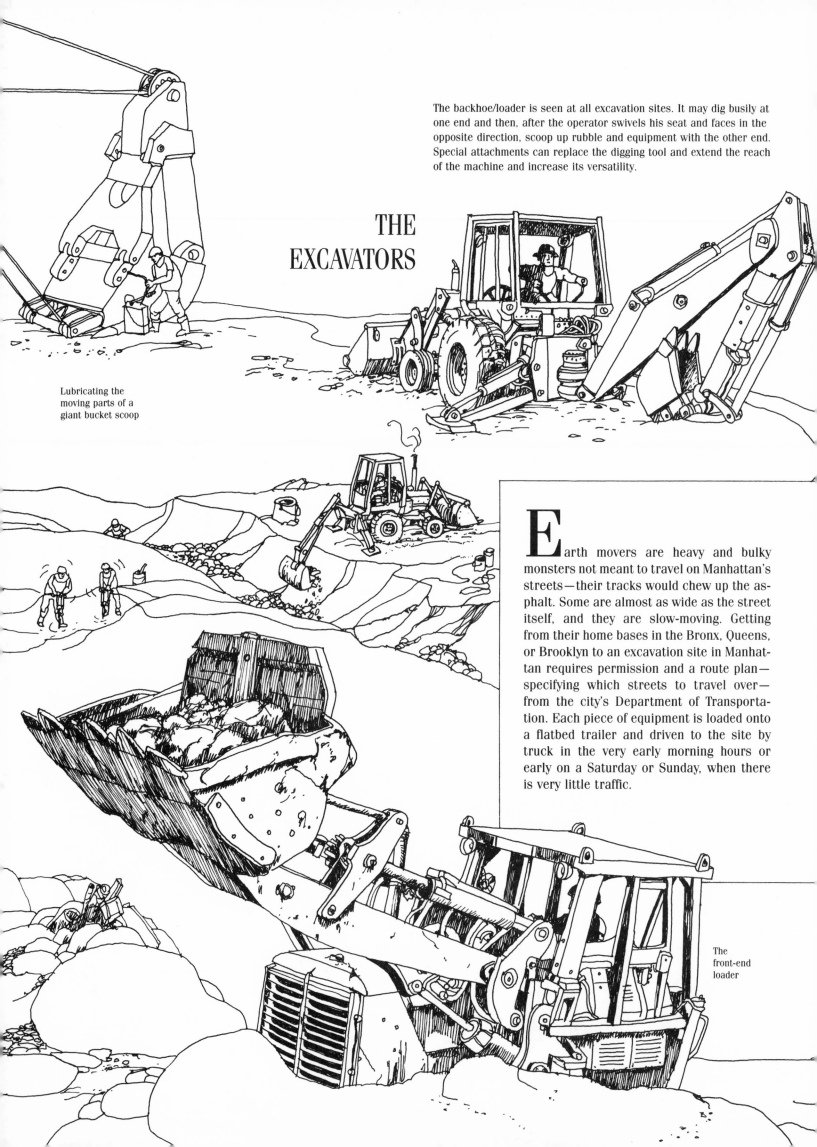

The backhoe/loader is seen at all excavation sites. It may dig busily at one end and then, after the operator swivels his seat and faces in the opposite direction, scoop up rubble and equipment with the other end. Special attachments can replace the digging tool and extend the reach of the machine and increase its versatility.

THE EXCAVATORS

Lubricating the moving parts of a giant bucket scoop

Earth movers are heavy and bulky monsters not meant to travel on Manhattan's streets—their tracks would chew up the asphalt. Some are almost as wide as the street itself, and they are slow-moving. Getting from their home bases in the Bronx, Queens, or Brooklyn to an excavation site in Manhattan requires permission and a route plan—specifying which streets to travel over—from the city's Department of Transportation. Each piece of equipment is loaded onto a flatbed trailer and driven to the site by truck in the very early morning hours or early on a Saturday or Sunday, when there is very little traffic.

The front-end loader

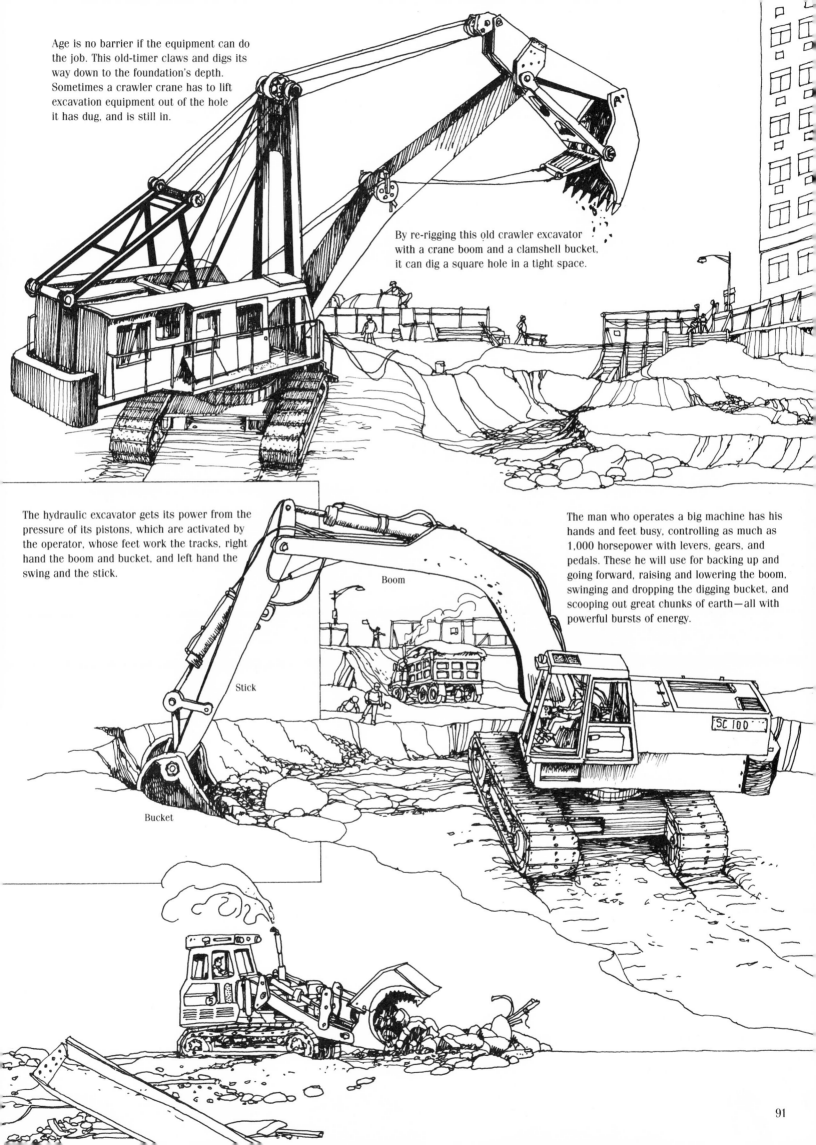

Age is no barrier if the equipment can do the job. This old-timer claws and digs its way down to the foundation's depth. Sometimes a crawler crane has to lift excavation equipment out of the hole it has dug, and is still in.

By re-rigging this old crawler excavator with a crane boom and a clamshell bucket, it can dig a square hole in a tight space.

The hydraulic excavator gets its power from the pressure of its pistons, which are activated by the operator, whose feet work the tracks, right hand the boom and bucket, and left hand the swing and the stick.

Boom

Stick

Bucket

The man who operates a big machine has his hands and feet busy, controlling as much as 1,000 horsepower with levers, gears, and pedals. These he will use for backing up and going forward, raising and lowering the boom, swinging and dropping the digging bucket, and scooping out great chunks of earth—all with powerful bursts of energy.

91

Dynamite is always under guard and is never left overnight at a construction site. The blasting caps and the dynamite are delivered in separate trucks. Each stick is numbered, registered, and accounted for.

DYNAMITE!

Dynamite was first developed in the 1860's by Alfred Nobel. It is a mixture of explosive material—usually nitroglycerine—with a nonexplosive material, in a stick form. This inert material helps to make it less sensitive to shock.

Today there are as many as 200 different explosive mixtures to choose from. Different mixtures, and different materials, give different results. Many explosives can be easily handled; they may even be broken in half, as when a stick and a half is needed for a more powerful blast. Even fire or shock won't detonate some of them.

Usually the blast holes are drilled in a spe-cific pattern so that the rock or old concrete will shatter in a predictable way. Even the blasting caps can be set to go off in a planned sequence, only fractions of a second apart, by the use of delayed-action blasting caps. These blasts, which sound like a single explosion, are in fact a series of small con-secutive blasts. By this means, the blasting will be controlled to achieve the maximum effect and make the clean-up quick and easy.

Before detonation, the explosive charges are all tamped down in the blast holes, the wire circuits are tested, and the heavy metal mesh mats are placed over the blast site.

The driller uses a jackhammer to drill a blast hole so the obstruction—whether old concrete foundations or solid rock—can be blasted apart and removed as rubble. He can drill down to a depth of 8 or 10 feet.

One man has the primer cartridge, or stick of explosive, ready to be inserted into the blast hole after another has made sure the hole is clean and straight. Then the primer cartridge is lowered to the bottom of the hole by its wires. Other charges will be tamped down solidly with the long wooden pole. Then the hole is filled with sand, dirt, or dampened clay on top of the explosives. These men are members of the Blasters, Drillers and Miners Union.

A wooden plug will cap the newly drilled hole until the time for blasting.

EXPLOSIVE CHARGE READY TO BE FIRED

Rock holds blasting wires in place

Packed-down sand and dirt

Charges of explosives

Primer explosive

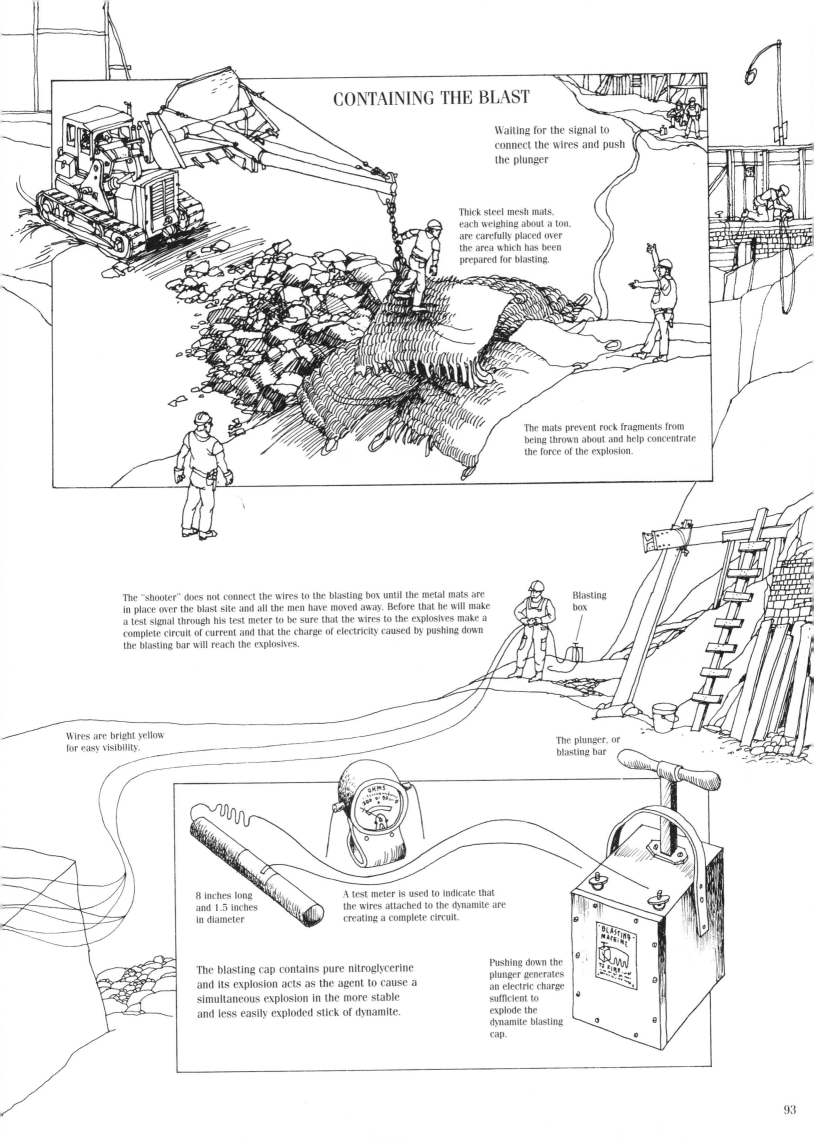

CONTAINING THE BLAST

Waiting for the signal to connect the wires and push the plunger

Thick steel mesh mats, each weighing about a ton, are carefully placed over the area which has been prepared for blasting.

The mats prevent rock fragments from being thrown about and help concentrate the force of the explosion.

The "shooter" does not connect the wires to the blasting box until the metal mats are in place over the blast site and all the men have moved away. Before that he will make a test signal through his test meter to be sure that the wires to the explosives make a complete circuit of current and that the charge of electricity caused by pushing down the blasting bar will reach the explosives.

Blasting box

Wires are bright yellow for easy visibility.

The plunger, or blasting bar

8 inches long and 1.5 inches in diameter

A test meter is used to indicate that the wires attached to the dynamite are creating a complete circuit.

The blasting cap contains pure nitroglycerine and its explosion acts as the agent to cause a simultaneous explosion in the more stable and less easily exploded stick of dynamite.

Pushing down the plunger generates an electric charge sufficient to explode the dynamite blasting cap.

STAND CLEAR!

One loud whistle . . . three minutes to dynamite explosion . . . two whistles . . . one minute to blast. All workers on the excavation site cease work and find a vantage point protected from danger. Three loud whistles . . . there is a dull, muffled boom as the metal mats on top of the explosion site rise a few feet, then settle back. A small puff of dust and smoke is briefly visible . . . a slight shock wave is felt. The whistle blows again, one long signal—it's the "all clear" and work resumes.

But what if a stick of dynamite didn't explode? With the wires disconnected, the sand and dirt can be blown out of the dynamite hole with an air hose. New wiring can then be tested by the galvanometer, which uses such a small amount of current that there is no danger of a blast. If necessary, a small charge of dynamite can be added to the hole, exploding both charges.

At strategic locations outside the excavation site, precision vibration sensing devices are placed to monitor and determine the force of each blast. A delicate needle, made to fluctuate by the blast, records a jagged line on unrolling graph paper. The man monitoring the recording device, by voice contact with the explosives expert, reports the effect of the blast as shown on the graph.

Too much force in the narrow confines of Manhattan is a danger. The excavation may already be deep, possibly next to the sub-basement of a towering skyscraper or a subway tunnel. Tricky work, and it must be done with the least disruption to nearby buildings, and to the people and traffic busily going about their business on the streets above. But without the explosives and the blasting, the removal of old foundations and the clearing of the site down to bedrock would be very difficult and slow work.

A sensing device is monitoring the blasting next to the Museum of Modern Art in order to ensure the safety of the priceless objects inside the museum. The device records an inked line or a series of dots on moving graph paper which the operator "reads" over a portable telephone to the men doing the blasting in the excavation below him.

> Permittees shall employ none but competent men, skilled
> in the work required of them and shall pay the prevailing
> scale of union wages to those so employed.
> —Rules and regulations for the issuance of
> Building Operation Permits, New York City

Manhattan's weather is a big factor in working in any type of outdoor construction. Workers encounter snow, rain, wind, heat, cold, ice, and perhaps fog.

The highest temperature ever recorded in New York City since records were first kept in 1869 was 106 degrees Fahrenheit, on July 9, 1936, and the coldest was on February 9, 1934, at 15 degrees below zero.

Construction workers do not have to work in all kinds of weather. Sometimes it is too cold, too windy, too dangerous. Even raising a load of steel Q-decking by crane on a windy day may be too dangerous—it might float out of control. In the cold, hands may lose their ability to feel. The work stops.

It may not be a man working, but a woman—for women are now employed as steam fitters, carpenters, sheet-metal workers, surveyors, and in other trades.

Many of the construction workers are journeymen, temporary workers for the duration of a particular job. New York City is a union city. Every worker is a member of a specific union with strict work rules governing what he or she can do, the material and tools each uses, and the number of hours in a workday. Every union has its own rules and its own representative, a shop steward, at each construction site.

The eight-hour workday may start earlier, with city approval, to meet specific problems, but citywide it starts at 7:30 or 8:00 A.M.; quitting time is at 3:30 or 4:00 P.M. For lunch, a half hour. Work on Saturdays or Sundays earns overtime. The union sets the pay scale and working conditions for its members. Yet sometimes a developer pays more than union scale to his ironworkers, and gives them one paid "rain day" a week, should bad weather stop work.

City rules state that every worker must be protected by New York State's Workmen's Compensation Law and the state's Disability Benefits Law. Sometimes a worker falls and is injured despite the city's safety requirements and the on-site safety man. If it is a rare fatal fall, all work ceases for the day.

HARD HATS

Sanitary facilities at construction sites are provided by portable, self-contained toilets, made of molded plastic. They can be moved about by forklift, or lifted by cables from overhead to any site desired.

Today's hard hats, required at all construction sites, are made out of tough lightweight plastic, and are shockproof. They frequently have attachments for hooking on ear and noise protectors.

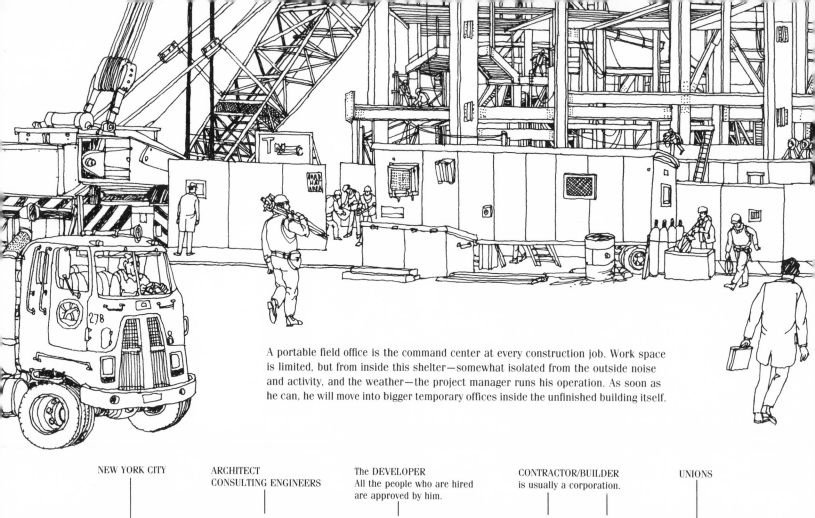

A portable field office is the command center at every construction job. Work space is limited, but from inside this shelter—somewhat isolated from the outside noise and activity, and the weather—the project manager runs his operation. As soon as he can, he will move into bigger temporary offices inside the unfinished building itself.

WHO DOES WHAT AT A CONSTRUCTION SITE

NEW YORK CITY

makes unannounced inspections during the construction and provides access to water and sewer lines.

ARCHITECT CONSULTING ENGINEERS

may have representatives at the site.

The DEVELOPER
All the people who are hired are approved by him.

His representatives visit the building site.

CONTRACTOR/BUILDER
is usually a corporation.

PROJECT EXECUTIVE
oversees several different construction jobs at the same time, at different locations.

UNIONS

A SHOP STEWARD represents each union on the job. Observes only; checks for safety.

Independent inspectors for all the different trades, such as steel, concrete, curtain wall, brick work, and spray fireproofing, are hired by the subcontractors but report to the project manager and project superintendent.

PROJECT MANAGER
has his office right at the construction site or in an office building nearby. He coordinates the flow of working drawings for each phase of construction, manages the money flow, and hires and pays the subcontractors.

Hires and controls the crane operator and the elevator hoist operator who are crucial in the delivery of material on an exacting time schedule. Even if only one man is working and he is above the sixth-floor level, there must be an elevator operator also working on the job.

MECHANICAL SUPERINTENDENT
works with the project superintendent and coordinates the work of the mechanical trades, such as the plumbers and electricians.

PROJECT SUPERINTENDENT
works with the project manager and supervises the actual construction. He and his assistants coordinate the work of the subcontractors.

An example of a major SUBCONTRACTOR

The STEEL FABRICATOR: Guarantees the job will be finished by a specific date. Gets the job by submitting a cost bid in competition with others. Must estimate his costs correctly in order to make a profit. Orders the steel, fabricates each piece to fit a specific place in the building's construction, and delivers it on schedule complete with working drawings of each piece of steel. Also hires the company that erects the steel and builds the framework of the building. Provides the independent surveyor for the precise erection of the steel.

SUBCONTRACTORS
do the construction for all the various trades.

The SUPERINTENDENT has some laborers who work directly for him, under a foreman.

FOREMEN direct the men in the performance of their job specialties.

The person who is responsible for the measurements determining that the building is built in the right place, to the exact depth, and is put up vertically and horizontally true, is the surveyor. Here he is sighting on the level rod in the excavation. By deducting the height of his instrument he can determine exactly how far below his cross-cut mark is the spot on which the level rod is resting. The cross-cut mark is the X mark cut into the sidewalk—his elevation reference point, to which he returns constantly to make sightings. His instrument is centered exactly over the cross-cut mark. He established this reference mark from a "bench mark"—a permanent elevation mark that is located nearby, but away from the construction site.

Cross-cut mark

The surveyor is involved in the building of a skyscraper from the very beginning. He or she establishes that the site's measurements match its description in his instructions, surveys the adjoining buildings, locates the placement of the utilities, and lays out the actual dimensions of the building-to-be. There are several surveyors on the construction site of a big building, working independently for different contractors.

A surveyor begins by cutting fixed *X* marks into the concrete sidewalks and other permanent places around the building site. These are his reference points from which to work and measure, and to which he can return continually. By setting his surveying instrument directly over a reference point and by consulting his log book for mathematical notations, the surveyor can sight horizontally and vertically and determine the position of points on the building relative to the building as a whole, as it is being built.

As the building rises higher and higher, his sightings and marks rise vertically, one above the other; they are absolutely crucial to the construction of the building.

It is impossible to build a skyscraper straight up, floor by floor, without adjustments—just imagine the problem of keeping the quarter-mile-high towers of the World Trade Center perfectly vertical. It is the surveyor's job to note any deviation from the vertical in the construction, and the construction workers must correct any discrepancy as they build.

THE SURVEYOR

The surveyor has different specialized instruments to look through, each of them giving him exact measurements—horizontally, vertically, and at angles. In one of them he sights through his telescope on a distant prism which sends back a reading of the distance between the two instruments. His instruments can give him measurements in hundredths of a foot. There are leveling devices on the instruments themselves and on the tripod legs, to properly position them. In use, the surveyor uses error-compensating readings to avoid mistakes. An example: first take a normal reading, then one with the telescope inverted. If two points are indicated, the middle distance between the two marks is the appropriate mark.

In addition to aligning the building vertically with his markings, the surveyor also gives an accurate marking on each floor, from which the necessary floor measurements originate, as directed in the blueprints. The tape measures and folding rules are in feet and in inches, or feet divided into hundredths of a foot.

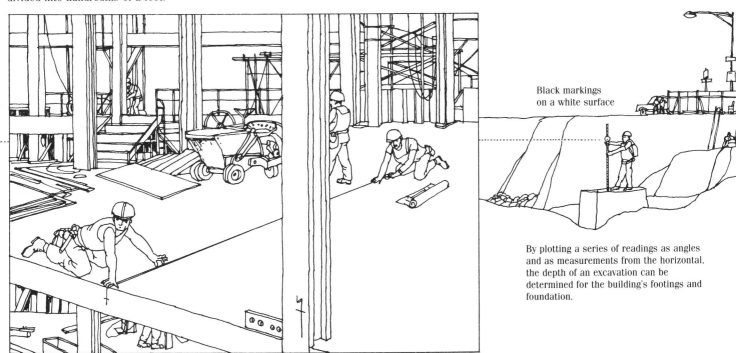

Black markings on a white surface

By plotting a series of readings as angles and as measurements from the horizontal, the depth of an excavation can be determined for the building's footings and foundation.

The surveyor has made a center mark on a newly built floor. By plotting the angles from that center mark, and by measuring the distances, the workmen know exactly where any holes are to be drilled and where the partitions and interior construction are to be placed.

SHORING UP THE OUTER WALLS

The New Yorker peering into any great excavation, curious to see what is going on, will find a busy confusion of workers, material, and machines, fascinating in their activity. It is all coordinated by unseen mechanisms—the working drawings and the work schedule—which tell what, where, when, and how.

Around the perimeter, out along the sidewalks, workers are beginning to build the foundation's outer wall. Whether the new skyscraper is to be of a steel frame construction, or of poured concrete, the underground foundation's outer walls will be of reinforced concrete. Wooden forms are built and interlocking steel forms are assembled where the new outer walls are to go up. Concrete trucks, engines idling, wait their turn to pour their loads into these prepared foundation forms.

Pigeons sometimes roost in exposed openings.

Surveyor marks

Steel from torn-down building, not yet removed

The surveyor makes periodic readings of his reference marks on adjoining buildings for the alignment and layout of the new building. His calculations determine when the excavation has reached the required depth.

Air-compressor hoses.

Pouring
concrete

Drilling in bedrock
preparatory to
blasting with
dynamite

These men are
members of the
Dock Builders
Union and are
called Dock
Builders.

Where old buildings
have just been torn
down there may be
vaults and openings
reaching out under
sidewalks. These are
filled in.

THE FOUNDATION

Who are the men and women who make the decisions that control all of this below-ground activity?

Their judgments are crucial to the quality of the building that will be constructed here. Upon its foundation are concentrated all the skyscraper's stresses and strains of weight, its internal tensions, external wind pressures, underground pressures of water, vibrations of man-made traffic and movement, and the forces of nature itself.

While other men with specialized abilities do the actual construction, the foundation engineers and the structural engineers are the experts with the educational background, the analytical skills, the experience, and the self-assurance to visualize and say how it is to be done. Their earlier counterparts built the ancient structures of Egypt, China, Greece, Rome, India, and those of other cultures that today amaze us with their size and complexity.

The Leaning Tower of Pisa, built in the 12th century amazes us too—tilted at an angle of more than 16 degrees from the perpendicular—with its foundation only about 10 feet deep.

It is only within this century that the scientific study of the properties of soils has made predictable results possible in the construction of foundations. Each job begins with an unknown variable. What has nature put out of sight underground? Is it dirt, hard rock, soft crumbly rock, glacial deposits, sand, unstable clay, water? What has man left there? Old foundation walls, debris from torn-down buildings, artifacts from the earliest days of Dutch rule in Manhattan?

How far down is it to bedrock? Sometimes in Manhattan it is just below the surface. Way back in 1916 test borings for the New York County Court House near City Hall went down 210 feet. The test borings were made on the former site of Collect Pond, filled in by the year 1815, and once Manhattan Island's largest freshwater pond.

Today's engineers make test borings, in a pattern all over the construction site, to determine what is underground. They do this before any excavating has begun, and while it is being done. They drill a hole, clean it, and go down again to collect a sample that has not been affected by the act of boring the hole. The sample is tested for its properties and its behavior under downward and sideways pressures, how it reacts to water, whether it can be shaped or molded, if it is stable and solid, and what it is composed of.

Any big excavation is a potential danger to nearby buildings, for the removal of large amounts of earth may lower the water table. This is the level below which the ground itself contains water in large or small amounts—in some parts of Manhattan it is only a few feet below the surface. This water can exert an upward pressure on buildings as well as a sideways pressure.

A lowered water table will allow the soil to be compressed. Buildings built years earlier with foundations designed for a stable base not on bedrock might sink or shift under their own weight. Water is sometimes pumped into an area adjacent to an excavation to keep the water table at its normal level, and to maintain the stability of nearby buildings as construction goes on in the excavation.

Today there is a worldwide exchange of information and innovative techiques to aid the foundation engineer. After he takes his soil samples and studies the architects' plans, he has to anticipate the problem areas and analyze all the possible ways in which to excavate and build the foundation. He recommends the most practical way to do this—which his experience also tells him is economical.

His foundation, with its basements, will be hidden from view—nonetheless, it is a spectacular part of Manhattan's skyscrapers.

Steel I-beams, called "soldier beams," are driven vertically down into the ground by a pile driver. Then, heavy removable wooden planks are slid down between the steel uprights, forming and acting as retaining walls during the excavation and the construction of the building's foundation.

When a developer digs in lower Manhattan there are archeologists peering into his excavation, and if they can, they are in there too, digging. They are looking for artifacts from Manhattan's Dutch and Colonial period, seeking to shed light on the city's past. It costs the developer money, and time taken from his work schedule, to cooperate with an archeological dig, but the city may say he has to, if the indications are that artifacts may be buried there. New York City has its own archeologist, with the Landmarks Preservation Commission, which conducts surveys of potential archeological sites and helps plan diggings.

Adding immeasurably to the sense of history in lower Manhattan are three glass-protected archeological displays of early Dutch and English New York. They are preserved in the outdoor plaza at 85 Broad Street, across from Fraunces Tavern. On this piece of land the Dutch built a tavern in 1641, which functioned as their first City Hall, called the Stadt Huys. Here also was the tavern built in 1670 by Francis Lovelace, second English governor of New York, appointed by Charles II. Lovelace's Tavern served briefly as the City Hall after 1697, when the Stadt Huys was torn down.

In 1979–80 a large-scale archeological exploration was made on the site, prior to the construction of a new skyscraper. From this important digging, much cultural material from the 17th through the 19th century was discovered. The resulting preserved underground exhibits reveal parts of the foundation wall of Lovelace's Tavern and an 18th-century well. Gray paving stones set into the plaza's walkways indicate the size and location of the tavern.

DIGGING IN LOWER MANHATTAN

The Museum of the City of New York is filled with treasures from the city's past. These include rarities dug up during excavations at about the same site 51 years apart. The bronze swivel gun with the initials of the Dutch East India Company incised on the barrel was dug up in 1967. These charred timbers from Adriaen Block's ship *Tyger*, which burned at the shoreline of lower Manhattan in 1613, were dug up in 1916. The cannon and the timbers were found near the excavation site of the World Trade Center, where two other cannon from the *Tyger* were unearthed in 1967. These disappeared and their whereabouts are unknown.

This famous old landmark of lower Manhattan, Fraunces Tavern, was originally built in 1719 as the Etienne Delancey residence. It was converted into a tavern in 1762 by Samuel Fraunces, who was present when George Washington said farewell to his officers here on December 4, 1783. The war was over. Only nine days earlier the British troops had left the city. Samuel Fraunces was a black man from the West Indies. His tavern, now a museum and restaurant, was reconstructed in 1907.

BULL'S LIVER AND OTHER PROBLEMS

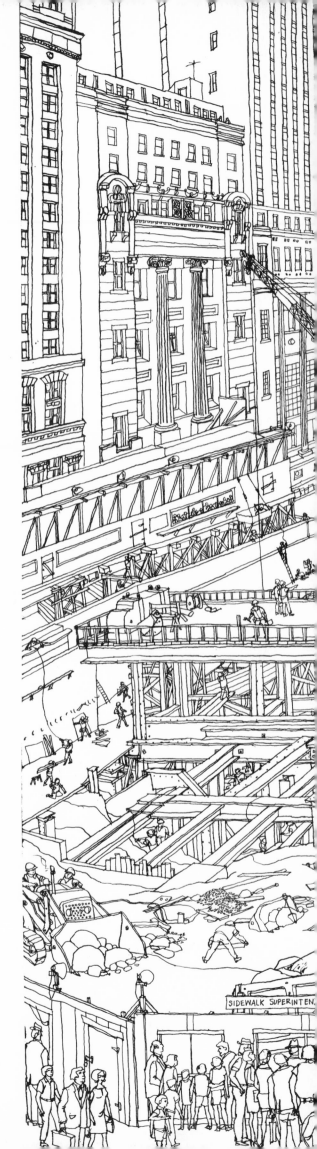

SIDEWALK SUPERINTEN.

The year is 1958. It has taken 22 tons of blasting dynamite and nearly two years of hard, dirty, and dangerous work by several hundred men to excavate and simultaneously shore up the outer walls of this 85-foot-deep excavation and foundation in lower Manhattan. It is to be the six-level basement of the Chase Manhattan Bank.

A major problem in the excavation of this site has been the unstable nature of some of the soil—a fine loose reddish sand on top of a layer of sandy silt, called "bull's liver," and also the sand overlying the bedrock. It is the headache of the men who dig and build foundations. If it is not contained during excavation and construction, its shifting about might undermine and cause damage to nearby streets, buildings, and the adjacent subways.

Underneath the bull's liver is hardpan, a compact formation of glacial till and boulders that is difficult to penetrate. Beneath the hardpan and above the bedrock, a sand layer frequently exists which will become "quick" and will flow into the excavation if not confined by sheeting. The problem of bull's liver can be effectively solved by driving vertical sheeting down through it.

Here, however, as it was not practical to drive sheeting through the hardpan to bedrock in order to confine the sand, the foundation engineers used a technique that was new in the 1950's—chemical soil solidification—to stabilize this unstable sand and silt. Pipes two inches in diameter were forced down as deep as 40 feet into the problem areas, in a planned pattern. Each pair of pipes came together at the base to form a Y shape, where calcium chloride and sodium silicate, after being poured down the separate pipes, were mixed. Within minutes, this mixture solidified and formed a hard stable material with the bull's liver. As the pipes were withdrawn upward, the mixture continued to be injected, forming and leaving in place vertical masses of solid rock-like material. This created a barrier four to five feet thick and allowed the digging to continue and the foundations to be built without danger of cave-ins.

During this early phase of construction, a crane toppled over into the hole, killing its operator. There was structural damage to some of the steel girders of the network of floor framing, requiring their replacement. The new steel girders had to be cut to exact lengths to assure a perfect connection with the steel foundation already in place. But this exactness made for tight maneuvering in fitting the steel pieces together. Just before positioning, the new steel girders were packed in dry ice, which caused the steel to contract and shortened their lengths. Quickly put in place, the steel girders expanded back to their original lengths, to an accurate fit.

Three steel tiers, seen here as platforms for the big crawler cranes, extend across the open foundation site. They are part of the building's permanent structure. The engineers have designed them to also function as cross-lot bracing, supporting the outer foundation walls during the excavation and underground construction.

AS THE CITY BUILDS

Forty-second Street is one of the most celebrated streets in American folklore, immortalized in song and by the movies as the stuff dreams are made of. It is alive with all the human variety the city has to offer. Wider than most cross streets, it can be walked easily from end to end in less than an hour. Its traffic flows in both directions, unusual for Manhattan.

At its Hudson River end there are people boarding the Circle Line boat for a ride around the island, inspecting the museum aircraft carrier *Intrepid*, visiting the Javits Convention Center, and arriving and departing daily at the Port Authority Bus Terminal. At the other end of the street, overlooking the East River, is the United Nations, with its delegates bringing their presence and influence to the city from all over the world.

In between, a glimpse of the sleazy under-side of Manhattan—its porno shops, karate-chop movies, and street hustlers. A few steps away Times Square beckons. At midpoint the magnificent Public Library and Fifth Avenue bisect the island neatly into east and west. The choice is yours.

Skyward you admire the unique spire of the Chrysler Building—you are now across the street from Grand Central Station, with its Park Avenue auto overpass. Crosstown buses, trucks, taxis, and autos whiz past you. A hundred thousand commuters arrive by train every morning and leave every night at Grand Central. Beneath the nearby streets different levels of subway trains rumble in from east and west, north and south, discharging and receiving 32 million passengers every year at this one, busiest, location.

Right here, construction is well under way for a new office skyscraper. It would be dif-

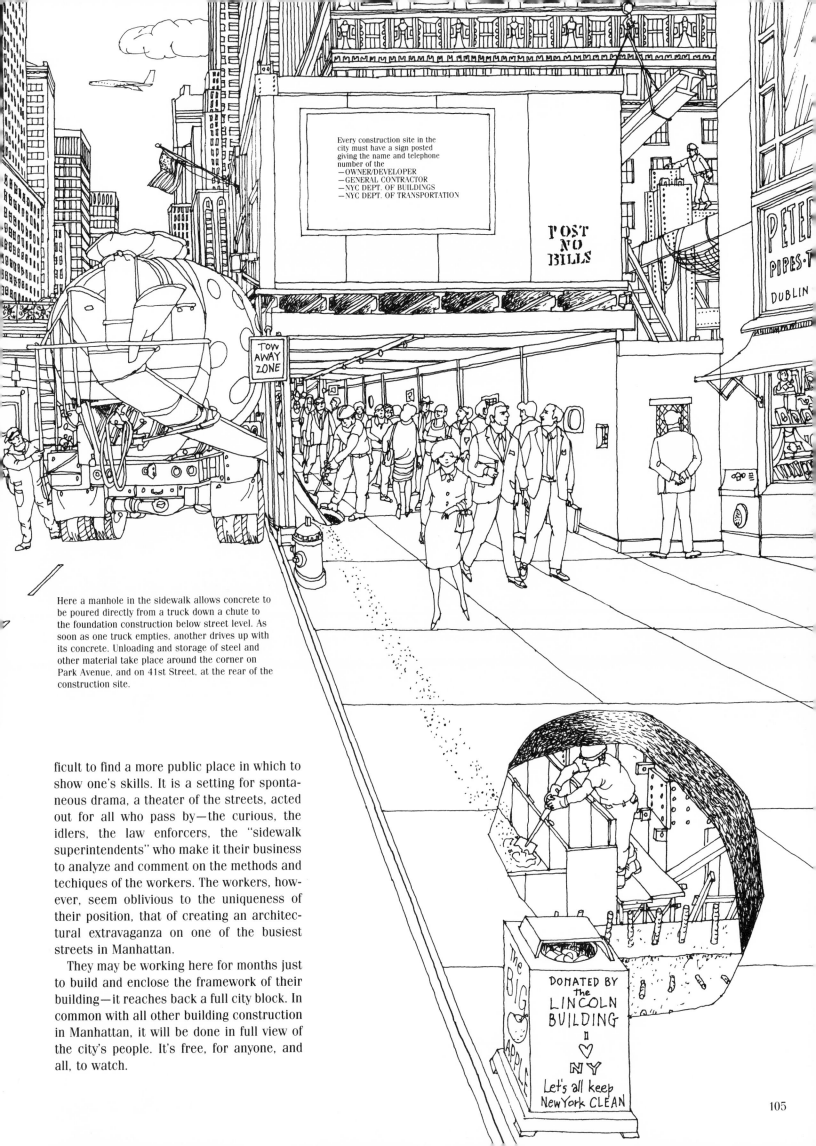

Every construction site in the
city must have a sign posted
giving the name and telephone
number of the
—OWNER/DEVELOPER
—GENERAL CONTRACTOR
—NYC DEPT. OF BUILDINGS
—NYC DEPT. OF TRANSPORTATION

POST
NO
BILLS

TOW
AWAY
ZONE

PETE
PIPES—T
DUBLIN

Here a manhole in the sidewalk allows concrete to
be poured directly from a truck down a chute to
the foundation construction below street level. As
soon as one truck empties, another drives up with
its concrete. Unloading and storage of steel and
other material take place around the corner on
Park Avenue, and on 41st Street, at the rear of the
construction site.

ficult to find a more public place in which to
show one's skills. It is a setting for sponta-
neous drama, a theater of the streets, acted
out for all who pass by—the curious, the
idlers, the law enforcers, the "sidewalk
superintendents" who make it their business
to analyze and comment on the methods and
techiques of the workers. The workers, however, seem oblivious to the uniqueness of
their position, that of creating an architectural extravaganza on one of the busiest
streets in Manhattan.

They may be working here for months just
to build and enclose the framework of their
building—it reaches back a full city block. In
common with all other building construction
in Manhattan, it will be done in full view of
the city's people. It's free, for anyone, and
all, to watch.

The
BIG
APPLE

DONATED BY
the
LINCOLN
BUILDING
II
♡
NY

Let's all keep
New York CLEAN

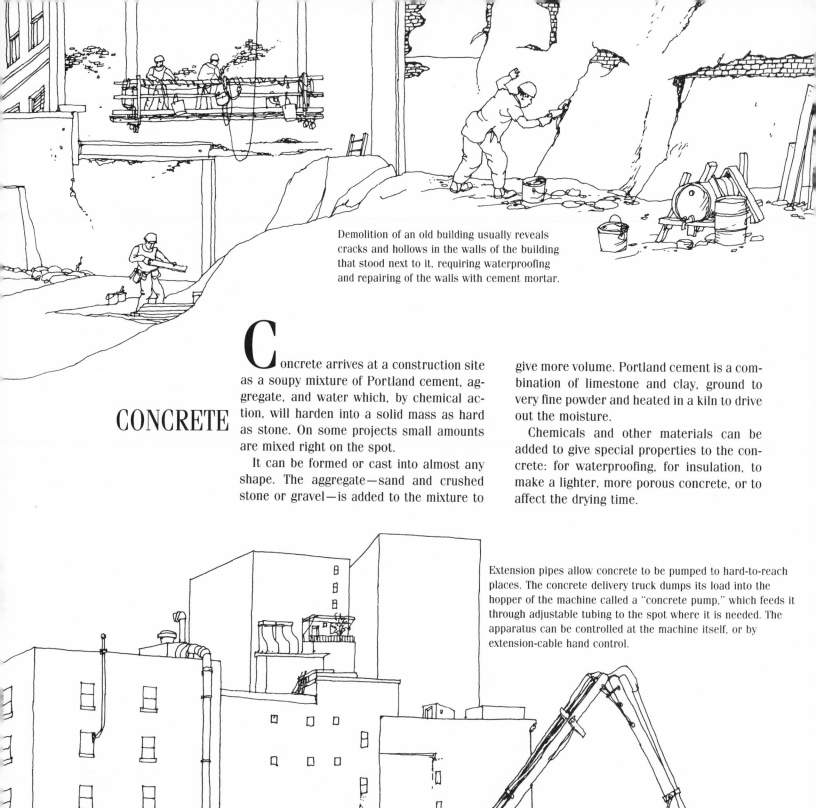

Demolition of an old building usually reveals cracks and hollows in the walls of the building that stood next to it, requiring waterproofing and repairing of the walls with cement mortar.

CONCRETE

Concrete arrives at a construction site as a soupy mixture of Portland cement, aggregate, and water which, by chemical action, will harden into a solid mass as hard as stone. On some projects small amounts are mixed right on the spot.

It can be formed or cast into almost any shape. The aggregate—sand and crushed stone or gravel—is added to the mixture to give more volume. Portland cement is a combination of limestone and clay, ground to very fine powder and heated in a kiln to drive out the moisture.

Chemicals and other materials can be added to give special properties to the concrete: for waterproofing, for insulation, to make a lighter, more porous concrete, or to affect the drying time.

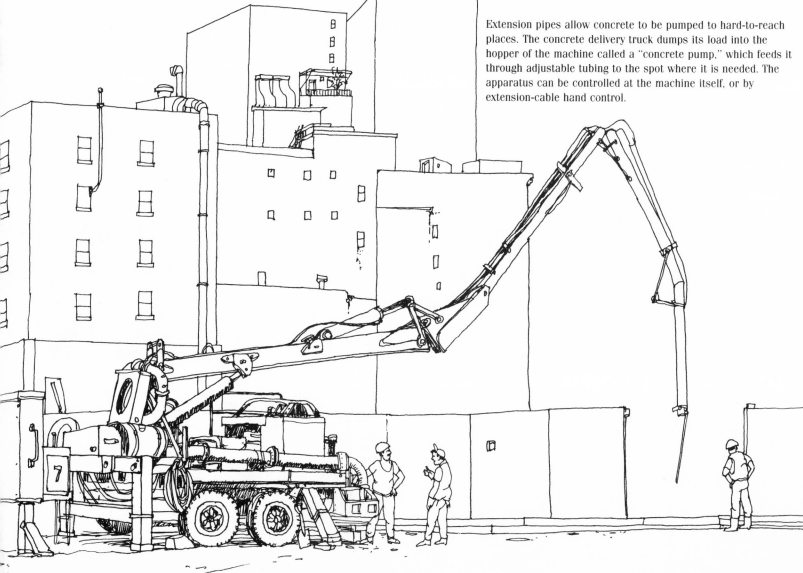

Extension pipes allow concrete to be pumped to hard-to-reach places. The concrete delivery truck dumps its load into the hopper of the machine called a "concrete pump," which feeds it through adjustable tubing to the spot where it is needed. The apparatus can be controlled at the machine itself, or by extension-cable hand control.

In addition to the bundles of prebent reinforcing bars that are already at the building site, a portable bending machine, powered by a gas engine, is set up. By shifting the controls on the metal table top, each steel reinforcing bar, or rod, can be individually bent to any required shape. Serrations, or deformations, have previously been pressed into the bars to increase the bond of the steel bars to the concrete.

The ingredients of the concrete are proportioned for specific uses. In the foundation of a skyscraper there is more sand and stone in the mix than cement. In the upper structure of the building more cement is used and less aggregate, since this allows the support columns and other parts of the building to be thinner, or reduced in bulk, without losing strength.

The amount of water in the mix is also carefully controlled—just enough to ensure maximum hardening, yet a sufficient amount to keep the concrete fluid and workable as it is poured and formed at the job site. Concrete, however, requires an additional ingredient to make high-rise construction practical.

Steel reinforcing bars—some are 2¼ inches in diameter and weigh 13.6 pounds per foot—are embedded in the concrete. When tied in clusters, or woven into a mesh of wires and bars, the steel bars give the hardened concrete the strength to withstand any vertical stress and strain as well as horizontal pressure.

The protruding ends of the steel bars seen at all concrete construction sites are for the connection of this reinforcement, by which a freshly formed concrete section is solidly bonded to the metal reinforcing of the rest of the concrete building. These bars must be placed in the areas of maximum tensile stress as determined by the engineers.

As this truck drove through the city's streets from the concrete plant to the construction site, its big drum rotated, coating each particle of sand and gravel with the cementing mix. Too long in the revolving drum, and it would harden too soon. It must arrive within an hour, freshly mixed, and the construction crew must be ready to use it in its proper place when it arrives. The ingredients, most likely, have come down the Hudson River by barge to the mixing plant on the West Side of Manhattan, right at the river's edge. A test cylinder is filled from selected batches of fresh concrete as they arrive at the construction site. If the concrete should prove not to be up to strength, the area already poured will have to be removed or strengthened with more concrete or with steel bracing.

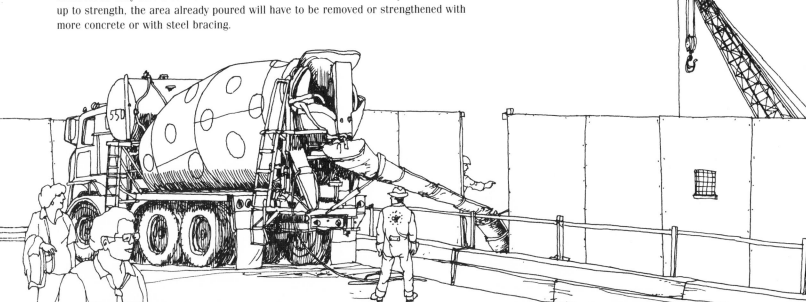

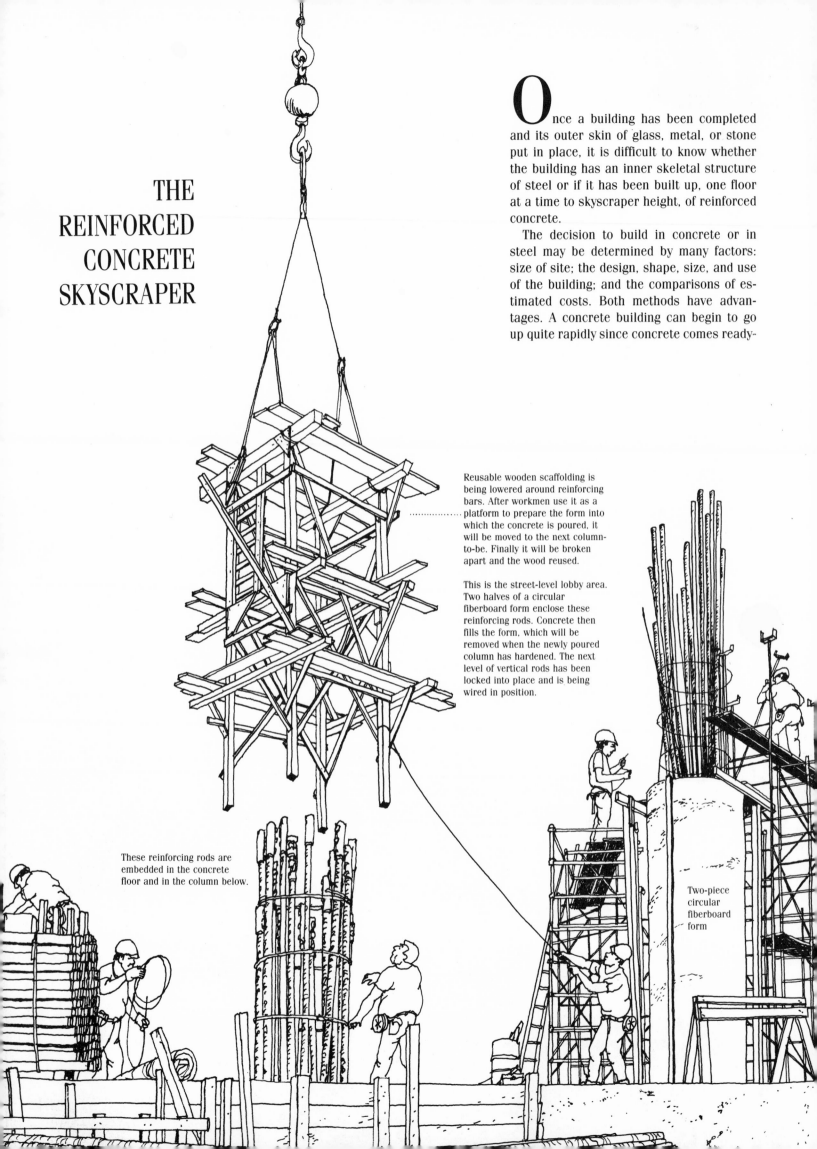

THE REINFORCED CONCRETE SKYSCRAPER

Once a building has been completed and its outer skin of glass, metal, or stone put in place, it is difficult to know whether the building has an inner skeletal structure of steel or if it has been built up, one floor at a time to skyscraper height, of reinforced concrete.

The decision to build in concrete or in steel may be determined by many factors: size of site; the design, shape, size, and use of the building; and the comparisons of estimated costs. Both methods have advantages. A concrete building can begin to go up quite rapidly since concrete comes ready-

Reusable wooden scaffolding is being lowered around reinforcing bars. After workmen use it as a platform to prepare the form into which the concrete is poured, it will be moved to the next column-to-be. Finally it will be broken apart and the wood reused.

This is the street-level lobby area. Two halves of a circular fiberboard form enclose these reinforcing rods. Concrete then fills the form, which will be removed when the newly poured column has hardened. The next level of vertical rods has been locked into place and is being wired in position.

These reinforcing rods are embedded in the concrete floor and in the column below.

Two-piece circular fiberboard form

New York's skyscrapers are most frequently box-like in shape, built on rectangular pieces of land, which is equally adaptable to steel or concrete construction. While an unusual elliptically shaped skyscraper has been built of steel on Third Avenue, irregular shapes, curved surfaces, and undulating walls are more easily achieved in concrete. The Guggenheim Museum, designed by Frank Lloyd Wright, while not a high-rise building, exemplifies such an irregularly shaped concrete building.

mixed. Steel must be fabricated and ordered months in advance, while the forms to shape poured concrete are built right on the spot, wherever needed, in any shape or size.

Enormous quantities of wood are needed in concrete construction, in the form of plywood sheets, and planks and beams of all sizes. The wood is used over and over again. Once the concrete has set within a form, the form is removed and reused, or dismantled, and the wood stockpiled.

At times—especially when the building is at street level—the piles of lumber, reinforcing bars, and prefab forms seem a jumble of confusion. The temporary nature of the wooden forms and supports used to shape the concrete columns and flooring makes them seem to be haphazardly placed. Yet the carpenters, integral to concrete construction, have built their wooden framing with precision. When all the wood is removed, the concrete form of the building is revealed, solid and exact in shape and built to the engineer's specifications.

FROM LIQUID MASS TO HARDENED SOLID

Once the concrete structure is built up beyond the street and mezzanine levels, the floors pile up on top of each other, usually with few structural variations.

Each floor goes up much the same way. The frameworks for the floor columns are built and poured. On top of the columns a temporary wooden floor is laid down—usually ⅝-inch thick plywood, its surface specially coated so concrete won't stick to it. All the circuits for electricity, telephone, and plumbing are laid out on this floor according to the blueprints. The ends of the conduits for the utilities are left sticking up above the floor level and are temporarily capped to keep concrete out.

Next, the wooden floor is covered by a network of steel reinforcing bars, woven into a grid of interconnecting metal. Concrete is poured onto the wooden floor framework until it covers the steel mesh to a depth of four to eight inches.

Floor after floor is made this way, with the wooden underfloor framework being disman-

"Chairs" are made in many sizes, and are heavy wire half-loop supports with plastic caps that separate and tie together the network of steel reinforcing bars, raising the bars to the correct height in the poured concrete.

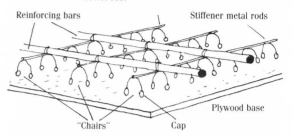

tled and reused over and over as soon as the concrete has hardened sufficiently.

Whole sections of plywood underflooring can be lifted by crane, leapfrogging the floors that have not yet hardened. As the plywood forms are moved out from under the newly formed concrete floor, wooden beams are forced between its underside and the floor below to support it while it finishes its hardening process. The concrete may still be warm to the touch—a result of the chemical action of the hardening process.

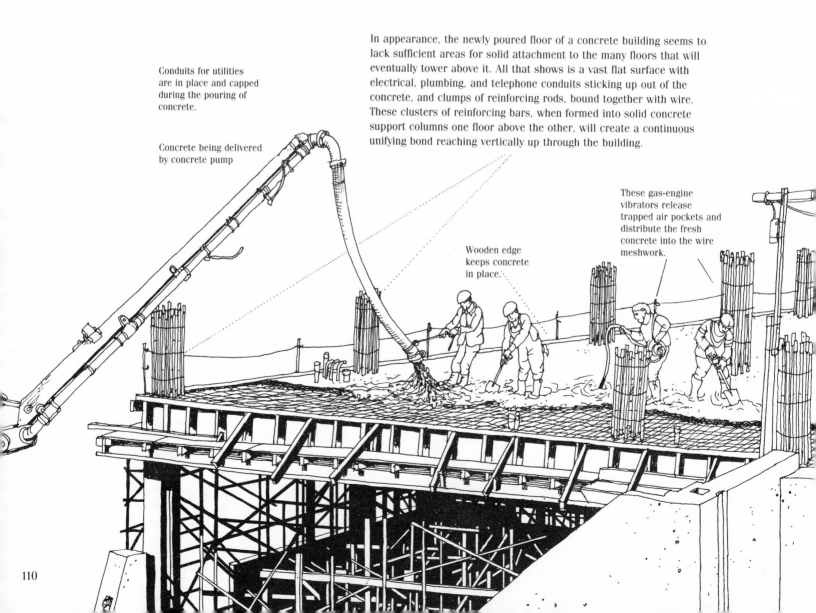

Conduits for utilities are in place and capped during the pouring of concrete.

Concrete being delivered by concrete pump

In appearance, the newly poured floor of a concrete building seems to lack sufficient areas for solid attachment to the many floors that will eventually tower above it. All that shows is a vast flat surface with electrical, plumbing, and telephone conduits sticking up out of the concrete, and clumps of reinforcing rods, bound together with wire. These clusters of reinforcing bars, when formed into solid concrete support columns one floor above the other, will create a continuous unifying bond reaching vertically up through the building.

These gas-engine vibrators release trapped air pockets and distribute the fresh concrete into the wire meshwork.

Wooden edge keeps concrete in place.

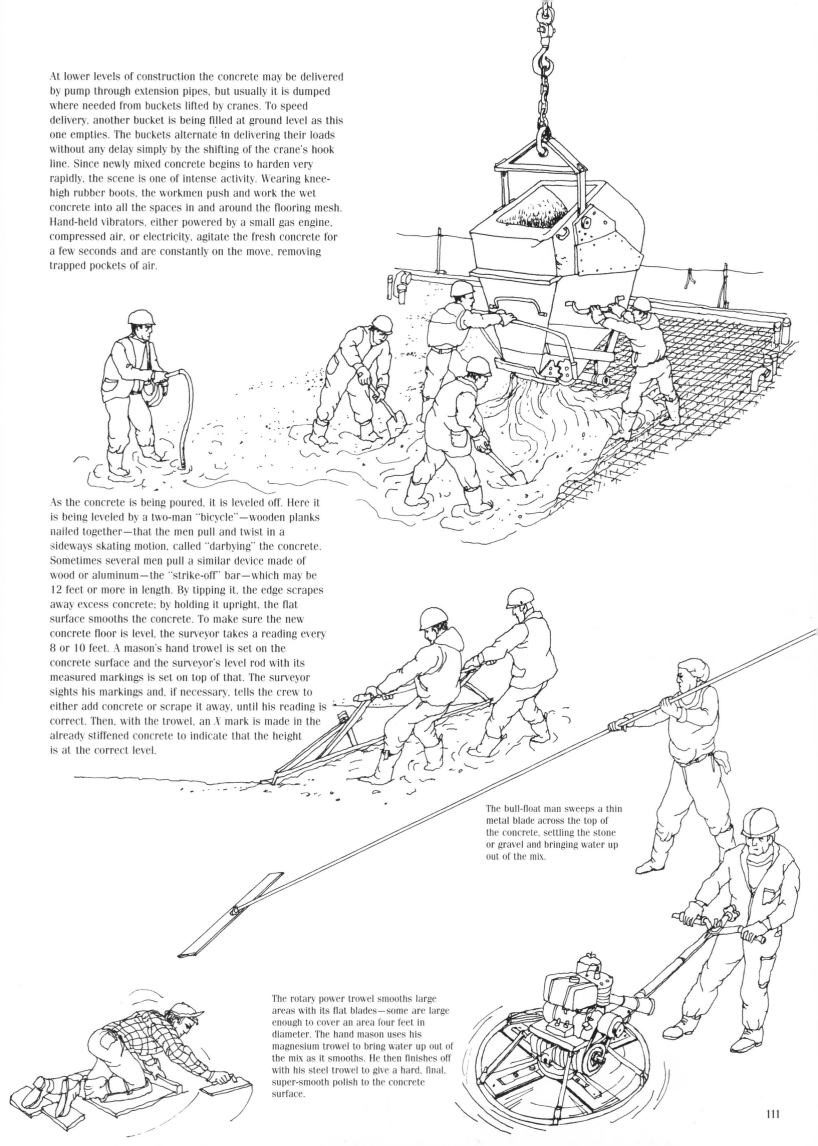

At lower levels of construction the concrete may be delivered by pump through extension pipes, but usually it is dumped where needed from buckets lifted by cranes. To speed delivery, another bucket is being filled at ground level as this one empties. The buckets alternate in delivering their loads without any delay simply by the shifting of the crane's hook line. Since newly mixed concrete begins to harden very rapidly, the scene is one of intense activity. Wearing knee-high rubber boots, the workmen push and work the wet concrete into all the spaces in and around the flooring mesh. Hand-held vibrators, either powered by a small gas engine, compressed air, or electricity, agitate the fresh concrete for a few seconds and are constantly on the move, removing trapped pockets of air.

As the concrete is being poured, it is leveled off. Here it is being leveled by a two-man "bicycle"—wooden planks nailed together—that the men pull and twist in a sideways skating motion, called "darbying" the concrete. Sometimes several men pull a similar device made of wood or aluminum—the "strike-off" bar—which may be 12 feet or more in length. By tipping it, the edge scrapes away excess concrete; by holding it upright, the flat surface smooths the concrete. To make sure the new concrete floor is level, the surveyor takes a reading every 8 or 10 feet. A mason's hand trowel is set on the concrete surface and the surveyor's level rod with its measured markings is set on top of that. The surveyor sights his markings and, if necessary, tells the crew to either add concrete or scrape it away, until his reading is correct. Then, with the trowel, an X mark is made in the already stiffened concrete to indicate that the height is at the correct level.

The bull-float man sweeps a thin metal blade across the top of the concrete, settling the stone or gravel and bringing water up out of the mix.

The rotary power trowel smooths large areas with its flat blades—some are large enough to cover an area four feet in diameter. The hand mason uses his magnesium trowel to bring water up out of the mix as it smooths. He then finishes off with his steel trowel to give a hard, final, super-smooth polish to the concrete surface.

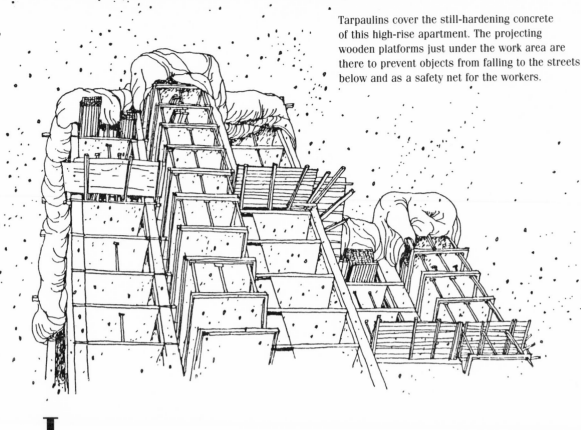

Tarpaulins cover the still-hardening concrete of this high-rise apartment. The projecting wooden platforms just under the work area are there to prevent objects from falling to the streets below and as a safety net for the workers.

SALAMANDERS

In cold, windy, or wet weather, canvas or heavy plastic tarpaulins cover and enclose the floors and areas where fresh concrete has been poured. Coke-fired heaters, called "salamanders," are kept burning day and night, giving off heat just under and around the area that has fresh concrete.

Trapped inside the area by the tarps, the heat rises and keeps the temperature of the floor above at the necessary level to achieve proper drying and hardening of the concrete. If moisture in the wet concrete were to freeze, it would cause cracking and weak-ening of the concrete. Extreme changes in temperature can also cause expansion and contraction in the concrete.

As the building's framework is built higher and higher, the exterior surfaces at the lower levels are readied for their outer facings.

Metal supports and fasteners for the outer wall were set in the concrete when it was poured. A wide variety of possibilities exist for this outer facing: glass panels, precast concrete sections, metal sheeting, or thin slices of stone or granite. It may be all brick, built up piece by piece.

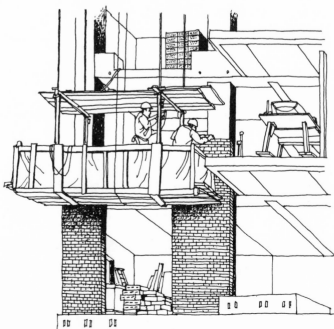

Suspended on wire cables and protected by a plywood roof, the masons work from a movable scaffolding as they build up the face of a building brick by brick—perhaps as high as 40 floors or more. The spaces between the reinforced concrete columns will be built up to window-frame height with precast concrete blocks. Thin strips of metal, inserted between the blocks and extending outward, act as anchors to hold the bricks in place. A wire mesh is also laid on top of every second layer of bricks to bind them in place with the cement. Between the bricks and the concrete blocks is an air space that acts as insulation. Metal stripping is then fastened to the inside of the concrete blocks; panels of sheet rock are fastened to this stripping to become the interior walls of the building.

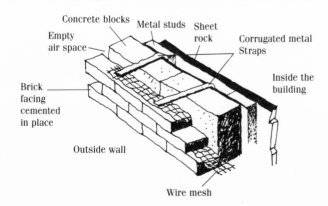

Concrete blocks
Metal studs
Sheet rock
Empty air space
Corrugated metal Straps
Brick facing cemented in place
Inside the building
Outside wall
Wire mesh

The city requires specific safety precautions: wire cables around open floors, railings around floor openings, outer platforms on upper floors, water standpipes, emergency elevators, properly situated loading ramps, street fences around the site, scaffolding over sidewalks, and cranes in approved positions.

The concrete floors are sufficiently solid to walk on in a few hours and will set thoroughly in 14 to 23 days. The wooden support beams are left in place for four weeks or more.

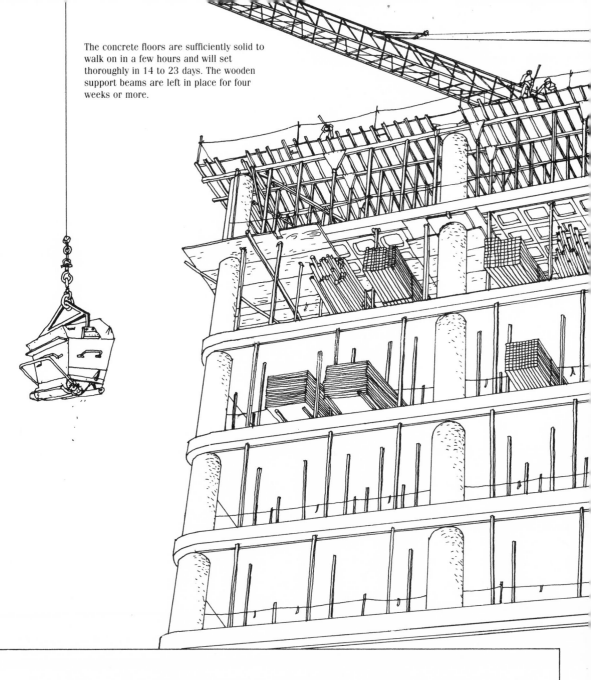

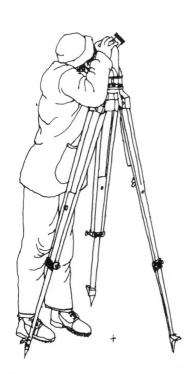

Unlike a steel building, where each floor is rigidly defined within the upright framework of metal columns and beams, the reinforced-concrete building requires the accurate placing of each new floor on top of the one just built. The new floor is poured concrete in a complex jigsaw puzzle of wooden forms, platforms, supports, steel reinforcing bars, and bracings. The wonder is that once the concrete has hardened, and the forms have been removed, the floor measurements are in agreement with the working drawings.

On the lower floors, the outer skin of the building will be put on, and the interior work begun. Flooring will be installed, partition walls erected, and drop ceilings hung below the concrete ceilings to hide wires, pipes, and ductwork. Stairways connect the floors. Elevators and utilities— water, sewage, electricity, air conditioning, heat, telephones—all have to be installed. Plasterers and painters finish off the interiors. It may take longer to complete the inside of the building than it did to put up its skeletal structure. The building's entrance, lobby, and ground floor are designed to enhance the entire building and will get special attention. When all is done, it will be impossible to tell whether the building is of steel-framework construction or has been built up, floor by floor, of reinforced concrete.

The surveyor keeps ahead of the construction with key measurements and markings that line up vertically on the building, one above the other, all in line with the ground-level reference point. To make a mark at the highest level, two surveyors work as a team: one at the reference point on ground level, the other holding a short measuring stick upright on the top level. Using hand signals, the ground-level surveyor directs the movement of the stick left or right until it is exactly on position, and the upper-floor surveyor marks it there precisely. They confirm the placement of the marking by voice, over walkie-talkies. All subsequent measurements on that upper floor will be taken from this mark.

THE BIG CRANES

The tallest crawler crane in use in Manhattan is as high as a 40-story building. It may weigh as much as 200 tons. And it can pick up a 50-ton load at street level and minutes later land it gently and safely on the exposed upper level of an unfinished building. It is the workhorse at many construction sites, wherever a self-contained revolving hoisting crane is needed.

One day it suddenly appears, full-sized and functioning on a city street. And just as mysteriously one day it disappears. Since it is too tall to be moved to or from its position, and too heavy and cumbersome to negotiate Manhattan's busy, narrow and crowded streets, what happened?

It all comes apart in sections.

These sections are the cabin, the solid-steel counterbalance weights behind the cabin, the jib at the very top, the bolted-together sections of the boom, the cables and their uprights, and the crawler pads. Each section can then be moved from a storage yard in the Bronx, or elsewhere, to the construction site.

To avoid traffic they are moved in the early hours, usually over a weekend, using a route worked out with city officials. Some streets have obstructions, and some are too weak for the weight.

The sections are moved on flatbed trailers; even the crane bodies with their eighteen oversized wheels and tires are on flatbeds. The crane sections with the heavy crawler pads are lifted onto a trailer bed, where they straddle steel beams.

The big cranes are too slow to move any real distance under their own power. Their wheels and treads are for maneuvering into position while working at the construction site.

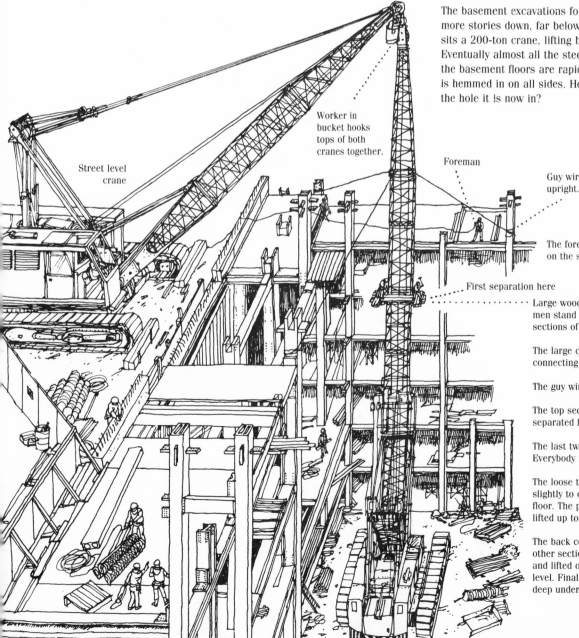

The basement excavations for big skyscrapers can reach six or more stories down, far below street level. Down at the very bottom sits a 200-ton crane, lifting beams and columns into place. Eventually almost all the steelwork of the foundation is in position, the basement floors are rapidly taking shape, and the crane itself is hemmed in on all sides. How to get this enormous crane out of the hole it is now in?

Worker in bucket hooks tops of both cranes together.

Street level crane

Foreman

Guy wires are attached above the separation to steady the upright.

The foreman is in voice contact with the crane operator on the street and directs the dismantling.

First separation here

Large wooden planks are placed between uprights, where men stand while knocking out the pins that connect the sections of the crane.

The large cotter pins are removed. Two pins with connecting rods are knocked out with big sledgehammers.

The guy wires are removed.

The top section is now tilted slightly so it is partly separated from the rest of the bottom of the crane.

The last two pins are knocked out.
Everybody is off the crane.

The loose top part is lifted by the street crane and moved slightly to one side, and then lowered to the basement floor. The pieces of this part are separated there and lifted up to the street individually.

The back counterweights are lifted off the cabin. Then the other sections, including the crawler pads, are removed and lifted out piece by piece by the crane on the street level. Finally the crane that seemed locked into place, deep underground, has vanished.

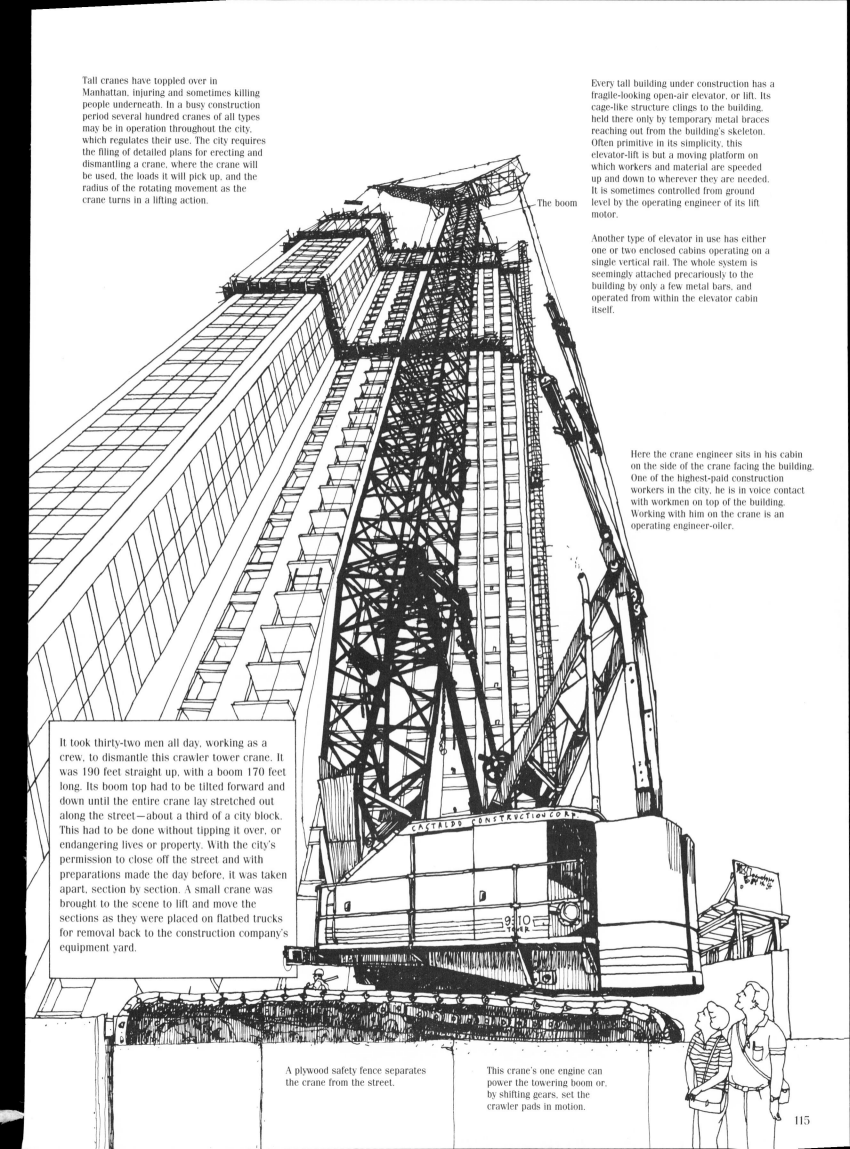

Tall cranes have toppled over in Manhattan, injuring and sometimes killing people underneath. In a busy construction period several hundred cranes of all types may be in operation throughout the city, which regulates their use. The city requires the filing of detailed plans for erecting and dismantling a crane, where the crane will be used, the loads it will pick up, and the radius of the rotating movement as the crane turns in a lifting action.

Every tall building under construction has a fragile-looking open-air elevator, or lift. Its cage-like structure clings to the building, held there only by temporary metal braces reaching out from the building's skeleton. Often primitive in its simplicity, this elevator-lift is but a moving platform on which workers and material are speeded up and down to wherever they are needed. It is sometimes controlled from ground level by the operating engineer of its lift motor.

Another type of elevator in use has either one or two enclosed cabins operating on a single vertical rail. The whole system is seemingly attached precariously to the building by only a few metal bars, and operated from within the elevator cabin itself.

The boom

Here the crane engineer sits in his cabin on the side of the crane facing the building. One of the highest-paid construction workers in the city, he is in voice contact with workmen on top of the building. Working with him on the crane is an operating engineer-oiler.

It took thirty-two men all day, working as a crew, to dismantle this crawler tower crane. It was 190 feet straight up, with a boom 170 feet long. Its boom top had to be tilted forward and down until the entire crane lay stretched out along the street—about a third of a city block. This had to be done without tipping it over, or endangering lives or property. With the city's permission to close off the street and with preparations made the day before, it was taken apart, section by section. A small crane was brought to the scene to lift and move the sections as they were placed on flatbed trucks for removal back to the construction company's equipment yard.

A plywood safety fence separates the crane from the street.

This crane's one engine can power the towering boom or, by shifting gears, set the crawler pads in motion.

115

How do you build an extremely narrow skyscraper just off Park Avenue in midtown Manhattan, one that is sandwiched between a tall office building and an old tiny brownstone? Because the developer of this building under construction has no air rights over these buildings on either side of his site, the crane is not permitted to swing out above either building. This concrete skyscraper reaches back from the street for about 100 feet, but is only 71 feet wide. At street level it has been built to the maximum width allowed, with a set-back beginning at the sixth floor. There is very little working space for unloading or storage at street level. This luffing tower crane, sometimes called a "kangaroo crane," working high above the building. requires no street space. It picks up and delivers materials anywhere and everywhere they are needed, and can swing in a narrow arc directly over its own building site. Some upright tower cranes have a moving counterweight that adds stability to their tower. As the vertical boom is lowered, the counterweight moves to the rear. As the boom rises to a more vertical position, the counterweight moves toward the center, since the weight load has also moved to the center.

Reinforced
concrete
counterweights

TOWER CRANES

The street-level crawler crane operator sits confined to his street-level cabin, his vision restricted to the space about him, and to the hoisting space directly above him.

Not so the tower crane operator. Perched out over open air, high above everything else, the operator in his tower cabin has an unparalleled view of the work activity going on below him. His tower crane has changed the way skyscrapers are built.

By concentrating all the hoist and control mechanisms of the crane on its upper structure, the tower crane requires a minimum of on-the-ground space for its supporting framework. In operation it can service and supply, unimpeded, a 360-degree workspace area, with precise control and speed of operation. Once in place, the tower crane's height is increased by its own self-climbing mechanism, and it keeps its advantage in height as the building itself increases in height during construction.

Tower cranes, which originated in Europe after World War II, come in big, bigger, and very big sizes—and with different design features. They all sway somewhat in the wind, and they twist and bend while carrying heavy loads.

The placing of the narrow upright tower crane on the building site is a matter of critical importance. Sometimes it rises up where the open elevator shaft will be, sometimes where the stairwell will be—often it is within the building itself, rising through openings left in the construction of the floors. When the crane tower is dismantled, these holes are filled in with construction to conform to the rest of the building.

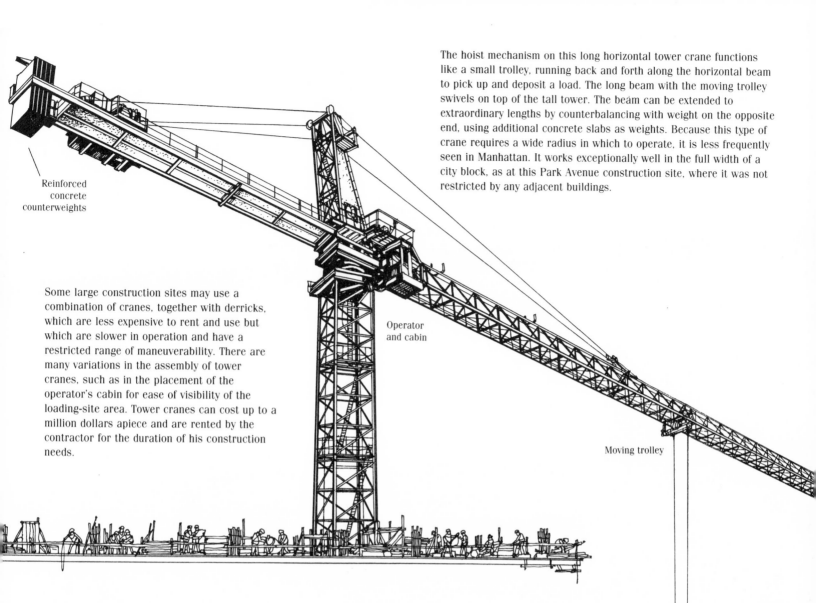

The hoist mechanism on this long horizontal tower crane functions like a small trolley, running back and forth along the horizontal beam to pick up and deposit a load. The long beam with the moving trolley swivels on top of the tall tower. The beam can be extended to extraordinary lengths by counterbalancing with weight on the opposite end, using additional concrete slabs as weights. Because this type of crane requires a wide radius in which to operate, it is less frequently seen in Manhattan. It works exceptionally well in the full width of a city block, as at this Park Avenue construction site, where it was not restricted by any adjacent buildings.

Reinforced concrete counterweights

Operator and cabin

Moving trolley

Some large construction sites may use a combination of cranes, together with derricks, which are less expensive to rent and use but which are slower in operation and have a restricted range of maneuverability. There are many variations in the assembly of tower cranes, such as in the placement of the operator's cabin for ease of visibility of the loading-site area. Tower cranes can cost up to a million dollars apiece and are rented by the contractor for the duration of his construction needs.

The tower-crane operator has to be an unusual man, not unnerved by the height, the vibrations, the solitude, or the responsibility of swinging tons of material out above the streets below, or out over the heads of his fellow workers.

It may take him half an hour or more to make the climb up, up, up the tall open-air ladder to get to his cabin. If there's a construction elevator working, he'll get a ride as high as it will go and then he has to somehow get out onto his tower crane ladder. He gets climbing pay for the time it takes him to make the long climb. Sometimes, if it's a short climb, he comes down to eat, or else he eats where he is. His bathroom is portable. He has an electric heater in his cabin to keep him warm. He is on the job early, before others have arrived. Sometimes his operating engineer partner, his oiler, takes over and handles the crane.

All tower cranes, whether long horizontal cranes or upright kangaroo cranes, are top-heavy mechanisms—tons of metal balanced on top of tall spindly support towers. Without proper balance they would topple, pulled over by the weight of the load they are lifting. To compensate for lifted weight, counterweight blocks of reinforced concrete are added to the side of the tower opposite the carried load, according to the need.

Within the cabin itself the operator is in voice contact with those below him, through a direct cable line and squawk-box intercom. Sometimes he cannot see over a wall or behind an obstruction. Then he operates his crane from voice directions or hand signals from below. Ironworkers inching steel beams into place give him hand signals.

His instrument control panel includes gauges that indicate the weight of the load he is lifting and the radius, how far out he can swing the load. A warning light flashes and a horn sounds if the load approaches allowable limits. Automatic devices reduce the hoist speed, or shut off the boom operation, if hoisting or lowering limits are about to be exceeded. His control mechanisms vary on different makes of cranes. On many, his hands control the levers that raise and lower the hoists and his foot pedals control the swing.

New York City requires that detailed plans be filed for each crane used in construction, specifying the type of crane, where and how it is to be erected and dismantled, the radius of its swing, and the pick-up areas at the site. Each piece of a tower crane has to be clearly marked in paint, giving the weight of the piece and showing the center of gravity. By placing the lifting sling at this center mark, the metal piece remains perfectly balanced as it is being hoisted.

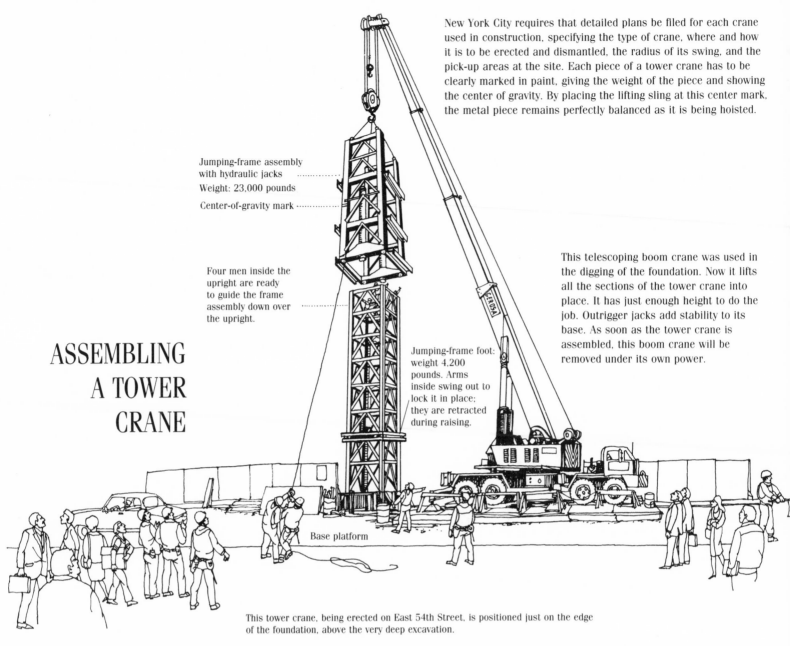

Jumping-frame assembly with hydraulic jacks
Weight: 23,000 pounds

Center-of-gravity mark

Four men inside the upright are ready to guide the frame assembly down over the upright.

This telescoping boom crane was used in the digging of the foundation. Now it lifts all the sections of the tower crane into place. It has just enough height to do the job. Outrigger jacks add stability to its base. As soon as the tower crane is assembled, this boom crane will be removed under its own power.

Jumping-frame foot: weight 4,200 pounds. Arms inside swing out to lock it in place; they are retracted during raising.

ASSEMBLING A TOWER CRANE

Base platform

This tower crane, being erected on East 54th Street, is positioned just on the edge of the foundation, above the very deep excavation.

First: at ground/street level, a heavy solid metal platform is bolted and welded into place with metal beams that were embedded in the concrete foundation wall. This platform must be absolutely level, or the tower crane above it will lean more and more off-center the higher it rises. The first 40-foot section of tower is bolted and welded to this base platform.

The jumping-frame foot is lowered into place and locked there.

The jumping-frame assembly is lowered onto the upright frame of the tower until it rests on the jumping-frame foot. Enormous steel bolts attach both together. The tower is now ready to receive the revolving upper-structure.

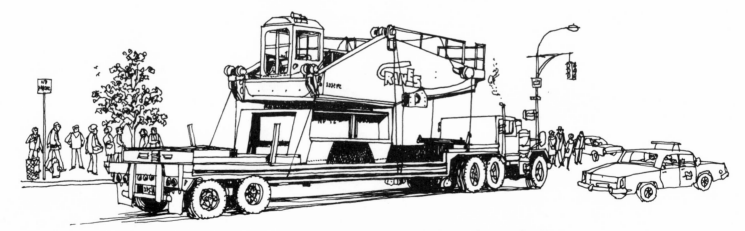

The upper-structure: the turntable base, with operator's cabin, the boom, and hoist mechanisms, arrive on flatbed trucks to be raised and locked into position.

Even though the assembly of a tower crane may be done in full view of the crawler crane operator, and it is he who raises the individual pieces of the tower crane into position, most of his directions come from the hand signals of the foreman in charge of the operation. From the East Coast to the West Coast the same set of more then twenty hand signals are used wherever cranes are operated.

RAISING THE CRANE'S HEIGHT

The tower crane grows in height as the building grows in height, by adding new sections to itself without being dismantled. It is astonishing to see.

The crane operator controls this "growing" process from inside his cabin. The jumping-frame assembly with its two large hydraulic jacks is the key to its climbing ability. These hydraulic jacks can raise the entire upper-structure of the crane about 14 feet, providing the opening for a new tower section.

ADDING THE NEW SECTION: FOR ILLUSTRATION PURPOSES THE NEW SECTION IS SHOWN HERE SUSPENDED AND WITH THE JUMPING-FRAME ASSEMBLY RAISED

In the sequence of assembly, the new section is lifted up from street level into a temporary position before the hydraulic jacks raise the jumping-frame assembly. The new section is brought in against the top opening of the frame assembly with two of its four legs resting on the I-beam extension, and its top is fastened to the pulley and the monorail beam. The crane's lifting slings, or cables, are removed; their job is done.

Inside the tower crane's framework ironworkers have attached the hydraulic lines and prepared the frame assembly for its slide upward. It rises slowly until it is at the correct height to receive the new section.

This section, suspended on the monorail beam, is now pulled inside the framework by the ironworkers until it rests on top of the tower's base frame. It is bolted into place.

The jumping-frame foot is released and is pulled up to a new height by the hydraulic jacks and again secured to the tower frame. It is now ready for future liftings.

Usually two or three new sections are added on the same day—it may be an all-day operation. Steel-beam bracing may also be welded out from the building's steel skeleton to the tower's frame, to provide support for the tower's increasing height. Finally the monorail beam is removed. When the height of the skyscraper's steel framework again reaches up to the tower's level, making the crane's job of raising steel and material difficult, the jumping process will be repeated, and new sections added.

This tower crane's engine is powered by diesel fuel. About once a week, or less often, the operator lifts a large tank of fuel up to his cabin level, lets it hang close to the cabin, and feeds the fuel into the crane's tank by gravity.

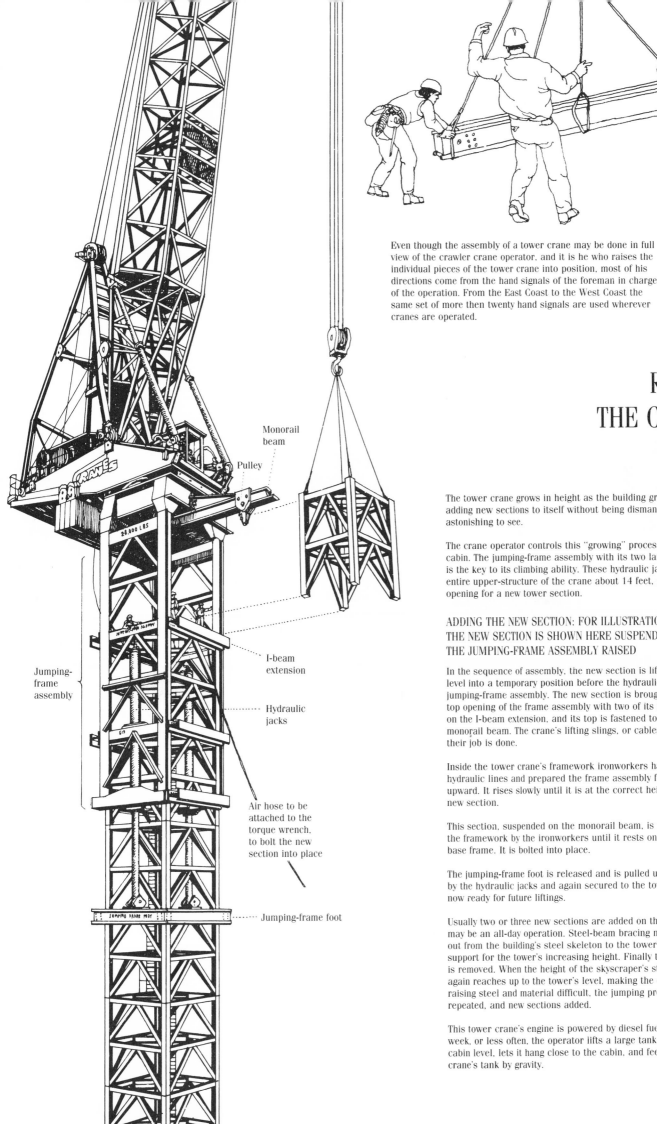

Monorail beam

Pulley

Jumping-frame assembly

I-beam extension

Hydraulic jacks

Air hose to be attached to the torque wrench, to bolt the new section into place

Jumping-frame foot

Manhattan has Central Park, Bryant Park, Bowling Green, and other oases of greenery to remind one that the island has not been completely covered over by concrete, asphalt, and buildings. Underneath all that construction there really is soil, capable of sustaining growing things. But with the cost of land in Manhattan sometimes well over $1,000 a square foot, any new greenery and growing soil have to be placed where they are by determined individuals. High above the city streets flowers bloom, shrubs grow, ivy clings to vertical wall surfaces, and tall trees cast their shade—on terraces, balconies, and penthouse extravaganzas.

PRIVATE PLACES PUBLIC SPACES

Office skyscrapers dominate the skyline of Manhattan, but apartment buildings of great height are also now commonplace.

Some penthouse apartments cost well in excess of two million dollars. These buildings may provide apartments with wood-burning fireplaces, wine cellars, whirlpool baths, saunas, steam rooms, servants' quarters, a waterfall in the lobby, video intercom security systems, 24-hour doormen, computer centers, lavish use of fine woods and marble, heated swimming pools, basement garages, and spectacular views of the city.

The new office buildings also offer special amenities to the public, in the form of public spaces. The old-style lobby, that passageway from the street to the elevators, is now often a social gathering space. It may be an atrium—an open space many stories high—a galleria, a plaza, or an arcade. Most invite tenants and passersby to visit, sit, eat, and shop.

Here the developer and his architect express their own sense of personal pride and creative ability by designing a space that is meant to be individual and different.

The IBM atrium is airy and welcoming with its bamboo plantings and opportunities for the visitor to sit and relax; the Trump Tower is opulent, and extravagant in its use of space and materials. Citicorp Center's atrium and plaza create their own lively neighborhood, busy and fast paced. The Equitable Center provides a branch of the Whitney Museum of American Art. Tiny in comparison, the Philip Morris street galleria also entices the public with its exhibitions of art from the Whitney. Wherever they're found, these public spaces add immeasurably to the human enjoyment of the city.

For the developer there is an added incentive. Under the zoning code he may be able to increase the height of his building, with more rentable space, in exchange for having provided this public convenience.

For the architects and engineers these great open street-level spaces are a test of their abilities. Not only must the supporting columns be designed to carry all the weight of the entire building above them, but the supporting beams spanning the open space must be capable of withstanding enormous stresses. Concrete has been used to spectacular effect in archways, domes, and complex structures, but there is one material that is preeminent in spanning great distances with a minimum of volume.

It is steel.

The steel skeleton of a big building is put together piece by piece, creating a lattice-work of metal in the open spaces above the city. The man who raises the steel beams, wrestles them into position, and bolts them solidly into place is the ironworker.

From the streets below he is seen walking along narrow beams of metal, in defiance of common sense.

There is nothing but his confidence, concentration, and sense of balance to prevent his falling hundreds of feet earthward to the streets of the city. The steel skeleton of the skyscraper is his handiwork.

STEEL

STEEL

Girders, columns, beams, trusses, sheet metal . . . all kinds of shapes and sizes . . . in steel.

The big pieces are trucked to the construction site resting on wooden blocks so the lifting cables or slings can be easily slipped under and around the heavy metal.

Such as the 125-foot-long girders, each weighing 70 tons, for the Marriott Marquis Hotel in Times Square.

Sixty thousand tons of steel for the Empire State Building.

More than 200,000 tons of steel for the World Trade Center.

Steel: iron ore melted at high temperature, alloyed with carbon.

The basic metal can be transformed into hundreds of different steels—each for a specific use—by the addition of minerals or chemicals, and by precise heat treatment. Beams, columns, and the other steel members of the skyscraper must be fabricated to the exact shape and size needed, and ordered months in advance of use. The steel may come from a foreign country or from a nearby state, depending on the cost and when it is needed.

Some high-strength steel used in the World Trade Center is rated to withstand an ultimate strain of 100,000 pounds per square inch. Few steel pieces require such strength, which is determined by the structural engineers and built into the metal exactly according to their specifications.

Now the steel has been formed and drilled according to the engineer's working drawings. It has been shipped to the ready yard—usually just across the Hudson River in New Jersey—until the day and hour it is needed.

Expansion section of truck

L egend attributes to the American Indian the ability to work at dizzying heights without fear. Many of the men who work the steel in Manhattan—all are called ironworkers—are indeed Native Americans. It is said that Canadian Indians first helped put up a high-water bridge over the St. Lawrence River, beginning this tradition of Native Americans working steel at great heights.

Manhattan's ironworkers are journeymen, moving from job to job, wherever work is available.

The top man is the connector. He is the man high up on a girder, usually with a partner, wrestling a dangling steel beam into place. With the pointed end of his spud wrench he lines up the holes so he can punch in a bolt to hold the beam in place. Then he shinnies out on the beam and releases the wire cables that lifted it into position.

Next, other ironworkers put in and ram tight the rest of the bolts with compressed air guns once they have made sure that the steel is level and true. Later, the decking gang puts down the corrugated steel floors. Overseeing it all is the foreman.

Down on the street level, wire cables are placed around another beam that's about to be lifted. The tag-line man hooks a rope to the end of the beam to guide it and keep it from swinging about as the crane lifts it skyward.

AND
IRONWORKERS

Each piece of steel arrives with painted-on numbers and letters that tell exactly where it goes in the construction. It must arrive when needed, on a tight schedule. It is loaded on the truck so it will arrive facing in the right direction. The ironworkers use their judgment to position the cables so the beam will balance safely while being lifted aloft. The rear section of this steel-carrying truck can slide back and forth, to make an expanded truck up to 85 feet long.

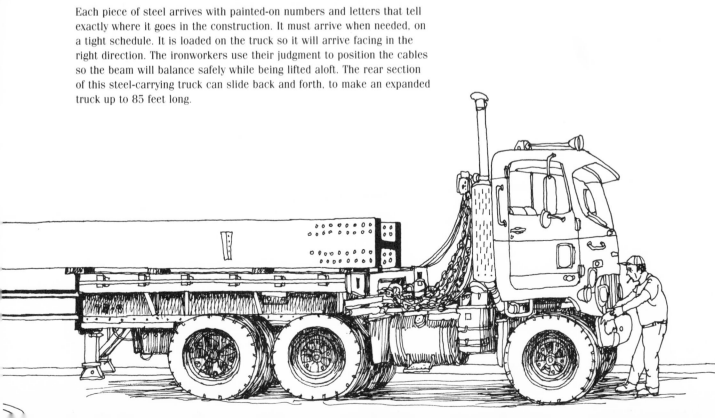

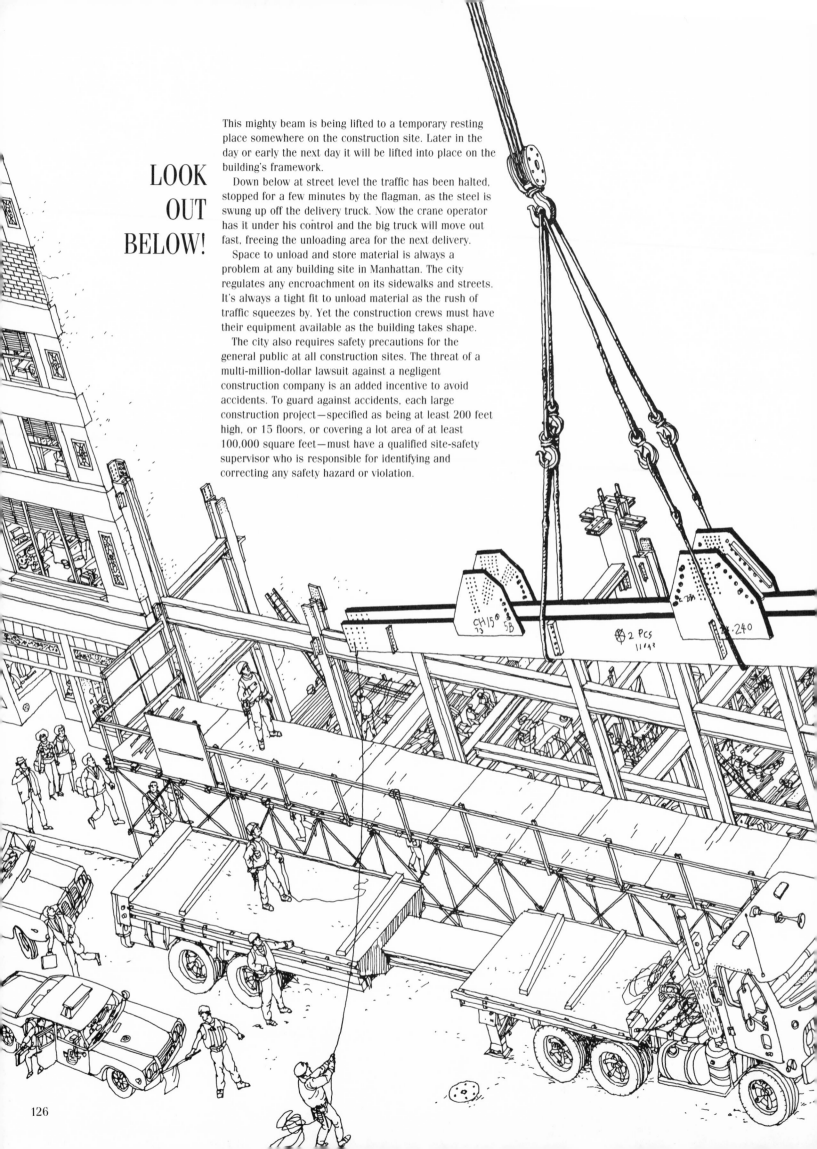

LOOK OUT BELOW!

This mighty beam is being lifted to a temporary resting place somewhere on the construction site. Later in the day or early the next day it will be lifted into place on the building's framework.

Down below at street level the traffic has been halted, stopped for a few minutes by the flagman, as the steel is swung up off the delivery truck. Now the crane operator has it under his control and the big truck will move out fast, freeing the unloading area for the next delivery.

Space to unload and store material is always a problem at any building site in Manhattan. The city regulates any encroachment on its sidewalks and streets. It's always a tight fit to unload material as the rush of traffic squeezes by. Yet the construction crews must have their equipment available as the building takes shape.

The city also requires safety precautions for the general public at all construction sites. The threat of a multi-million-dollar lawsuit against a negligent construction company is an added incentive to avoid accidents. To guard against accidents, each large construction project—specified as being at least 200 feet high, or 15 floors, or covering a lot area of at least 100,000 square feet—must have a qualified site-safety supervisor who is responsible for identifying and correcting any safety hazard or violation.

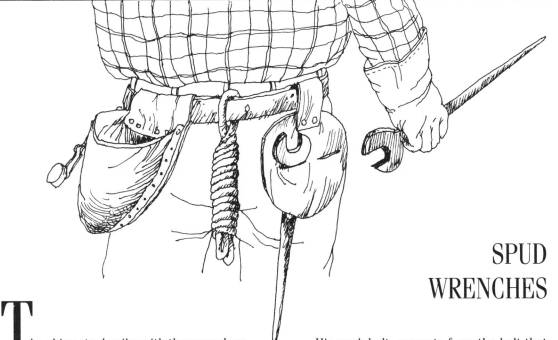

SPUD WRENCHES

The shiny steel spike with the wrench on one end is the ironworker's indispensable tool—his spud wrench. It comes in different sizes, to fit the need. It is polished to a high finish by constant handling. The tapered end is jammed into empty bolt holes to force a beam or girder into position so a bolt can be inserted into the lined-up holes. Then, with the wrench end, the ironworker tightens the nut on the bolt.

His spud wrench is not a straight piece of metal: the wrench end is offset, allowing hand room when tightening a nut. Usually two spud wrenches hang from his belt to meet that day's requirements.

His work belt, separate from the belt that holds up his pants, may weigh as much as 30 pounds or more. His leather or canvas pouch is his carryall. Nuts and bolts, clamps to lock wire cables together, anything he'll need, all go into his pouch. The coiled rope is his safety rope, used to tie himself to a support in an especially dangerous work position.

His friction lighter, or striker, hangs from his belt. It's used to light an acetylene torch if he has to trim away a bit of excess metal, which happens from time to time. The wonder is that it doesn't happen more often. Blueprints are drawn in New York City for steel that is fabricated and drilled with holes hundreds, perhaps thousands, of miles away.

When the heavy metal arrives in Manhattan and is hoisted into position high up on the building's skeleton, it has to fit. The ironworker's job is to wrestle it into position, and to bolt it in place. Sometimes a hole has to be enlarged with a tapered reamer, right on the job.

There are times when a loud clanging hammering noise reverberates through the city's streets. Very rarely it might be a dropped wrench bouncing off steel beams on its way down to a lower level. More likely, two large pieces of steel do not line up exactly, and a drift pin is driven in to align the holes. Then the ironworker pounds the metal beams or columns with a heavy sledgehammer. He must move the metal beams just enough for the pin to be loosened and the bolt inserted and rammed home.

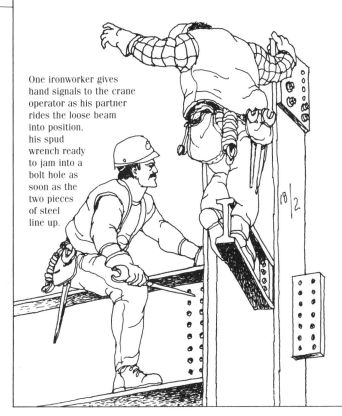

One ironworker gives hand signals to the crane operator as his partner rides the loose beam into position, his spud wrench ready to jam into a bolt hole as soon as the two pieces of steel line up.

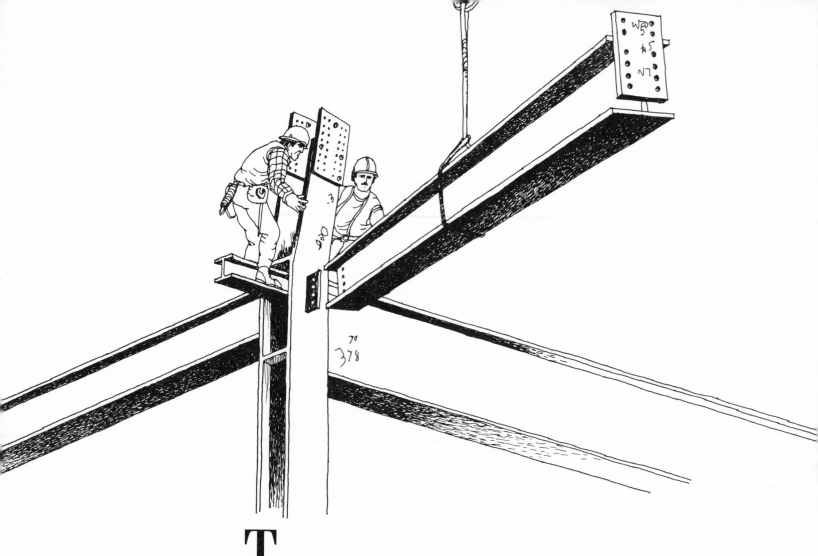

FROM BEAM

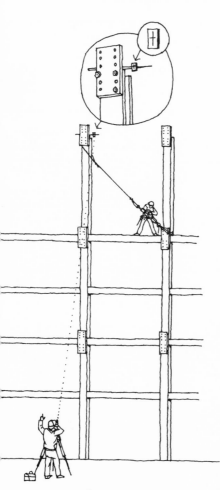

Two ironworkers, connectors working as a team, are at a new height, the highest yet of the building's steel framework. They have just temporarily bolted two horizontal beams to the upright column where they are perched. About them, at their level, are more tops of unconnected steel columns.

Now it is time to join these columns together by bolting horizontal beams to their tops, creating a new floor level of the building's construction.

Below the ironworkers lie the beams that are to be lifted into place. They were placed there earlier when and where space was made available, in accordance with the time schedule. The foreman has consulted his drawings and checked the numbered markings on each piece of steel at this lower level. There are shouted words—the beams are facing in the right direction but are not in the correct order for lifting by crane. There is quick action as loud curses fill the air. Other ironworkers attach cables to the out-of-place beam, guide the tower crane operator with hand signals, and get the sequence right.

A new beam is hoisted to the men waiting above. One ironworker has guided the beam end into place, while the other has inserted his spud wrench in one of the predrilled holes, lined up the two pieces of metal, and shoved in a bolt. His partner walks the suspended beam to its opposite end, forces it into position, and puts in a temporary bolt. They signal for the next beam. They may stay up on the beams, moving along each time they create a new place from which to work, until all the upright columns of that section have been connected.

The columns and beams are now connected and the "bolters-up" have put bolts in all the rivet holes. They are still called rivet holes even though rivets are no longer used this way. The nuts on the bolts are loosely tightened. But are all the uprights perfectly vertical? And all the horizontals true? To assure that this is so is the job of the surveyors, with their precision instruments. It is also the job of the "plumbers-up" to check the positioning of the columns and beams. They will have to physically adjust any piece of metal that is out of plumb. They stretch heavy wire cables with giant turnbuckles between the upright columns of steel. The surveyor's crosshairs, fastened to the top of the column upright, must line up with the surveyor's sight to have the steel upright truly vertical. His hand signals tell the ironworker to loosen or tighten the turnbuckles, until perfect alignment is achieved. One way to determine a true vertical is with the plumb bob—a pointed weight suspended on a string or wire—in use since the days of the ancient Egyptians. When any piece of metal is found to be off-line the turnbuckles are adjusted and the wire cables stretched taut, holding the columns true while the bolts are tightened.

These steel columns, which have just been temporarily bolted, are each two floors tall. They will now be checked for vertical alignment and be permanently bolted, welded, and inspected. Steel Q-decking will be laid on top to provide a floor on which to store the steel for the next upper levels.

As the crane lifts steel up to the new top level, stores it there, and then positions each piece for the ironworkers to temporarily bolt in place, the floor just below is being worked on. It was bypassed. Now it is its turn to be permanently bolted, welded, inspected, and to get its Q-deck flooring. This jumping of floors speeds up the construction of the building's framework.

The four-inch layer of concrete for the floors will be poured on top of the Q-decking later, from the bottom floor on up to the top.

TO BEAM

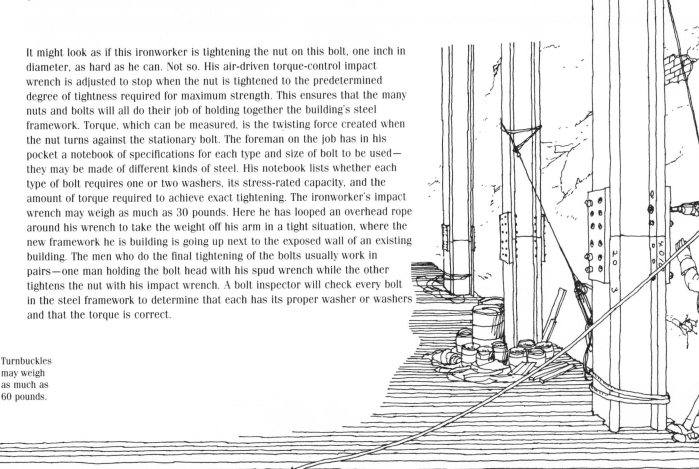

It might look as if this ironworker is tightening the nut on this bolt, one inch in diameter, as hard as he can. Not so. His air-driven torque-control impact wrench is adjusted to stop when the nut is tightened to the predetermined degree of tightness required for maximum strength. This ensures that the many nuts and bolts will all do their job of holding together the building's steel framework. Torque, which can be measured, is the twisting force created when the nut turns against the stationary bolt. The foreman on the job has in his pocket a notebook of specifications for each type and size of bolt to be used— they may be made of different kinds of steel. His notebook lists whether each type of bolt requires one or two washers, its stress-rated capacity, and the amount of torque required to achieve exact tightening. The ironworker's impact wrench may weigh as much as 30 pounds. Here he has looped an overhead rope around his wrench to take the weight off his arm in a tight situation, where the new framework he is building is going up next to the exposed wall of an existing building. The men who do the final tightening of the bolts usually work in pairs—one man holding the bolt head with his spud wrench while the other tightens the nut with his impact wrench. A bolt inspector will check every bolt in the steel framework to determine that each has its proper washer or washers and that the torque is correct.

Turnbuckles
may weigh
as much as
60 pounds.

All ironworkers have learned the art of welding in the third year of their apprenticeship. Not all choose to be certified to weld. Many do, and not only erect the steel, but weld it and cut it. There are also welders who do nothing but weld. They follow closely behind the ironworkers who bolt up the steel. While the welder can adapt his electric arc welding torch to cut away metal, here he is using a cutting torch. Instead of electricity, it uses a mixture of acetylene gas and oxygen. Here he is burning off a slight misalignment where two pieces of metal are to be joined. The welder must control the amount of heat and flame and the tempo of his work—neither too fast nor too slow—when using either the arc welding or the cutting torch. In very cold weather he uses a torch to preheat the metal parts to be welded, since the cold metal has contracted and would create stresses in the weld if not heated adequately prior to the moment of welding.

THE WELDER

Welders can be seen anywhere on the building's skeleton, with the blinding light from their arc welding rods showing where another permanent bond is being joined in the steel beams and columns.

Welders are enveloped in protective clothing: large leather gauntlet gloves, leather aprons, and shoulder and arm guards. These prevent painful skin burns from the blinding arc of electricity given off at the tip of the welding rod. Special eye goggles and protective head masks protect their eyes and faces, for the electric arc gives off invisible untraviolet and infrared rays as well as intensely brilliant light.

The arc welder gets his low voltage, yet concentrated electricity, from a portable generator. It is so powerful that it can create a temperature of 10,000 degrees Fahrenheit at the tip of the slender welding rod, which melts and flows at the joining of the separate pieces of steel to create a permanent bond.

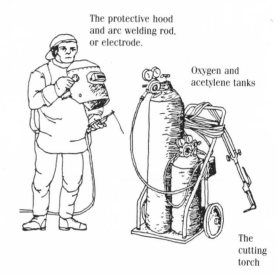

The protective hood and arc welding rod, or electrode.

Oxygen and acetylene tanks

The cutting torch

The electric current from the generator flows through the cable to the electrode in the welder's hand. It jumps a short gap as an arc to the piece being welded on the building's steel framework. The current passes harmlessly through the building's framework back to another terminal in the generator, completing the circuit of electricity.

The finished welds are each tested for imperfections with a portable ultrasonic device that sends high-frequency sound impulses through the metal. Any air pockets or imperfections in the weld show up on a testing meter, requiring that the weld be redone.

The steel framework for this IBM headquarters is still only a few stories high, but the safety precautions include taut guard wires around the top edge and a safety net strung beneath the overhang, where the building's entrance will be. The welders work in precarious positions, kneeling on wooden platforms called "floats" which hang from ropes and defy logic by not tipping over. Wherever it is possible to do so, wooden planks or metal decking are placed beneath workers erecting and working on steel. Safety rules state that this precaution should be no more than 30 feet, or two floors, below the workers.

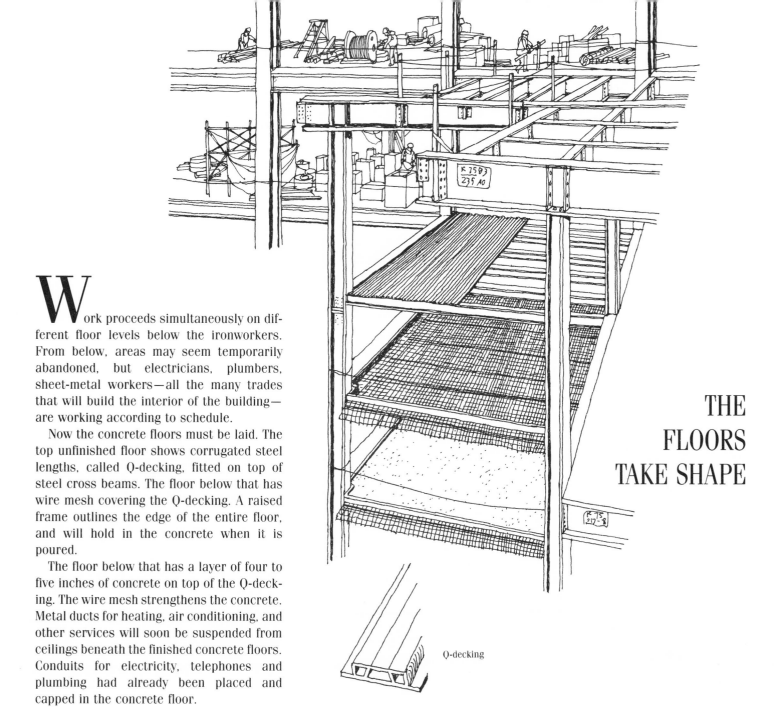

W ork proceeds simultaneously on different floor levels below the ironworkers. From below, areas may seem temporarily abandoned, but electricians, plumbers, sheet-metal workers—all the many trades that will build the interior of the building— are working according to schedule.

Now the concrete floors must be laid. The top unfinished floor shows corrugated steel lengths, called Q-decking, fitted on top of steel cross beams. The floor below that has wire mesh covering the Q-decking. A raised frame outlines the edge of the entire floor, and will hold in the concrete when it is poured.

The floor below that has a layer of four to five inches of concrete on top of the Q-decking. The wire mesh strengthens the concrete. Metal ducts for heating, air conditioning, and other services will soon be suspended from ceilings beneath the finished concrete floors. Conduits for electricity, telephones and plumbing had already been placed and capped in the concrete floor.

Q-decking

THE FLOORS TAKE SHAPE

Steel won't burn but it may warp and buckle in a fire of intense heat. For its protection, the steel framework is spray-coated with a fireproofing compound that reduces the possibility of structural change due to fire. Asbestos was once used for fireproofing but is now forbidden as a health hazard. Instead, a cement-like solution is mixed with water as it is being applied; it is sprayed on to coat the metal.

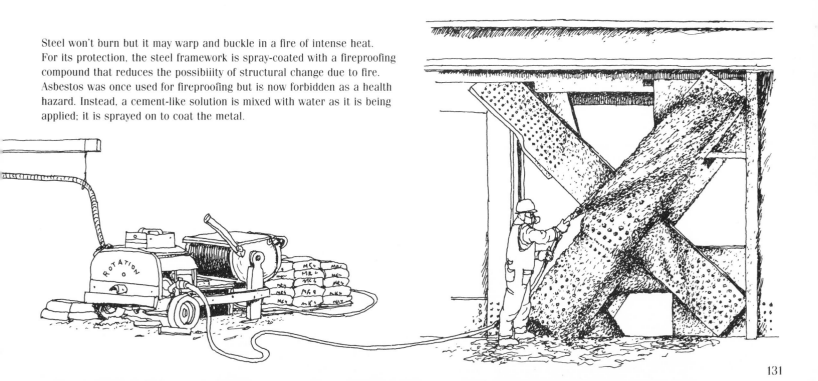

In 1954, thirty-six workmen working in six-man crews completely enclosed a 22-story building on Park Avenue in 10 hours by bolting prefabricated 2-story-high aluminum panels directly to the skyscraper's framework. It took nearly 700 panels to do the job.

THE OUTER SKIN

Since the outer surfaces of today's skyscrapers do not have to support the weight of the building, they may be thin sheets of glass, thin slabs of granite or stone, panels of aluminum, stainless steel, ceramic tile, or prefabricated concrete. This outer skin, or curtain wall, is suspended in front of the structural frame. It is bonded by special adhesives and bolted to the framework of the building, whether the building is of reinforced concrete or of steel construction.

The choice of which material to use can be based on esthetic reasons, as well as on the cost of the materials, ease of installation, and future maintenance.

Architects may set up test panels of the material they plan to use at the job site, to judge its visual effect and to test its desirability. The marble used for the curtain wall of the IBM Building in 1983 cost $8.6 million. It came from a quarry in Canada and was chosen carefully for its color, beauty, and resistance to weather.

In addition to keeping out rain and snow, the outer skin must act as insulation, keeping out heat in summer and cold in winter. It should also act as a soundproofing wall,

minimizing street noises from the outside. It must meet standards of fireproofing. For example, aluminum will melt in extreme heat, so it requires additional safety precautions: steel fasteners and a fire-resistant back-up panel.

There is a wide range of anchoring devices and methods of installation. In some buildings grids are formed by attaching metal strips vertically to the building's framework and fastening horizontal pieces between these verticals. Wall inserts, and then the windows, are installed in the resulting open spaces.

In other buildings large panel units, often with window openings, are fastened directly to the building's structure to form a continuous outer surface.

All outer-skin materials are dependent on their anchorages, which fasten them to the building and by which the weight of the outer skin is transferred to the building itself. The weight of each piece, of whatever material, is never stacked one on top of the other. Rather, it is crucial that each piece be independently supported by its own devices connecting to the building's frame.

A flatbed truck delivers these four pre-assembled granite outer wall panels. Each section weighs several tons and contains sixteen thin slices of granite, bolted and secured to the section's own reinforced concrete backing. The concrete back is designed to be supported by the steel framework of the building and will be fastened by locking devices. Here, these outer wall panels are about to be lifted by slings from a crane. Man-made concrete precast panels are lifted by means of wire loops embedded within the panels. The loops are cut off once the panels are bolted to the building.

Veneer of marble

Concrete backing

Fastening holes

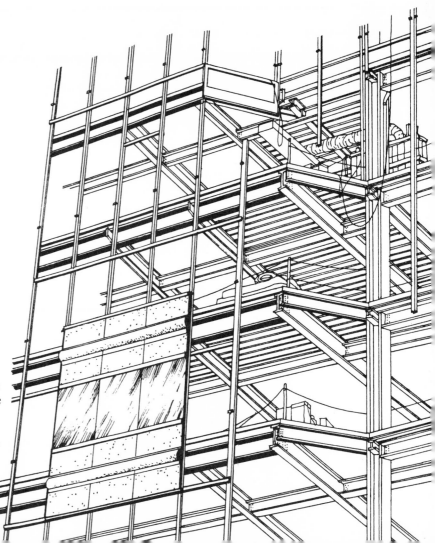

INSIDE FACE OF PRECAST PANEL

AN EXAMPLE OF A
LOCKING ARRANGEMENT

Precast panels are reinforced
internally by steel rods.

This steel locking device is used
to support the weight of the
panel and is embedded in it.

Adjustable bolts
position the outer face
of the panel flush with
the other panels.

FLOOR SURFACE:
concrete poured on top
of steel Q-decking

Shims: thin strips
of steel to adjust
height

Outer edge of building

Welded to the steel frame of the building

Colored access mark scored
into concrete floor by surveyor.
Measurements are made from this mark.

Positioning a five-ton slab of precast stone—actually a man-made conglomerate of
reinforced concrete and stone—into its proper place high above the city's streets requires
delicate care. Suspended in space by the crane above, the stone is eased into place, lined
up with its anchoring devices, and loosely bolted in position at the correct height, in
alignment with all the other panels at that floor. The stone erectors, who must serve a
three-year apprenticeship, adjust the bolt connectors. The panel must be level. Its outer
face must be flush with the outer surfaces of all the other panels. It must be at the
proper distance away from the building's frame. Its weight must rest on its main weight-
bearing connection. It must never be in shear—a twisting pressure that creates unequal
and excessive tension and strain on any steel fastener.

Once the panels are locked in place, the
outside joints are sealed with a caulking
compound. On the inside, in addition to
insulation, fireproofing barriers are installed.
These are especially needed to prevent fire
from spreading up or down, between floors.

Metal anchorages for outer panels are
embedded in concrete buildings as the
concrete is poured. They were nailed inside
wooden forms, exactly as indicated on the
working drawings, as the wooden forms
were built. When the concrete hardens, the
forms are removed, exposing the anchorages
that are ready and in place for the bolting or
welding of each panel.

Along with the development of strong lightweight-metal outer wall
panels has come the use of glass as a major visual element in
skyscraper design. Many of Manhattan's skyscrapers appear to be
giant glass boxes. These strong wind-resistant glass outer walls may
be tinted for the comfort of those inside the building, may be glare-
reducing, or may have a mirror-like surface to reflect the sun's rays
and act to insulate the interior of the building. Large glass sections
may be an inch thick. The men who handle such pieces use suction-
cup hand grips to lift and hold the glass; or when the size and weight
of the glass requires too many men for ease of installation, a multiple
vacuum-cup arrangement is attached to the glass. This frame-like
gripper can be mounted on a forklift attachment and operated by an
air-hose connection and vacuum gauge control to move the glass into
its proper place.

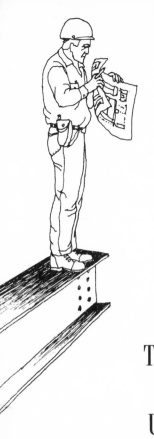

TRADES
AND
UNIONS

Once the framework of a building has been erected, whether it is of steel or of concrete construction, and the outer skin has been put in place, it looks as though most of the work has been done. On the lower floors, office workers may have already moved their equipment and furniture in and are going about their business.

Yet up above their heads, on other levels, very little may be ready except for the floors and the outer walls. It may take as much time or more to complete all the interior work on a skyscraper as it did to build the foundation and erect the framework.

Now that the vital services are in—utilities that are hidden: heat, air conditioning, electricity, water, plumbing, telephones—a wide variety of men and women workers finish off the interior details. Room partitions have to be installed, plastering, painting, paneling has to be done, tile and carpeting put down, toilet facilities constructed, doors hung, lighting fixtures connected—all the carefully done detail work that hides the basic structure of the building and puts the finishing touches on the completed skyscraper. Perhaps sixty or seventy different trades and unions will be involved in the construction of a major large building in Manhattan.

Manhattan construction is practically all unionized. Most construction workers are journeymen; they do not work for a specific company, they work from job to job. Their union is their link between work and unemployment, between management and worker. If a worker needs a credit reference to get a mortgage and buy a house, he gets it from his union. Most importantly, the union is the worker's bargaining agent to establish working conditions.

Whatever a construction worker receives for his labor is written into a contract his union has made with the contractors who are responsible for getting the job done. Each union has its own type of contract. There may be sick leave—in some trades it is five paid sick days a year—hourly wages, vacation pay, a retirement fund, overtime and double-time stipulations for work done outside normal hours. Vacation pay may be built up in different ways by different unions. Operating engineers who work the big cranes put weekly stamps into their work books. A full book earns a vacation payment from a fund to which contributions have been made by the contractors who have used the engineer during the year, whether or not the vacation is taken.

In some unions, when a worker finishes a job he reports back to his union, where he, or she, is put on the ready list. When his turn comes up, the union tells him where to report for work. In other unions the worker "shapes the job"—finds his own work, shows his union card, and goes to work if there is a job opening. At the job site he is represented by his union shop steward. The steward is there to assert his union's position in any work dispute, to mediate with other shop stewards in resolving any problems, and to look out for hazardous working conditions. Every union with workers at a construction site has a shop steward at that site. No worker may do any task outside his union specialty.

Some unions have apprentice programs, some have on-the-job training. Beginners work their way up to full pay during the first years of work. Many workers have followed fathers, or family members, into specific trades.

How does one learn to work at great heights, in exposed positions? Not just iron-workers and the men who build the wooden forms for concrete construction work at great risk, but many others lean out over the edge of buildings high above the city at one time or another. From a construction fore-man to a one-time visitor to the upper reaches of an unfinished building it may be, "Follow me, but if you get hurt I don't know you." From the beginning worker, "It's not so bad if you start at ground level and work your way up, one floor at a time, unless you're really working out over the edge. Mostly you're too busy to worry—three concrete floors like this in a week—that's sweating. Sometimes it's scary when you're on the ground and you look up to where you've been. It's what you get paid for."

An indication of the variety of trades and professions that are involved in putting up Manhattan's tall buildings.

DANGER HARD HAT AREA

ARCHITECTS
BLASTING OPERATORS
BOILERMAKERS
BRICKLAYERS
BUILDING INSPECTORS
BULLDOZER OPERATORS
CARPENTERS
CEMENT AND CONCRETE LABORERS
CEMENT FINISHERS
CEMENT MASON-TENDERS
COMPRESSED-AIR WORKERS
CRAWLER CRANE OPERATORS
    AND OILERS
CURTAIN AND DRAPERY WORKERS
DEMOLITION CREWS
DOCK BUILDERS
DRAFTSMEN
DRILLERS
ELECTRICIANS
ELEVATOR BUILDERS
ELEVATOR OPERATORS
EXCAVATION LABORERS
FIRE-ALARM INSTALLERS
FLAGMEN
FOAM-INSULATION APPLIERS
FOREMEN
FOUNDATION ENGINEERS

GAS FITTERS
GLAZIERS
HOD CARRIERS
HOIST ERECTORS
HOIST OPERATORS
JACKHAMMER OPERATORS
LABORERS
LATHERS
MACHINISTS
MARBLE FINISHERS
MASONS
MECHANICAL ENGINEERS
METAL LATHERS
METAL POLISHERS
ORNAMENTAL IRONWORKERS
PAINTERS
PAPER HANGERS
PIPE FITTERS
PLASTERERS
PLUMBERS
RIGGERS
ROOFERS
RUBBER, CORK, AND
    LINOLEUM INSTALLERS
SAFETY SUPERVISORS
SCAFFOLDING ERECTORS
SECURITY GUARDS

SECURITY SYSTEMS
    INSTALLERS
SHEET-METAL WORKERS
SHOP STEWARDS
SITE ENGINEERS
SOILS ENGINEERS
STATIONARY ENGINEERS
STEAMFITTERS
STEEL KING LABORERS
STONEMASONS
STRUCTURAL ENGINEERS
STRUCTURAL IRONWORKERS
SUPERVISORS
SURVEYORS
TELEPHONE INSTALLERS
TERRAZZO FINISHERS
TILE FINISHERS
TIMBERMEN
TIMEKEEPERS
TOWER CRANE ENGINEERS
TRUCK DRIVERS
VENETIAN-BLIND
    INSTALLERS
WATERPROOFERS
WELDERS
WINDOW CLEANERS

As the workers build, they generate great amounts of trash—inside the building as well as at curbside. The big trucks, first to arrive at the excavation site when digging began, are among the last to leave as the building is completed, carting away the debris from the final clean-up.

One way to get to the top of the Empire State Building is to run up, as has been done every year since 1976 in the annual Valentine's Day Run-Up sponsored jointly by the Empire State Building and the Road Runners Club of New York City. There are 1,575 steps to the 86th-floor observatory, each 7.5 inches high, with a landing and reverse direction halfway between each floor. The race is by invitation only, not for the weak-hearted and usually limited to fifty runners, both male and female. Best men's time: 10 minutes, 59.7 seconds; best women's time: 13 minutes,19 seconds. The express elevator to the 86th-floor observatory takes less than a minute. A visitor's brochure states that there are seven miles of elevator shafts in this famous skyscraper. Rockefeller Center's elevators travel nearly two million miles in a year—with more than 400,000 passenger rides in a day. Their fastest elevators go nonstop to the 65th floor in 37 seconds.

UP
AND
DOWN
. . . AT 20 MILES
AN HOUR

It seems faster than 20 miles an hour as you drop straight down 106 floors in one of the express elevators at the World Trade Center. Your ears pop. You are in a large elevator. You entered on one side and will leave through doors on the opposite side. You and your fellow passengers eye each other cautiously, realizing you are all hurtling down the tallest elevator shaft in New York City, empty space beneath you.

The elevator core of a building is much more than just the space in which passengers go up and down. By its construction—a rigid vertical box-like structure that extends upward uninterruptedly from the basement to the upper floors of the skyscraper—it can provide structural support for the entire building.

Concrete walls enclose it to make it fireproof and, in doing so, strengthen it. Its specialized metal framework, constructed in exact alignment for the smooth operation of the elevators, adds rigidity. Its box-like shape may be a stabilizing factor in combating any swaying motion caused by high winds. It may be a central column, designed to add support to each of the floors of the skyscraper, as in the construction of the World Trade Center.

The elevator and its placement is one of the necessities in the design and construction of a skyscraper, determined in the early planning stages of the building. How many people are expected to use your building? How do you provide for their rapid and efficient movement up and down without wasting valuable space—space that can be used as rent-producing offices?

The World Trade Center did it by creating three elevator zones, one on top of the other, in each of its two towers. The first zone extends from ground level up to the 44th floor sky lobby, the middle zone from the 44th floor up to the 78th-floor level, the top zone

from the 78th sky lobby to the top of the building.

These sky lobbies are really transfer lobbies. Traveling at speeds of 1,600 feet a minute, express elevators with a capacity of fifty-five passengers each speed from ground level to the 44th- and 78th-floor lobbies, where one transfers to local elevators to reach the floors between sky lobbies.

In the elevator core of each building there are thirty-six open shafts, some with three elevators operating in them. Special express elevators speed nonstop between ground level and the 107th-floor observation deck in the South Tower and the club restaurant in the North Tower. There are four giant freight elevators in each building.

Today, in all large buildings, computerized controls automatically dispatch elevators to floors as microprocessors analyze the traffic volume during peak and off-peak hours. Gone are the days, not long ago, when the individual elevator operator controlled the timing and used hand controls to bring the elevator to a halt, sometimes just missing proper alignment of the elevator and floor.

With the appearance of push-button elevators shortly after the end of World War II, a whole segment of city life disappeared. Now even the voice that announces the floor is recorded and automatically activated. The floor alignments are perfect and smoothly done. Electronic sensors within the elevator cabin can detect unusual conditions, stopping the elevator at the nearest floor. And engineers are at work to further improve what started out essentially as a box suspended, raised, and lowered by cables, guided by vertical rails. Elisha Otis would be impressed; the company he founded is still in business—the largest elevator maker in the world.

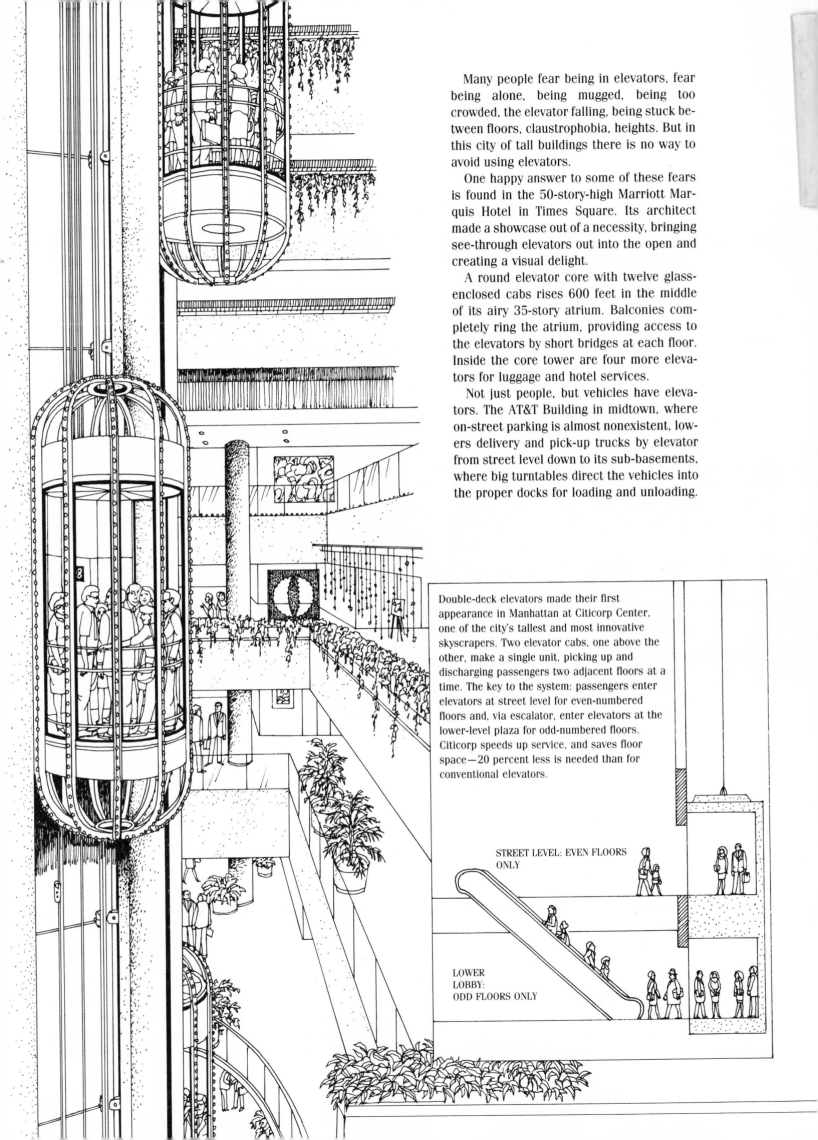

Many people fear being in elevators, fear being alone, being mugged, being too crowded, the elevator falling, being stuck between floors, claustrophobia, heights. But in this city of tall buildings there is no way to avoid using elevators.

One happy answer to some of these fears is found in the 50-story-high Marriott Marquis Hotel in Times Square. Its architect made a showcase out of a necessity, bringing see-through elevators out into the open and creating a visual delight.

A round elevator core with twelve glass-enclosed cabs rises 600 feet in the middle of its airy 35-story atrium. Balconies completely ring the atrium, providing access to the elevators by short bridges at each floor. Inside the core tower are four more elevators for luggage and hotel services.

Not just people, but vehicles have elevators. The AT&T Building in midtown, where on-street parking is almost nonexistent, lowers delivery and pick-up trucks by elevator from street level down to its sub-basements, where big turntables direct the vehicles into the proper docks for loading and unloading.

Double-deck elevators made their first appearance in Manhattan at Citicorp Center, one of the city's tallest and most innovative skyscrapers. Two elevator cabs, one above the other, make a single unit, picking up and discharging passengers two adjacent floors at a time. The key to the system: passengers enter elevators at street level for even-numbered floors and, via escalator, enter elevators at the lower-level plaza for odd-numbered floors. Citicorp speeds up service, and saves floor space—20 percent less is needed than for conventional elevators.

STREET LEVEL: EVEN FLOORS ONLY

LOWER LOBBY: ODD FLOORS ONLY

The Empire State Building has proved itself to be a remarkably stable structure. When the B-25 bomber crashed into it in 1945 it tore a hole in the building almost twenty feet square at the 78th and 79th floor level. This was followed by a great burst of fire. Occupants reported that the building seemed to move at the impact, but the damage was repaired without any noticeable effect at all.

In 1938 and 1940 studies were made in the building to measure any movement that might be caused by high winds, and it was tested again in the late fifties. As a measuring device Minneapolis-Honeywell used a light beam from the 85th floor down to the 6th floor and found very little deflection—less than a quarter inch off center.

SKYSCRAPER STRESS

Do skyscrapers bend, or sway, in strong winds? They can, and they do, but usually so slowly and in such small measurements that the motion is imperceptible to the building's occupants. It is part of the structural engineer's responsibility to design elements into the building that will eliminate or reduce such motion.

To analyze wind stress on a skyscraper, a scale model of the proposed building čan be tested in a computerized wind tunnel. Many of Manhattan's tallest buildings, such as the World Trade Center, IBM, AT&T, and Citicorp, have been tested in this way, some in a Boundary Layer Tunnel where different zones of wind turbulence can be duplicated—the wind pressures at the top of a skyscraper can vary from those at lower levels of the building.

Some models are made of a rigid material for testing wind pressures against the surfaces of the building; some are flexible, to tell how the building bends in the wind. Because other tall buildings nearby will have an influence on the wind patterns, the testing is done with scale models of these other buildings in their proper positions. The entire model can rotate as computers and sensors make readings, and smoke patterns give visual understanding of the way the design features of the building affect the wind currents. The final analysis can help determine whether the building needs additional bracing, adjustment in its height or design features, and what effect it will have in creating street-level turbulence.

New structural materials and stronger steel have reduced the overall weight of today's skyscrapers, making them more susceptible to stresses caused by strong winds. Too much sway may cause a feeling of uneasiness in the occupants and might cause damage to the building itself. On occasion, additional steel bracing has had to be added to completed structures in Manhattan to provide more strength to the building's framework.

Older buildings, such as the Empire State Building and the Chrysler Building, were built of heavier steel and materials than those currently used, and have a more rigid framework than today's skyscrapers.

Bracing the building's framework is one way to minimize sway. Another way is to use a "dampening" device that will slow down sway motion and make it imperceptible, so that people in the building are unaware of any movement.

In the Citicorp Building skyscraper on Lexington Avenue, one of the tallest skyscrapers in the world, this is done by means of a 400-ton block of concrete up on the 59th floor. This block rests on a platform and is connected to the frame of the building by arms that move like shock absorbers, or pistons.

When the building begins to sway because of strong winds, oil is pumped onto the platform and "floats" the 400-ton block. The block countermoves to the building's sway, transmitting inertia through the pistons, slowing the building's motion. Then the oil drains off and the "tuned mass damper," as it is called, rests until the computer again floats it in response to more swaying.

The twin towers of the World Trade Center, reaching almost a quarter of a mile into the sky, present enormous flat surfaces to the winds of lower Manhattan. To control swaying motion, each tower has 10,000 devices installed in the framing systems of its floors. Made from a special material which resists movement by creating friction, these devices act as brakes on any swaying motion in the towers.

Tall buildings are not only buffeted by high winds—they also cause high winds. When wind is blocked by a skyscraper, it can follow the building downward, to end up whirling about pedestrians at street level. Also, as wind is compressed between rows of tall buildings, it increases its velocity. When the wind whistles down onto some Manhattan streets and whips around the sharp corners of a building, it can create a whirling, spinning effect, blowing debris up in the air, and sending pedestrians, hats, and umbrellas flying.

Spectacular photos have been taken of lightning striking the top of the Empire State Building. It has been hit hundreds of times since it was built, once nine times in less than half an hour. Yet no damage has been done to the building and none of its occupants has been in danger or inconvenienced. The lightning charge, in a fraction of a second, harmlessly follows a path from the building's metal topmast down through the steel structure into the ground below. Scientific studies into the nature of lightning itself have been made at the Empire State Building since the mid-1930's.

Few studies about the nature of lightning were available in 1913 when the Woolworth Building was being built. As it was to be the world's tallest commercial structure, no chances were taken. Copper wires were connected to the copper roof, and run down inside the structure and into the ground below to carry any lightning charge harmlessly into the ground.

What happens now that skyscrapers are built of reinforced concrete and do not have steel skeletons that might act as carriers to ground a lightning charge? The cold-water piping system will act as a ground if properly prepared and connected to a mast or lightning rod.

THE AT&T BUILDING

This most unusual construction, two enormous steel boxes in a building's foundation, is for a most unusual skyscraper—the AT&T headquarters on Madison Avenue. Very tall, 647 feet, and narrow for its height, the building occupies the width of a full city block, from 55th to 56th streets.

Its gift of public spaces at street level is monumental, with two open-air pedestrian plazas, built at either end of the building, and a glass covered pedestrian arcade at the rear. One enters the building itself through a 70-foot-tall arched entrance at the center of the building. Fourteen granite-clad columns in each plaza soar 60 feet into the air, supporting the building above. It is at this high level up above the street, its sky-lobby level, that the office tower and work areas of the building begin. A shuttle elevator runs from the street to this sky-lobby level, where express and local elevators service the building.

The design of this skyscraper, which has been likened to a tower perched on stilt-like columns, required unusual engineering solutions to the problem of maintaining the building's structural integrity.

Why build two enormous steel boxes in a skyscraper's basement? They are called "shear tubes."

Shear—torsion—is the twisting motion created in a building's structure by the action of wind pressure against the building's surface. It begins at the top of a building and increases in intensity as it moves downward. This pressure could cause a fluttering motion in a tall narrow building.

These two shear tubes are shown here during construction. They will be encased in concrete—some of the concrete will be 2.5 feet thick—and fastened to the ⅜-inch-thick steel plates by steel stud connectors projecting from the plates. These shear tubes will extend from the foundation base up through the building into the sky lobby 77 feet above street level.

Any wind-shear forces against the building will be directed, by design, to these two tubes and dissipated downward into the foundation bedrock without affecting the skyscraper's stability.

This building has been noted for its beautiful granite surface—a pink stone with flecks of gray, ranging from almost black to white, quarried near Branford, Connecticut. Unlike the granite facing sometimes used on tall buildings, where a thin veneer of stone is bonded to a concrete slab backing and fastened to the building as a unit, these granite pieces are solid. Most pieces are two inches thick; some are five inches thick. They are heavy and require a strong anchoring system, with each piece individually anchored to the building.

Granite is rigid and unyielding, but there is movement in steel structures. So provision had to be made to accommodate any movement between the building's frame and the stone itself by using vertical steel support tubes with expansion joints. The granite panels do not butt against each other but are positioned and anchored three-eighths of an inch apart to allow for slight movement. The joints between are filled with a flexible silicone sealant. The granite is not polished but finished rough to enhance the beauty of the stone and to create variations of light and shade as one looks at the skyscraper.

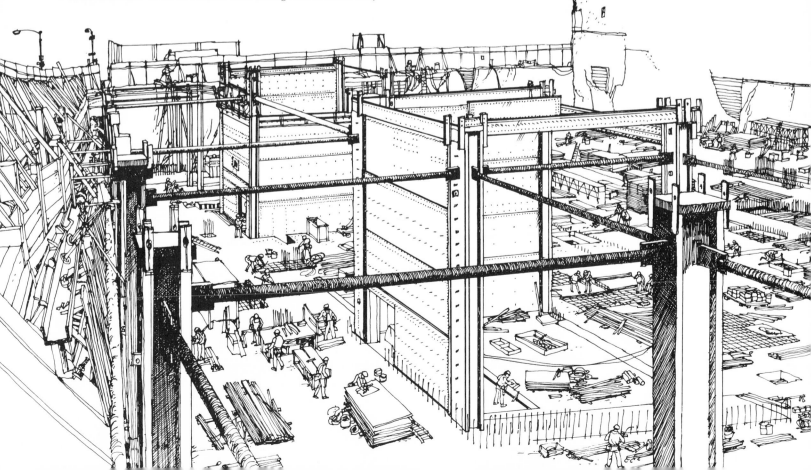

ACROPHOBIA ... FEAR OF HEIGHTS

Some visitors to the observation towers of Manhattan's famous skyscrapers feel uneasy and some almost feel terror when, though safe behind guard rails, they look down at the tiny figures and autos on the streets far below. There is a word for this sensation, *acrophobia*—fear of heights. It is a very real fear.

The men who build these skyscrapers seem to have no fear: surefooted, they walk on slender beams day after day with nothing to hold on to and with great open spaces beneath them. It is dangerous work and what they do is spectacular. Yet they are never known by name or as individuals unless by accident.

There are individuals who, upon seeing a tall building or a great height, see a challenge. If they succeed in meeting the challenge, they may capture the imagination of the nation. They may also incur the wrath of the authorities because of the danger, the cost, and the disruption of normal activities that they cause.

Three men who saw Manhattan's tallest buildings—the twin towers of the World Trade Center—as a direct challenge, did so in very different ways.

The open observation deck on the South Tower is surrounded by an electrified fence topped with barbed wire. The parallel tracks guide the window-washing machine.

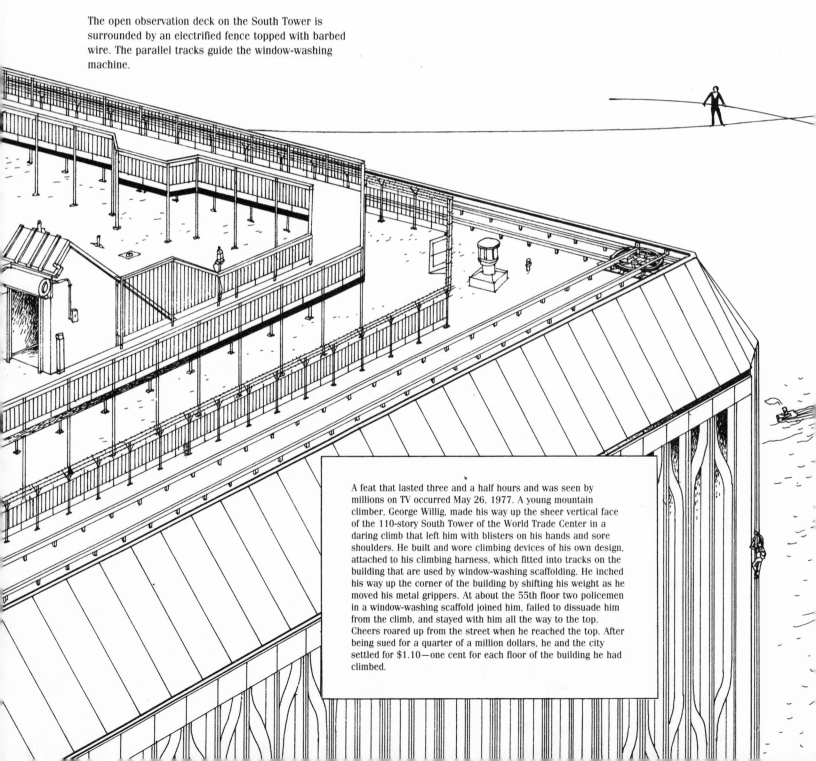

A feat that lasted three and a half hours and was seen by millions on TV occurred May 26, 1977. A young mountain climber, George Willig, made his way up the sheer vertical face of the 110-story South Tower of the World Trade Center in a daring climb that left him with blisters on his hands and sore shoulders. He built and wore climbing devices of his own design, attached to his climbing harness, which fitted into tracks on the building that are used by window-washing scaffolding. He inched his way up the corner of the building by shifting his weight as he moved his metal grippers. At about the 55th floor two policemen in a window-washing scaffold joined him, failed to dissuade him from the climb, and stayed with him all the way to the top. Cheers roared up from the street when he reached the top. After being sued for a quarter of a million dollars, he and the city settled for $1.10—one cent for each floor of the building he had climbed.

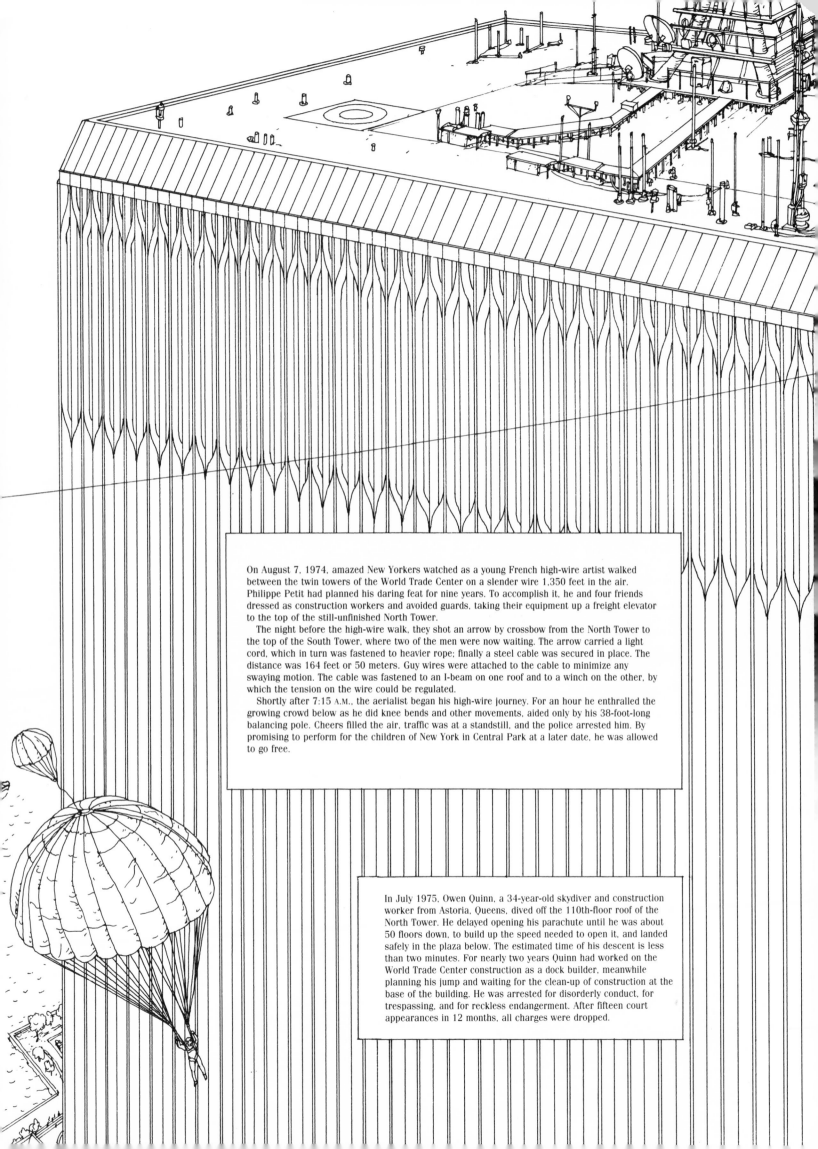

On August 7, 1974, amazed New Yorkers watched as a young French high-wire artist walked
between the twin towers of the World Trade Center on a slender wire 1,350 feet in the air.
Philippe Petit had planned his daring feat for nine years. To accomplish it, he and four friends
dressed as construction workers and avoided guards, taking their equipment up a freight elevator
to the top of the still-unfinished North Tower.

The night before the high-wire walk, they shot an arrow by crossbow from the North Tower to
the top of the South Tower, where two of the men were now waiting. The arrow carried a light
cord, which in turn was fastened to heavier rope; finally a steel cable was secured in place. The
distance was 164 feet or 50 meters. Guy wires were attached to the cable to minimize any
swaying motion. The cable was fastened to an I-beam on one roof and to a winch on the other, by
which the tension on the wire could be regulated.

Shortly after 7:15 A.M., the aerialist began his high-wire journey. For an hour he enthralled the
growing crowd below as he did knee bends and other movements, aided only by his 38-foot-long
balancing pole. Cheers filled the air, traffic was at a standstill, and the police arrested him. By
promising to perform for the children of New York in Central Park at a later date, he was allowed
to go free.

In July 1975, Owen Quinn, a 34-year-old skydiver and construction
worker from Astoria, Queens, dived off the 110th-floor roof of the
North Tower. He delayed opening his parachute until he was about
50 floors down, to build up the speed needed to open it, and landed
safely in the plaza below. The estimated time of his descent is less
than two minutes. For nearly two years Quinn had worked on the
World Trade Center construction as a dock builder, meanwhile
planning his jump and waiting for the clean-up of construction at the
base of the building. He was arrested for disorderly conduct, for
trespassing, and for reckless endangerment. After fifteen court
appearances in 12 months, all charges were dropped.

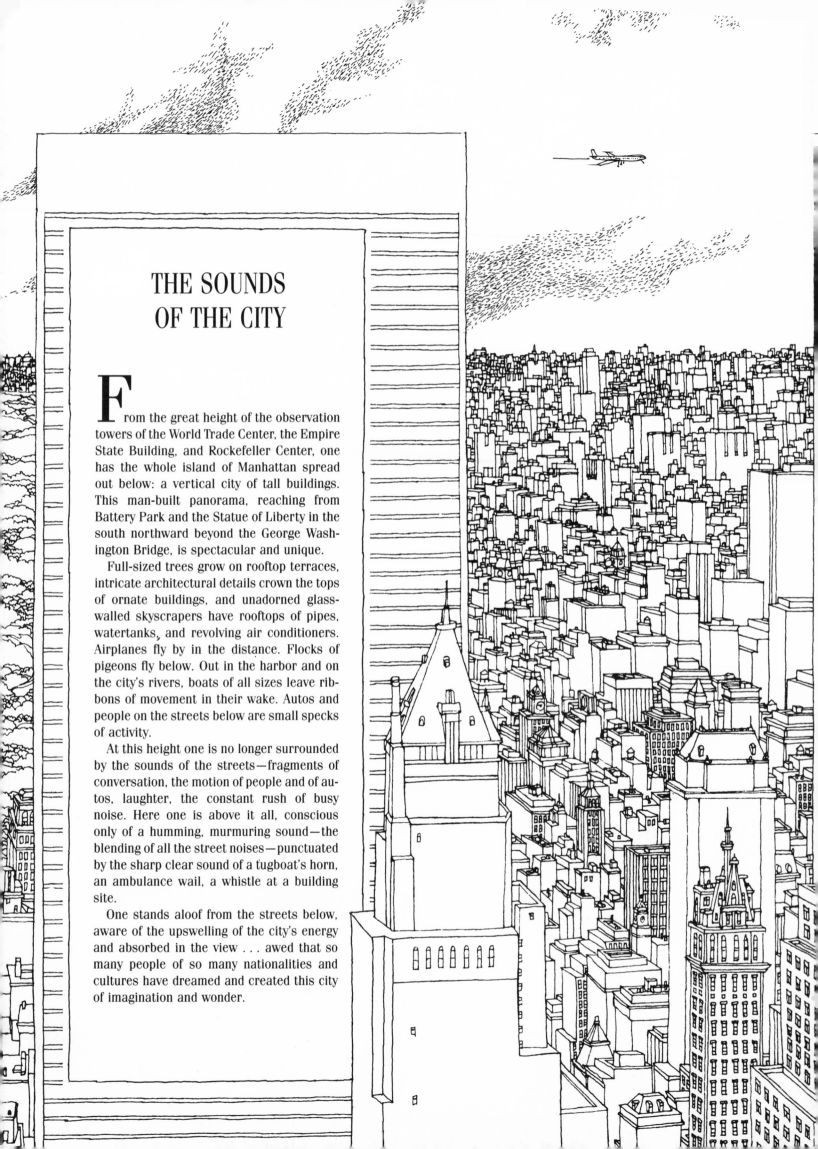

THE SOUNDS
OF THE CITY

From the great height of the observation towers of the World Trade Center, the Empire State Building, and Rockefeller Center, one has the whole island of Manhattan spread out below: a vertical city of tall buildings. This man-built panorama, reaching from Battery Park and the Statue of Liberty in the south northward beyond the George Washington Bridge, is spectacular and unique.

Full-sized trees grow on rooftop terraces, intricate architectural details crown the tops of ornate buildings, and unadorned glass-walled skyscrapers have rooftops of pipes, watertanks, and revolving air conditioners. Airplanes fly by in the distance. Flocks of pigeons fly below. Out in the harbor and on the city's rivers, boats of all sizes leave ribbons of movement in their wake. Autos and people on the streets below are small specks of activity.

At this height one is no longer surrounded by the sounds of the streets—fragments of conversation, the motion of people and of autos, laughter, the constant rush of busy noise. Here one is above it all, conscious only of a humming, murmuring sound—the blending of all the street noises—punctuated by the sharp clear sound of a tugboat's horn, an ambulance wail, a whistle at a building site.

One stands aloof from the streets below, aware of the upswelling of the city's energy and absorbed in the view . . . awed that so many people of so many nationalities and cultures have dreamed and created this city of imagination and wonder.

Topping out . . . a celebration of Manhattan's newest skyscraper.

The very topmost piece of the building's steel has just been fastened into place—and atop it, in keeping with tradition, waves the Stars and Stripes. And next to it, for reasons long since forgotten, but perhaps of Norse origin, is tied a fir tree. The workers will celebrate their hard-won achievement—with drinks and sandwiches.

Way off to the north they can see the George Washington Bridge . . . and way off to the south, the Statue of Liberty. Far below are the streets and the people, millions of fellow New Yorkers, endlessly on the move—the vibrant liveliness of the great city.

. . . Manhattan.

ACKNOWLEDGMENTS

Invariably the people involved in the planning and construction of the buildings, and those working for the city and for the utilities, have been helpful. I regret not having asked more individuals for their names; some preferred to remain anonymous. If by chance someone reads this and recalls his or her own contribution, my thanks to you. Most especially to Elmer Richards and George Tamaro of Mueser Rutledge Consulting Engineers, who offered their time, knowledge and help and to my son Neil, with his invaluable word processor and assistance.

To John Hughes and Mary Layton of the Port Authority of New York and New Jersey, Alan Ritchie of John Burgee Architects with Philip Johnson, Frederick B. Davidson of the Battery Park City Authority, John Leeper, Sol Olsher and Frank Rohauer of HRH Construction Corp., Chuck Appel and Martin Gitten of Con Edison, William Heard of Otis Elevator, Bevin Maguire of Rockefeller Center Management Corp., Felix Sanchez and Paul Leontzwick of NYNEX, Edward Stegeman of Empire City Subway, William Rosado and his associates, Ronnie Pollicino and his crew. To John Hunt and Harold Manchester especially, and to Ed Schussler and all those who put up 527 Madison Avenue.

To Fred Liebmann, Ralph Lamo, Fred Sturges, Bruce Kahan, Wallace Rosenwach, Dana Gunter, Jim Duggan, Robert McGiveron, Tim O'Brien, Don Casamassina, Philippe Petit, George Willig, Owen Quinn, William Reidy, John Brennan, Lillian Alaya, Dr. Sherene Baugher, Dr. Nick Isyumov, and many others, thanks.

To the City of New York and its Department of Environmental Protection for its many books and pamphlets, and to the city's own bookstore, Citybooks, where in addition to codes and regulations, one can buy a sixty-five pound cast-iron "Seal of the City" that once was part of the West Side Highway.

I made extensive use of both the Central Research Library and the Mid-Manhattan Branch of the New York Public Library. The portion of the Ratzer Map of 1767 and the portion of the Viele Map of 1874 are both from the Map Division; the 1797 watercolor by George Holland of Broad Street is from the I. N. Phelps Stokes Collection; the line engraving of the cast-iron store front from Badger's Catalog is from the Art, Print and Photographs Division; and the line engraving showing cast-iron construction, 1858, is from the General Research Division. All of these are from the Astor, Lenox and Tilden Foundations of the New York Public Library, with help from Anna Bartmon. The library's technical and historical books, and the microfilm records of the *New York Times* and of technical journals were invaluable.

The Museum of the City of New York has been very helpful, especially for its displays of the early Dutch settlers on Manhattan Island. The Teunis Tomasen mentioned in the text, also known as Teunis Tomassen Quick, is an early ancestor. Thanks to Terry Ariano for her help with the Museum's Print Collection. Also to Martha de Montaño of the Museum of the American Indian, and to Katherine Naylor of the New York Historical Society. The drawings of the men working on the Empire State Building are imagined, based on photographs taken by Louis Hine, courtesy of George Eastman House and Coralee Aber.

147

SOURCES

PAGE

6–7   "Mantles of Feathers . . . of good Furres." J. Franklin Jameson, editor, *Narratives of New Netherland, 1609–1664.* (New York: Charles Scribner's Sons, 1909), p. 19.

"This is a very good Land . . . Land to see." Ibid., p. 17.

"of the bark of trees." I. N. Phelps Stokes, *The Iconography of Manhattan Island,* vol. 1, p. 10.

"delivered to him at thirteen inches to the foot." Ibid., vol. 2, p. 247.

"at his own pleasure . . . cannot be prejudiced thereby." Berthold Fernow, editor, *The Records of New Amsterdam from 1653 to 1674.* (New York: The City of New York, 1897), p. 207.

"Isaac de Forest registers at the office . . . guiders for the job." Stokes, *Iconography,* vol. 4, p. 94.

"with provisions and drink until the work is completed." Ibid., vol. 4, p. 115.

10–11   "Scituate upon the Island commonly knowne by the Name of Manhatoes." Ibid., vol. 4, p. 240.

12–13   "at which all negro and Indian slaves . . . took their stand." David T. Valentine, *Manual of the Corporation of the City of New York,* vol. 1849, p. 353.

14–15   "in the morning the American troops marched . . . and took possession of the city." Ibid., vol. 1870, p. 826.

16–17   "by which it was provided that no master. . . . to make satisfaction in some other way." Thomas E. V. Smith, *The City of New York in the Year of Washington's Inauguration 1789* (1889; reprint ed., Riverside, Conn.: Chatham Press in cooperation with the U.S. Dept. of the Interior, National Park Service, Federal Hall National Memorial, New York City, 1972), p. 100.

"every negro, mulatto, or mestee who was a slave. . . . punishable by 40 shillings fine." Ibid., p. 122.

18–19   "a four storey brick house. . . . twenty-eight feet four inches wide." Ibid., p. 27.

20–21   "To some it may be a matter of surprise. . . . Harlem Flat will be covered with houses." Valentine, *Manual of Corporation of the City of New York,* vol. 1866, p. 759.

"the Mayor draw on the city Treasurer . . . as a compliment to the workmen." Ibid., vol. 1853, p. 469.

22–23   "The city is now undergoing its usual annual metamorphosis . . . to its utmost extent." Philip Hone, *The Diary of Philip Hone,*

1828–1851 (New York: Dodd, Mead & Company, 1889, 1927, 1936), p. 41.

"The spirit of pulling down. . . . once in ten years." Ibid., 395.

24–25   "The cast-iron frame of the building. . . . which may be ornamented to any taste." James Bogardus, *Cast-Iron Buildings, Their Construction and Advantages,* pamphlet (New York, 1858).

26–27   "energy of 8,500 incandescent lamps." *Harper's Weekly,* January 18, 1890.

32–33   "A type of construction . . . carries all stresses directly to the foundations." *The Architectural Record,* August 1934, p. 114.

"An iron bridge truss stood on end was the solution of the problem." *New York Times,* May 21, 1905, p. 6.

"the earliest example of skeleton construction . . . date 1888–9." Ibid.

36–37   "unfortunately for the science of construction . . . skeletons cased with masonry." *The American Architect and Building News,* vol. 77, no. 1396, 1902.

"For many reasons this building is unique. . . . twentieth; 10 feet 6 inches." "American Local History," booklet, the New York Public Library, p. 91.